THE ROLE OF RELIGION

IN CARIBBEAN HISTORY

From Amerindian Shamanism to Rastafarianism

BY
PATRICK "POPS" HYLTON

Edited by Klaus May

Copyright © 2002
by
Patrick "Pops" Hylton

ISBN: 0-9726053-0-4

Library of Congress Control Number: 2002094998

Billpops Publications
P. O. Box 2349
Washington, D.C. 20013

www.billpops.com

Printed in the United States by
Morris Publishing
3212 East Highway 30
Kearney, NE 68847
1-800-650-7888

Table of Contents

It is easier for a camel to enter the eye of a needle than for a rich man to enter the kingdom of God.

Jesus Christ

If you don't know where you come from, it's difficult to assess where you are. It's even more difficult to plan where you are going.

Rev. Joseph Lowery

If we consider ourselves fully human, then we are compelled to struggle relentlessly to remove all obstacles that impede the creation of a world that is fully human.

Klaus May

In order to succeed, colonization required that the imagination of the colonized be conquered. Europeans demonized Africans, treating African cultures as objects of ethnographic study and rendering their differences monstrous in order to impose European governance on the continent. When it became clear that the Africans could not be annihilated, the Europeans tried to create a class of "new men". To make them *civilized*, or *Christian*, or *évolus*, or *asimilados*. Africans were separated from their folktales, lullabies, riddles, dances, and masquerades. In this way, Africans lost the bogeymen that their communities had fashioned to ward off danger: wild animals, disease, neighboring communities, slave traders. . . . . Africans instead adopted the bogeymen of their conquerors and colonizers: in large measure, themselves.

Muhonjia Khaminwa

Table of Illustrations

FOREWORD AND ACKNOWLEDGMENTS

This work is the product of several years of study and interaction with adherents of and institutions representing many of the religions and denominations in the Caribbean. It incorporates the beliefs and opinions of the working people on Caribbean and world affairs, personal knowledge derived from my relationships with pioneers and some of the younger adherents of the Rastafari Movement, as well as my own direct acquaintance with the ceremonies, rituals, and some of the practitioners of Kumina, Pukumina, Revivalism, Shango, Bongoism and other religious expressions.

It is intended as a modest investigation into the role of religion in the lives of the Caribbean people from the pre-Columbian period to the present, particularly during the periods of their greatest tribulations: invasion, plunder, genocide, abduction, enslavement, colonization and racial oppression. It is an investigation that attempts to provide answers to many questions and an insight into some of the concerns, values and contradictions of the people. In a word, this investigation provides a perspective of the collective spirit of the people.

Religion is very deep-rooted among the Caribbean people. It is manifested in their talking, singing, eating, drinking and in virtually every artistic, social and political activity. The historical role played by religion in the struggles of the people has been so influential that any socio-political analysis or any contemporary political movement that fails to take this fact into account will undoubtedly be committing a grave error.

i

Religion represents a great deal more than a collection of sermons, writings and dogmatic literature. It is an organized, institutionalized and systematized form of articulating, manifesting, witnessing and evidencing socioeconomic, political, cultural and historical values. Further, a distinction can be made between "vulgar theology" which apologizes for, acquiesces and participates in the exploitation and oppression of humanity, and "liberation" theology which recognizes the inseparable unity between the material and spiritual needs of the people and struggles to realize their fulfillment.

This book does not compare the several religions and sectarian denominations with a view to determining which or whose deity is more in conformity with "the truth". It does, however, concede to each religion or denomination its respective philosophical claim and measures its impact, positively or negatively, on the lives of the people it seeks to attract to its fold. Hence, it is the practical manifestation rather than the idealizations and theoretical expressions of the respective religions that are of greater interest to this author. In other words, what were the social practices or the posture of each religion or sect in relation to the issues of territorial plunder, the wanton rape, servitude and genocide of Amerindians, African enslavement, the African Slave Trade, the Abolition Movement, colonialism, racism, and so forth?

I acknowledge with appreciation the editorial contribution and intellectual and moral support unstintingly provided by my friend Klaus May. I am grateful to my wife, Winnie Hylton, for her support, encouragement, and tolerance. I extend appreciation to my friend Melissa "Damali" Pullins for her assistance and encouragement; Dr. Jacques Homiak and Florence Johnson for their assistance with the illustrations; Dr. Jean Purchase-Tulloch for proofreading the text; Ras Irice Clarke for his consultative assistance with the chapter on Rastafarianism; Pamela Prue for arrangement and organization of the illustrations, text and cover design; and my son, Salim Hylton, for his artistic contribution to the cover design.

I am indebted to Theresa Charles and Ann Thomas of Grenada and Clare Brewster of Barbados whose personal experiences with, and profound belief in Shango, Shouterism and Obeah did not only serve as a source of education but also as a reaffirmation of the cultural unity of the Caribbean people. I extend my appreciation to my friend Dr. Carlos Nelson for his valuable criticisms, to Dr. Barry Chevannes whose critical commentaries undoubtedly contributed to an improved manuscript, and to Ken Ford, Fenton Ferguson, Horace Campbell and Ainsley Vaughn of Trinidad-Tobago and Jamaica respectively who were all early sources of encouragement to me.

Patrick Hylton

INTRODUCTION

The conquest and colonization of the Americas, like Asia, Africa and Australia, were accomplished with the gun and the bible. Historically, religion has been used to rationalize and consolidate military conquests, preserve empires through mental enslavement of the conquered, and destroy resistance by debasing and vulgarizing the culture of the subject peoples. Those among the vanquished who refused to submit to the alien faith were treated as social outcasts and – depending on the level and effectiveness of their resistance – as outlaws. This was the role played by the culture of the European ruling classes in the Caribbean and the New World. The institution entrusted with its propagation was the Christian Church – Roman Catholicism and Protestantism.

On the other hand, the religion of a conquered people deprived of economic, political and military power can become the principal instrument of resistance against the conquerors. As a tool of struggle, it serves as the chief communicator, educator and guardian of the people's identity. Religion, in this context, becomes revolutionary – inspiring and galvanizing the people; providing them with leadership; giving them strength and comfort in the quagmire of unrelenting adversity; and mobilizing, organizing and protecting the culture for future generations. Such was the role of Shamanism and the religions of the African people in the New World in general and the Caribbean in particular.

The role of the European Christian Church, however, has been markedly different. Its history has always been explicitly political and seemingly antithetical to the nihilism and materialism of the private social "ethos" and "aesthetics" of the leisure class.

Yet the political-theological focus of the Church has been less upon the private discrete ethics of those who rule, than upon the social values reflected among the ruled. Thus, for instance, the Church has historically condemned "sensuality" (especially sensualistic music) among the people, while professing to find the "higher" ethical virtues in the rulers and the owners of property.

The Church "closed its eyes" to the prostitution and social injustices carried out by big business and military and political leaders against the people and commended the perpetrators for their "virtuosities". It excoriated the poor for their vices, but disregarded their virtues. It demanded obedience and obeisance to the higher authorities, while acquiescing and participating in the vices and corruption of the higher authorities. It assiduously accumulated wealth for itself, but counseled poverty and resignation for the people. It remained silent in the face of wanton cruelty and tyranny, but displayed impatience with public disobedience to unjust authorities.

The political and religious history of the Caribbean, as obscure and "exotic" as it appears to Westerners, is not pleasant. While it is a story of the long travails in the wilderness of poverty and ignorance, it is not yet the story of a united sovereign community which others feel obliged to respect. It is precisely because of the region's unpleasant history that such painstaking efforts have been employed by the colonizers and neo-colonizers to bury it in obscurity and propagate instead, especially to gullible tourists, romantic myths about piracy, plantation life, and religious proselytizing.

All these efforts, however, have failed to obscure the

historically documented fact that from 1492 to the present the Caribbean and its people have been victims of continuous oppression and suffering. The aboriginal inhabitants were almost completely annihilated, their way of life destroyed, and their land and its wealth appropriated by the European conquerors. Poor European workers and prisoners of war were condemned to a life of servitude in the new land. The white pioneer small farmers, utilized by the ruling families of Europe and North America to eliminate the Amerindians, were themselves evicted from the land and transformed into proletarians, sharecroppers and a host of social undesirables.

The African continent was devastated and its people condemned to slavery. Tens of millions were transported to the New World as commodities to create wealth and a life of luxury for the European and American ruling classes and the hierarchy of the Christian churches. Subsequent to the abolition of African slavery, Chinese, East Indian and Javanese laborers were brought in as supplemental beasts of burden through their contract of indenture, and as unwitting players in the colonizers' strategy of "divide and rule."

Thus, the economic development of Western Europe and the United States was achieved at the expense of the Amerindians, Africans, Asians and poor Europeans. It was realized through genocide, plunder, human enslavement and other forms of exploitation now universally denied, but once justified as features of progress. The soil of the region is saturated with the blood of millions of its martyrs and its waterways still hold in their bosoms the remains of numerous ships and their plundering crews, the bones of shackled slaves, and vast quantities of ill-gotten treasures. Between the seventeenth and the first half of the nineteenth centuries the ruling families of Britain, France, Spain, Portugal, the Netherlands, the United States, Denmark, Sweden and other European countries made a fortune from the commerce in African slaves and from sugar, cotton and tobacco produced by slave labor. Until the nineteenth century when large-scale sugar production in Brazil and the Near East and beet sugar production in Europe gained control of the sugar market, the Caribbean was the principal source of wealth for Western Europe. Slavery, sugar, and cotton in the Caribbean facilitated the rapid growth of the Industrial Revolution, the birth of manufacturing, shipping, financial and military complexes in Western Europe and the United States, and in the conquest and colonization by Europe of Africa, Asia and the Pacific region.

The wars of the seventeenth and eighteenth centuries (the American War of Independence and the Anglo-French Wars of the 1790s excepted) and the condonation of the high-profit institutions of piracy (buccaneering and privateering) and slave trading were the standard expressions of primitive accumulation of capital. These were activities in which the Christian churches themselves were no minor players. The struggle for economic and political supremacy among the European states found its complement in the competition between the Christian Churches – Roman Catholicism and Protestantism – both of which sought to reconcile the crimes of their ruling classes and their own iniquities with the social justice principles of Jesus Christ.

The advent of the Non-Conformist denominations

(Methodists, Baptists, and Moravians) in the second half of the eighteenth century not only broadened the field of competition among the Christian Churches, but also sharpened the rivalry between them and simultaneously exposed their spiritual fraudulence. The Non-Conformist Churches, persecuted by the Established Churches (Roman Catholicism, Anglicanism, Presbyterianism, the Dutch Reformed Church, and Lutheranism) and the plantocracy, found a natural ally in the industrialists and financiers whose further expansion was held back by the plantation system and the institution of slavery.

To break the power of the plantocracy and its religious allies, the industrialists and the Non-Conformists threw their support behind the Abolition Movement. Thus, the abolition of African slave labor was as important to the industrialists and financiers, Methodists and Baptists, as it was to the African slaves. It represented the victory of industrial over agrarian capital; the creation of a new, vast, lucrative market for the industrial capitalists; the emancipation of the Non-Conformist Churches from ecclesiastical tyranny; a change in the form of exploitation from chattel to wage slavery; and the transformation of the slaves into emancipated unequals.

The post-Emancipation period was marked by the further institutionalization of racism; the passage of iniquitous legislation and regulations to compel the ex-slaves to remain on the plantations as a source of cheap labor and as a captive consumer market; and the implementation of economic and social measures calculated to create a wedge between poor Europeans, Africans, Mulattoes, Mestizos and Asians. The Christian Churches were entrusted with the education of the colonized – with the task of creating, without coercion, a submissive, hard-working, god-fearing, and law-abiding laboring class, and a class of social functionaries with an undying loyalty to colonialism, neo-colonialism and Western culture and concept of social organization.

The educational system was in accordance with the class and racial supremacism fostered by the colonizers. Its purpose, so well outlined by the psychiatrist and political theorist, Frantz Fanon, of Martinique, in his masterpiece, *The Wretched of the Earth,* was essentially the degradation of the cultural heritage of the ex-slaves and other non-white peoples; the glorification of the culture and accomplishments of the Europeans; and the inculcation of the colonized, especially the Africans, with a feeling of worthlessness and contempt for their races, customs and creative abilities.

The destruction of African civilization by the Europeans and the continent's subsequent economic decay were propagandized by the destroyers and cited as "further evidence" of the African people's inferiority. This blatant misrepresentation, a vital element of the colonial educational system, was so devastatingly effective that Caribbean and North and South American people of African descent generally deemed it an insult to be called Africans, and those with a lighter shade of color considered themselves superior to their brothers and sisters with a darker shade.

This philosophy of racism was articulated by the leading historians, social scientists, statesmen, theologians, philosophers, geneticists, anthropologists, novelists and other writers and was adopted by the ruling classes of Europe and the United States as justification for the exploitation and oppression of the non-white peoples of the world. And this theory of the superiority of the Teutonic and "Aryan" people over all others and their assertion of a "moral", "natural" and "god-given" right to impose their concept of economic, political, social and juridical organization on the rest of humanity has remained a central feature of the ideologies of the Western states.

The victory of the industrial capitalists over the plantocracy was followed by the removal of restrictions on foreign products into the "mother-countries." Caribbean planters who had previously benefited from these restrictions were severely affected by their removal. Many of them became bankrupt; numerous estates were abandoned; and the people of the region experienced several decades of intense economic hardships. At the same time local industrial production and competition remained forbidden by the provisions of the Navigation Acts which restricted local manufacture.

The development of industrial and financial monopolies toward the end of the 19th century sounded the death knell for the free enterprise system and intensified the political and military conflicts among the European and North American ruling classes. The US commercial and industrial interests in the Caribbean is almost as old as the republic itself. US capital began to permeate the Caribbean economy from as early as the turn of the 19th century. The conquest of Cuba and Puerto Rico by the United States in 1898, its occupation of the Dominican Republic and Haiti in 1915, its seizure of the Canal Zone from Colombia, and its purchase of the former Danish Caribbean (St. Croix, St. Thomas,

St. John) two years later, served to transform it into a leading economic and political force in the region. The hold exercised by the US ruling class over the Caribbean became even tighter at the end of the First World War and, by the end of the Second, it had become the pivotal economic and political force in the entire region.

Such is the unpleasant historical legacy that Western writers and commentators have painstakingly tried to bury in obscurity, while simultaneously transmutating the Caribbean odyssey into a white-washed story of "progress". They confuse and obfuscate the injustices perpetrated against the people under such misleading and nebulous terms as "balance of power", "democracy", and "economic freedom" without showing how these concepts, policies and practices apply to and benefit the masses of the people.

They conceal the unpleasant truths of the people's history in the subterranean passages of sociological, anthropological, ethnological, and other "scholarship". Through the liberal use of aesthetic data, they seek to establish a new foundation and starting point for an understanding of Caribbean politics. The evidence of this concealment is laid bare with the slightest penetration of the facade that enshrouds the political and economic history. However, an understanding of the people's religious and cultural history not only helps to illuminate the region's economics and politics but also exposes the social and political contradictions of the religions themselves.

SECTION ONE

THE ROLE OF CHRISTIANITY
IN CARIBBEAN HISTORY

Christianity, a religion that professes the ideas and principles of Jesus Christ, accompanied the European conquerors to the New World as the institution that would ostensibly bring civilization to the "heathen savages." When Columbus set out on his first voyage in 1492, his instructions from the Spanish monarchy were to take by force anything that did not belong to Christians. Amos Fiske noted:

> He was to seize on the way anything that might belong to the "heathen", as a preliminary to their conversion, simply because the "heathen" were assumed to have no rights of possession, and not because the previous existence of the property was unknown. The so-called "right of discovery", as superior to the right of possession, was a peculiar conception of fifteenth-century Christianity.[1]

To appreciate this seemingly paradoxical behavior of the Christian Church and State, as well as the arrogance of Pope Alexander VI who divided the world between Spain and Portugal in 1493, a few brief statements on the historical evolution of Christianity is appropriate.

During the first, second, and third centuries, A.D., Christianity was a mobilizing, organizing and galvanizing force among the poor, oppressed and enslaved peoples of the Middle East, North Africa and Europe. It was a nonviolent but profoundly revolutionary creed that boldly defied the secular and religious might of the Roman Empire. For its militant advocacy, thousands of its adherents were fed to the lions in the empire's arenas, crucified, cremated, or otherwise brutalized. In time, their commitment, steadfastness, and perseverance won them many converts. However, Christianity's revolutionary character had begun to experience an erosion as increasing numbers of wealthy Romans and imperial officials became converts. Ultimately, the Emperor Constantine (306-337) himself became a convert and adopted Christianity as the official religion of the Roman Empire. The religion was subsequently stripped of its remaining revolutionary elements and transformed into the ideological and institutional arm of imperial Rome.

Christianity became known as Roman Catholicism in the Western Roman Empire and in the Eastern Roman Empire,[1] the Orthodox Church. During the Middle Ages, Roman Catholicism, was the backbone of feudalism; the official censor of both religious and secular thought; and the accuser, judge, jury and executioner of alleged infractors of its prescribed rules of religious and social conduct. Numerous religious and secular thinkers who dared to

---

[1] The Roman Empire had become so immense and difficult to administer that in A.D. 293, the Emperor Diocletian divided it into two - Eastern and Western. The Western Empire with its capital at Rome was overrun several times between the years 410-455 A.D. by the Goths, Visigoths, the Huns, and the Vandals. The Western Empire officially came to an end in A.D. 476 when the last emperor of Rome, Romulus Augustulus, was ousted from power. The Eastern Empire with its capital at Byzantium (renamed Constantinople by the Emperor Constantine), the Byzantine Empire, lasted for another one thousand years until its conquest in 1453 by the Muslim Ottoman Turks. In the Byzantine Empire, Christianity developed as the Christian Orthodox Church and in the West, Roman Catholicism. After the destruction of the Western Roman Empire, Roman Catholicism continued to exist in the fragmented territories and in the Holy Roman Empire established by Charlemagne in A.D. 800.

question the Church's interpretation of the scriptures and theology were fed to the flames by the leaders of the Church and later the Inquisition. Giordano Bruno, for example, was burnt at the stake by the Inquisition for expressing the belief that the world was heliocentric; [2]while Galileo Galilei, on pains of death, was obliged to repudiate a similar thesis.

The organization of the Church reflected the same type of hierarchical structure and social stratification as the feudal states. Under the system of primogeniture, the first son would inherit the kingdom, dukedom, earldom, and so forth, and the second and third sons would enter the army or the Church. The ordination of the sons of the aristocracy had nothing to do with ecclesiastical inclination or "religious vocation". It was simply a question of social background.

Birth, not religious devotion, dedication, nor longevity of meritorious service was the distinguishing factor between cardinals, archbishops, abbots, bishops, and friars. The cardinals, abbots and bishops were usually members of the aristocracy; the monsignors came from the gentry; and the friars from the laboring classes. The Catholic Church, like other subsequent Christian denominations, promoted the concept of women's inferiority and inequality among women. Thus, women could not hope to serve in any other capacity than that of nuns, although the daughters of prominent families

---

[2]Bruno and Galilei scientifically proved that the sun was the center of the universe (heliocentric), which contradicted the teachings of the Roman Catholic Church, namely, that the earth was the center of the universe (geocentric). Bruno refused to recant and was burnt at the stake. Galilei repudiated his thesis and lived.

could aspire to become Mothers Superior.

So inseparable was the unity between Church and State – between Roman Catholicism and feudalism – that an assault against the one was simultaneously an assault against the other. Consequently, when the young emerging capitalist class began its struggle for political supremacy against the feudal order, it chose the more vulnerable of the two partners – the Church – whose greed, corruption, arrogance, intolerance and oppressiveness had produced widespread hatred among the people of Christendom. The capitalists and their theological allies – Martin Luther, Professor of Theology at the University of Wittenberg; Huldreich Zwingli, Pastor of the Munster Church in Zurich; John Calvin, a French theologian in Geneva; George Wishart and his lieutenant, John Knox, of Scotland, et al – were able to mobilize the serfs and workers who resented the payment of tithes (one-tenth of their earnings) to the Papacy in Rome; the offering of indulgences by priests as commutation of penance for wealthy "sinners" in exchange for generous monetary contributions; the working people's condition of virtual servitude to the barons[3] and guildsmen which the Church sanctioned and profited from; and their state of landlessness because of the Church's ownership of vast territorial holdings.

The emerging capitalist class was also able to win the support of philosophers and scientists whose ideas, inventions and

---

[3] Besides being tied to the land as the virtual slaves of the barons, the serfs were obliged to accept a host of affronts to their dignity. These included the right of the baron to be the first to have sexual intercourse with their wives on the night of their marriage. This social and legal practice, which was sanctioned by the Church, became known as the "Right of the First Night."

theories had been ruthlessly suppressed by the Church because of their failure to conform to its interpretation of the scriptures. In the sixteenth century Calvinism won victories in Switzerland, the Netherlands (Dutch Reformed Church), and Scotland (Presbyterianism); but its adherents in France (the Huguenots) were liquidated by the feudal Bourbons in the late sixteenth and seventeenth centuries. Martin Luther's ideas created a schism among the German aristocracy. The peasants, under the banner of Lutheranism, staged an armed revolt in an attempt to ameliorate their condition. As a result, Lutheranism temporarily triumphed in Germany as a revolutionary religion until it was adopted by the German aristocracy at the Peace of Augsburg in 1555 and transformed into an instrument for oppressing the peasant majority. The aristocracy of Norway, Sweden and Denmark also adopted Lutheranism as its new faith.

Anglicanism, the product of Henry VIII's struggle against the Papacy to win the complete allegiance of his subjects, ownership of church property and, consequently, to be head of his own country (Church and State), constituted a very limited break with Roman Catholicism. Henry was less concerned about the ceremonies and rituals of Roman Catholicism than about Papal infringement on English sovereignty. The refusal of Pope Clement to grant Henry an annulment of his marriage to Catherine of Aragon[4] to enable him to marry Anne Boleyn, provided Henry with the excuse he desired to break the power of the Papacy in his

---

[4] It was virtually impossible for Pope Clement de Medici to grant Henry an annulment of his marriage to Catherine, inasmuch as Catherine was the aunt of Charles I, King of Spain, who was also Charles V, Holy Roman Emperor, who had defeated Pope Clement on the battlefield and was at that time holding him prisoner.

country. However, it was, in essence, a political break, not a spiritual one – a break with the Papacy rather than with Roman Catholicism.

To be sure, the Pope was no longer head of the English Church and the people were no longer required to pay tithes to Rome. The English king now replaced the Pope as head of Church and recipient of tithes. Henry's "Reformation", except for brief interludes during the reigns (1553-1559) of Mary Tudor and (1653-1658) Oliver Cromwell, was continued by his successors, but to the present day the distinction between Anglicanism and Roman Catholicism remains more formal than substantive. Under Elizabeth I, the Church of England embraced both Catholic and Protestant elements. The understanding was that the Anglican Church followed the *via media* or middle way between the extremes of Protestantism and Catholicism.[2] Just as the political struggle against the aristocracy was characterized by indecisiveness, so was the English religious Reformation. Indeed, this indecisiveness on the part of the British bourgeoisie has resulted in the retention of the aristocracy – a superfluous and extremely expensive anachronism – whose trappings and pageantry still hold the capitalist ruling class enthralled.

Therefore, to the extent that Calvinism, Puritanism (a sect that demanded a more substantive and clearer distinction between Anglicanism and Roman Catholicism), Lutheranism, and the Dutch Reformed Church struggled against feudo-clerical bondage in Europe, they were revolutionary. However, they came to the Caribbean and the New World, in general, in the capacity of aggressors, oppressors and consolidators of empires – the institutions that sought to reconcile plunder, pillage, massacres, and human enslavement with the social justice ethics of early Christianity.

Like Roman Catholicism in the Spanish, Portuguese and French Empires, Protestantism became the alter ego of the British, Dutch and Danish Empires – the partner whose jurisdiction encompassed spiritual, cultural and intellectual suppression of the Amerindian and African peoples. Roman Catholicism and Protestantism had a vital stake in exploitation and oppression and were among the principal beneficiaries of colonialism and human servitude, investing in and profiting from the Amerindian and African Slave Trade, exercising dominion over numerous and vast plantations and hundreds of thousands of slaves. Hence, the greed, corruption, arrogance and disdain for human rights that characterized Roman Catholicism in Europe were painfully manifested by both Catholics and Protestants in the Caribbean and the New World.

Roman Catholicism
(The Spanish Catholic Church)

The Roman Catholic Church of Spain was no more interested in "civilizing" and "saving" the souls of the "heathen savages" than were the conquistadores. The exceptional Dominican friar, Bartolomé de las Casas, wrote extensively about the greed of the Spanish priests; about their acquiescence in the enslavement and extermination of the Amerindians; and about the virtual repudiation of the canons of St. Augustine and Judaeo-Christian ethics in general. A considerable number of priests from the several Catholic Orders – Dominicans, Carmelites, Franciscans, Jeronimites, and Hieronymites – came to the New World during the sixteenth century. For the most part, they became participants in, or at best, passive onlookers at the plunder, rape, enslavement and genocide of the Amerindians. Vast areas of land were appropriated by the Church for the establishment of monasteries, convents and plantations with the labor of Amerindian slaves.

Martín Fernandez de Enciso, in about 1513, argued that God had apportioned the Indies to the Spaniards in much the same way that he had given the Promised Land to the Jews.[3] Just as the slaughter and enslavement of the Canaanites by the Israelites, in their conquest of Canaan by force of arms, met with God's approval because the Canaanites were "idolaters", so was the slaughter and enslavement of the Amerindians by the Spaniards. According to Enciso:

> The King of Spain might very justly send men to require those idolatrous Indians to hand over their land to him for it was given him by the Pope. If the Indians would not do this, he might justly wage war against them, kill

them and enslave those captured in war, precisely as Joshua treated the inhabitants of the land of Canaan.[4]

An appreciable amount of idealism, however, punctuated the otherwise universal arrogance, cruelty and barbarism of the Spanish colonizers. Nicolás de Ovando was ordered by the monarchy, among other things, to organize the Amerindians into villages and that anything taken away from them should be paid for according to its worth. Captain James Southey cites some of these orders:

> The superintendents of the villages were to induce them to wear clothes, and to have them taught the common arts of life. A church was to be built in each village, and particular care taken to convert the natives to Christianity. A school-room was to be built, and the children of each village, twice every day, to be instructed in reading, writing, and the doctrines of the church.[5]

None of the above orders, which were concomitant with the order to appropriate the lands of the Amerindians and reduce to slavery those who refused to adopt Roman Catholicism as their religion, were obeyed by the Spaniards. In fact the Spaniards who first came to the New World were not interested in tilling the soil or teaching the catechism to the Amerindians. They were restless and in search of adventure and glory. And above all, they were hungry for gold, silver, and precious stones. When Columbus departed from Haiti in December 1492 to explore Jamaica and Cuba, he instructed his lieutenant to leave the Amerindians alone and to report on the island and its products. These instructions were flagrantly disobeyed. Selden Rodman noted:

> The Spaniards needed food -- Las Casas wrote that "one Spaniard ate more in a day than a whole family of

natives would consume in a month" -- and to get it they resorted to whippings and enslavement. It is amazing that in this most fertile of countries the Spaniards never did become independent of imported food supplies. Why? "Although the soil is very black and good, ...they have not yet found the way nor the time to sow; *the reason is that nobody wants to live in these countries.*" Only Columbus himself and a few idealists thought in terms of a permanent colony and of Catholicizing the natives; the rest of the Spaniards were out for gold and only gold.[6]

In 1513, Diego Columbus, annoyed by the absence of gold in the islands of the Bahamas, Curacao, Aruba and Bonaire, declared them *islas inútiles* (useless islands). This decree served as an indirect sentence of enslavement or death to the "useless" people who inhabited these islands. Within a few years the inhabitants were rounded up by Spanish slave traders and sold to the owners of the mines and encomiendas (land consisting of entire villages along with its inhabitants) in Hispaniola. Leading members of the Roman Catholic Church in Hispaniola profited from this lucrative trade.

Although conversion of the Amerindians was, in many ways, rendered ineffective by the greed of the Spanish conquistadores and adventurers, a significant number of Church leaders worked in concert with the secular leaders and were the beneficiaries of their treachery to the Amerindians. However, there were other members of the Church, albeit a small minority, who protested against these acts of wanton cruelty. Fr. Antonio Montesinos, a Spanish priest in Santo Domingo, conducted a valiant struggle against the inhumanity of his countrymen. He castigated the Spanish conquerors for their acts of evil against the Amerindians and questioned their right to appropriate their lands and rule over them. Montesinos was rebuked by the Spanish monarch, but his courageous advocacy had sparked a debate in Spain which ultimately led to the promulgation of the *Ley de Burgos* in 1512, providing, among other things, the termination of the sale and enslavement of Amerindians and the right of the Amerindians to be paid for their labor. The law, however, did not bring to an end the prevailing practice.

The first missionaries to Curacao, Aruba and Bonaire, the Hieronymites, appealed to Cardinal Cisneros in Spain to investigate with a view towards terminating the abuses and deprivations inflicted on the Amerindians by the Spanish conquerors. In Cuba, Bartolomé de las Casas and his Franciscan friend Father Rentería waged a courageous struggle in the Spanish Cortés on behalf of the Amerindians. Bartolomé de las Casas is worthy of special mention. He first came to the New World with Columbus on his third voyage in 1498. Four years later he returned with Nicolás de Ovando who was appointed Governor of the Indies by King Ferdinand and Queen Isabella of Spain in 1501. Within the next ten years, he became the first priest to be ordained in the New World; served under Diego Velasquez who, like Ovando, was a principal in the genocide of the Amerindians; amassed a small fortune for himself; and was the owner of a large number of Amerindian slaves. He then experienced a spiritual metamorphosis which resulted in the complete transformation of his life. He gave up his material possessions; liberated his slaves; and became the indefatigable advocate of the Amerindians and the outspoken critic of the barbarity and inhumanity of his fellow Spaniards. For his zealous defense of the Amerindians, he was dubbed a "fanatic" by his detractors. It should be pointed out, however, that it was Las Casas who, in an attempt to save the Amerindians, recommended to the Spanish monarch, Charles V, African slavery as a substitute.

> The subject of Las Casas' fanaticism, which occupied him for the remaining fifty years of his very long life, was the inhumanity and most unchristian treatment of the Indians by his fellow country-men – a state of affairs which the good bishop did much to alleviate but was powerless to change. His horrendous error, committed in 1517 as the clinching argument in a plea to Charles V to save the Indians from slavery, was to suggest that their liberation be made palatable by giving every Spanish resident in the Americas the right to import twelve Negro slaves. In Las Casas' defense – he himself made none, retiring into a monastery for eight years to expiate his shame – it may be said that slavery was already an established institution in Europe, that Africans in small numbers had already been brought to Hispaniola by Ovando as early as 1503 to work the mines, and that an ecclesiastical point still unresolved was whether a man with black skin could have a "soul."[7]

In 1526 Juan Martínez de Ampúes, a wealthy and influential soldier in Santo Domingo, was appointed factor and made a special appeal to the Spanish monarch on behalf of the Amerindians of Curacao, Aruba and Bonaire. King Charles V placed the islands under the protection of Ampúes and prohibited any further abduction and enslavement of the population. Ampúes was successful in recovering a few hundred Amerindians who had been abducted and enslaved in Hispaniola. Included in the royal order, however, was the stipulation that Ampúes should have a number of priests accompany him to the islands to administer to the "spiritual needs" of the Amerindians. Cornelis Goslinga noted:

> During the first three decades after their discovery, when the islands formed part of the ecclesiastical realm of

Santo Domingo, little or no effort was made to convert the inhabitants or instruct them in the Roman Catholic faith. But in 1526, with the appointment of Ampúes as factor, it was stipulated that he take with him two priests to assume spiritual leadership over the Indians. If the natives refused to accept the Christian doctrine and clung to their former cult, they were to be sold forthwith into slavery.[8]

Thus, the naked terror and the threat thereof, which the Spanish conquerors applied against the Amerindians to dispossess them of their possessions were also used to strip them of their religion and culture. Pursuant to the above referenced instructions, a chapel was erected in the island of Curacao in 1527. However, until the seventeenth century when the Dutch captured the islands, very little was achieved by the priests, many of whom abandoned the area for the lucrative colonies of Mexico and Peru.

In the island of Cuba the Jeronimite Order of Monks, in whose charge some of the remaining Amerindians had been placed for protection and spiritual guidance, was extremely abusive of that trust. When Diego Columbus returned to Hispaniola as governor in 1520, he found the Indians being abused by the priests to whom they had been turned over for religious instruction.[9] The priests, like their secular counterparts, were hungry for gold. In Puerto Rico, as elsewhere, the Spanish monarch received one-fifth of all the wealth stolen from the Tainos. In 1511, the royal fifth was 10,000 pesos. In 1515, with the discovery of a new gold mine, the royal fifth was increased to 25,000 pesos. And by 1520, in spite of the dwindling native population, the royal fifth was estimated at 80,000 pesos a year. From 1509 to 1539, 286,963 pesos in gold were exported to Seville, an enormous sum of money in that period.[10]

Motivated by greed, they objectively repudiated their trust

by working the Amerindians to the bones in order to enrich themselves. In 1542 Las Casas' efforts on behalf of the Amerindians culminated in the promulgation of the *New Laws* which abolished Amerindian enslavement and the inhumane treatment of the native population in the New World. By then the Amerindian population had already been so severely decimated that only a relatively small number actually benefited from the decree. In spite of the *New Laws*, Amerindian slavery was clandestinely carried on even by priests.

Cuba's economic development was delayed by the avarice of the Roman Catholic Church which demanded one-tenth of all goods produced. The ecclesiastical foundations accumulated, by the middle of the seventeenth century, a capital amounting to the then phenomenal sum of four million dollars ($4,000,000.00).[11] The cruelty of Spain's secular and clerical representatives in the New World was a nearly universal phenomenon. Here and there someone recanted or, like Bartolomé de Las Casas, refused to sacrifice the principles of his religion to the expediency of the plantation economy.[12] The Taino Amerindians, numbering several million in 1492, had been reduced to a few thousands by the time Spain's rivals came to the Caribbean in the second decade of the seventeenth century. Quisqueya (Hispaniola) and Borinquen (Puerto Rico) alone had populations in excess of 3,000,000)[13] and 600,000)[14] respectively. Indeed the Roman Catholic Church of Spain (a few of its representatives being worthy exceptions) must share with the conquistadores the guilt for this dreadful crime against humanity.

Roman Catholicism
(The French Catholic Church)

The colonization of the Lesser Antilles and the Guianas by Spain's rivals brought Roman Catholicism face to face with its "heretic" foes -- the Lutheran Church and the Reformed Church of the Netherlands, the Church of England (Anglicanism) and the Church of Scotland (Presbyterianism). Roman Catholicism, however, was strengthened by the advent of the French Roman Catholic Church. This did not mean that there was unity between the French and Spanish Catholics. They were bitter enemies because the economic and political contradictions between them greatly outweighed the spiritual commonality. In fact, the French colonist D'Esnambuc entered into an alliance with his English counterpart, Thomas Warner, to divide and settle the island of St. Christopher (St. Kitts) in defiance of Spanish claim thereto. Roman Catholicism was also strengthened by English and Irish Catholics fleeing persecution from their native countries.

A measure of religious tolerance existed in the early stages of French colonialism. This was largely due to the fact that a large number of Huguenots (French Calvinists) were among the first colonists, Huguenots like Gaspard de Coligny occupied powerful positions in the French court, and the Edict of Nantes (1598) had guaranteed freedom of conscience to them. However, as the French became more secure in their conquests, especially after the massacre of the Callinagoes (Carib Amerindians) in St. Kitts, Guadeloupe, Martinique, and Grenada, the level of tolerance waned. Accordingly, when the Edict of Nantes was revoked in 1625, all non-Catholics were forbidden to settle in the French colonies and those who were already living there were expelled. Some came and lived quietly until they were discovered by the authorities and deported. Others came and remained when enforcement became lax.

From then on, the Roman Catholic Church dominated the religious and intellectual life of the colonies. Its various religious orders owned thousands of slaves whom they forcefully baptized. The slaves not only served as laborers on the plantations but were also expected to strengthen fortifications in the colonies during attacks by rival European powers. Hence, like the Spanish Roman Catholic and the Protestant Churches, the French Catholic Church was a direct participant and beneficiary of the institution of slavery.

French Catholics, like their Spanish counterparts, proclaimed as their "primary and sacred duty" the Christianization of the Callinagoes, Tainos, and African slaves. Yet the French clerics, especially the Carmelites, were among the biggest landowners and slavemasters, and paid scant attention to their "sacred duty" of baptizing and instructing the slaves as provided by the **Code Noir** (1685) of Louis XIV. Some Jesuits and Dominicans made significant but unsuccessful attempts to evangelize the Africans and Amerindians. Their efforts were unrewarding because the Africans and Amerindians had their own religions which they were not anxious to renounce in favor of the religion of their enemies.

The French clergy were exempt from the payment of taxes and, except in Saint Domingue, the salaries of the priests were paid by the French Crown. While every white man who had no sugar was obliged to pay 6 francs in taxes for himself and for each of his slaves or free engages, the priests were entirely exempt from these payments. At the same time, the French Crown demanded and received one-third of all confiscations and fines; 2,000 pounds of sugar per year from every cabaret; and one percent of the value of all merchandise arriving in the colonies.[15]

The efforts of those priests who took their vocation seriously and tried to win converts among the Callinagoes were a dismal failure. Pere (Father) Jean Baptiste Labat underscored those failures in his *Memoirs*:

> Everything done up to the present to educate and convert the Caribs has failed. For more than thirty years our Order has maintained missionaries who have studied their language and lived among them. The missionaries have taught them the catechism and prayers, and have neglected nothing to win them to Christianity, but all their work has been fruitless. Fathers Raymond, a Breton priest, and Phillipe de Beaumont, both priests of our Order in Provence de St. Louis, lived in Dominica for five-and-twenty years without doing more than baptize a few children as they were dying, and a few adults morally certain to die within a few moments.[16]

The Jesuits in St. Vincent fared no better among the Black Caribs. Yet, instead of appreciating and conceding the fact that the Amerindians, like Europeans, had their own social organizations and institutions, as well as their own conception of the relationship between humanity and nature and between humanity and god, these priests arrogantly dismissed the universal rights of humans by concluding that it was a waste of time trying to proselytize the Amerindians because of their "superstitiousness and indifference" to things spiritual. Labat stated:

> The priests knew only too well the native wickedness of the Indians, their inconstancy and their indifference which even now still makes them regard the most solemn ceremonies merely as games. Thus when Caribs ask to be baptized it is only to get the presents which their godfathers give them. They invariably return to their vomit so as to get baptized again, and this sacrament can be repeated as often as you care to offer them a glass of rum.[17]

Between 1651 and 1654 the Callinagoes of Grenada were massacred by the French, and in 1664 the first Catholic mission was established in the island by Dominican priests. In his commentaries on the invasion and massacre of the Callinagoes of Grenada, Rev. Thomas Coke wrote:

> Du Parquet, [Governor of Guadeloupe and leader of the expedition - PH] according to his account, having collected about two hundred of his fiercest desperadoes, caused them, in conjunction with their commanders, to receive the *holy sacrament* on their embarkation; estimating, most probably, the success of their enterprize, by their ardor to serve god in embruing their hands in savage blood. On their arrival in Grenada, a cross was erected; and the banditti were compelled to kneel before it, and join in devout prayer to God for success in those murders which they were about to perpetrate.[18]

The "indifference to things spiritual," attributed to the Callinagoes by the Capuchin priests, was more in keeping with the disposition of the French settlers in the colonies. Pere Labat vividly described this state of irreligiosity among the settlers of Saint Domingue:

> I cannot help saying that I was much scandalized by the little respect shown by the people for their religion. They came to church laughing and chaffing each other as if they were about to see some show or entertainment. Especially was this the case with those on the outside of the church, who leant on the top of the fence and spoke to each other much louder than I preached, continually introducing the name of God in their conversation in a manner I could not tolerate. I warned them to stop talking three or four times as gently as I could, but as this did no good, I was obliged to complain to some officers, who compelled them to keep silent.[19]

Pere Labat made this observation during a visit to the island in 1695 and it remained the general picture throughout most of the eighteenth century. The indifference and uncooperativeness of the colonists and administrators of Haiti to religious matters rendered the priests dispensable. The activities of most priests, as a consequence, became largely secular. Even when the calibre of the colonists improved, religion was a minor concern, business and pleasure pushing it well into the background.[20] Indeed even religious activities such as Mass, baptism, burial and marriage ceremonies were more economic than spiritual, as specific fees were associated with their performance. The performance of the Roman Catholic Church in Haiti (Saint Domingue) was dismal; but the achievements of the priests in the other French colonies was somewhat different. The Jesuits established five parishes in Martinique; the Capuchins seven; and the Jacobins or Peres Blancs seven. The Religieux de la Charité had all the hospitals, and the Ursuline nuns had a convent and a school.[21]

> Priests who showed interest in the souls of the slaves were regarded as subversive; in fact the Jesuits were expelled for precisely this in 1764. "The safety of the Whites," a Governor wrote home at the time, "demands that the Negroes be kept in profound ignorance." In such an atmosphere, it is not surprising that the priests accommodated themselves to local mores. A report to the Vatican charged some of them with leading lives "so indecent . . . . that the citizens and Negroes have lost all the sentiments of religion which the Jesuits gave them."[22]

The irreligious disposition of the settlers corresponded to the material conditions prevailing in the colonies. Until the turn of the seventeenth century when they were superseded by the free enterprise system, piracy and plunder were the principal means of accumulating wealth. They provided a life of luxury for the royal families of Europe, the governors, merchants, planters, and social functionaries in the colonies. Many of the early governors were themselves ex-pirates who continued to finance "privateering" expeditions and to share in the booty. Members of the clergy were also known to have shared in the plunder of the pirates. Even Pere Labat himself reportedly partook of the spoils and enjoyed such an excellent relationship with the buccaneers that he earned the nickname *Priest of the Buccaneers.*

In his *Memoirs*, Pere Labat acknowledged this relationship and spoke highly of the generosity of the buccaneers who shared their plunder (including at times church ornaments stolen from his fellow Catholics in the Spanish colonies) with him and the French clergy. Eaden cited Pere Labat's own account of the ceremony that was given to a crew of buccaneers whose ship had arrived in the harbor in Martinique. He wrote:

> The Mass of the Virgin was celebrated with all solemnity, and I blessed three large loaves which were presented by the captain and his officers, who arrived at the church accompanied by the drums and trumpets of their corvette. At the beginning of Mass, the corvette fired a salute with all her cannons. At the Elevation of the Holy Sacrament she fired another salvo, at the Benediction a third, and finally a fourth when we sang the Te Deum after Mass. All the filibusters contributed 30 sols to the sacristy, and did so with much piety and modesty. This may surprise people in Europe where filibusters are not credited with possessing much piety, but as a matter of fact they generally give a portion of their good fortunes to the churches. If church ornaments or church linen happen to be in the prizes they capture, the filibusters always present them to their parish church.[23]

Under such circumstances, it was inevitable that the intellectual and spiritual life of the colonies would reflect the same deformities as the material life.

At the outbreak of the Haitian Revolution in 1791, most of

the clergy took flight to the Spanish colony of Santo Domingo or went into hiding in Haiti. For the next decade the country was engulfed in intermittent warfare. Religion, a matter of very low priority in more stable and peaceful times, took a definite back seat during this period. When Toussaint L'Ouverture came to power, he restored some measure of calm to the country and revived the economy. Believing the Church to be an institution that could contribute to stability and the restoration effort, he made many overtures to the priests to return and reestablish themselves in the country. James G. Leyburn wrote:

> His constitution of May 9, 1801, states that "the Catholic religion, apostolic and Roman, is the sole religion publicly professed." To obtain priests he besought the return of many who had fled the slave insurrection; he likewise turned to France, but France at this time was less than ardent in religion; nor were French priests likely to wish to come to an island ruled by blacks, particularly one which Napoleon was quite obviously planning to subdue.[24]

When Jean-Jacques Dessalines, the first ruler of independent Haiti, assumed the mantle of leadership in 1804, he spared the lives of many priests, notwithstanding the understandable rage and hatred he felt for Whites following the brutal and wanton massacre of thousands of Africans by the French Generals, Jean Baptiste Rochambeau and Victor Le Clerc, in their attempt to reimpose slavery on the Haitian people. Like Toussaint, he too sought a restoration of Roman Catholicism in Haiti, albeit with certain reforms. These included his "right to fix the limits of jurisdiction of each priest and to nominate, even to appoint cures to the vacant parishes."[25]

However, of greater concern to the Church than jurisdictional limits was the provision in Dessalines' constitution of May 1805 regarding the separation of Church and State. For the

Roman Catholic Church, which had hitherto enjoyed the privileges of being the Established Church this was a serious setback. The Church also rejected the provisions, which granted to illegitimate children the same rights as legitimate ones; and which not only sanctioned divorce, but also made it easier to obtain in Haiti than anywhere else in the Western World, to wit, by mutual consent, application by one party to the marriage, or simple allegation of incompatibility of temperament or character.[26]

Dessalines' successors, Henri Christophe and Alexandre Petión, revoked some of these provisions and, although they were not practising Catholics, made numerous attempts to appease the Catholic Church and to have it reinstated as the official religion of the country. All of their efforts, however, were rebuffed by the Vatican which refused to recognize either the Haitian state, or the provisions of its secular constitution, and it declined to allow priests to enter the country.[27] The rift between the Haitian state and the Papacy, which was more political and racial than religious, lasted for fifty-five years. During this period, Roman Catholicism, which did not have deep roots in the country before the schism, suffered a serious doctrinal erosion. Even among the ruling class, its main adherents, the doctrine had begun to incorporate non-Catholic elements. The beneficiary of this schism was Vodun which became the religion of the working masses.

Roman Catholicism in Haiti (1805-1860) had reached a level of social and moral degradation. There were no archbishop, cures, or canons; only priests. And their knowledge of the ceremonies and rituals of the religion was no better than that of their congregations. In fact the priest who did not operate as a hustler or an outright swindler had become a rare exception. Leyburn wrote:

> There were seventy so-called priests in the country in
> 1840. Some of them had once been in holy orders but

were now unfrocked: they found in Haiti not only a haven but a fertile field for gain. In addition to these religious renegades came adventurers who knew just enough of ritual and theology to use the priestly garb as a cover for easy graft. Both groups encouraged crude superstition with a view to making money. They baptized houses, boats, and doorposts, and blessed fetish charms or amulets, all for a fee. Immorality was flagrant, and many of the "priests" had mistresses and children. The debauchery of some was so notorious that Secretary-General Inginac had publicly to rebuke them and even to banish a few from the country.[28]

Such was the state of Roman Catholicism in Haiti when President Fabre Geffrard signed the Concordat with the Vatican in 1860. Roman Catholicism's role in Haiti since that time will be discussed later.

As noted previously, a minority of the Spanish and French Catholic clergy made a valiant attempt to fulfill the Church's sacred mission. The majority, however, constituted a group of scheming, avaricious and ruthless exploiters who tried to cover up their ecclesiastical betrayal with platitudinous proclamations. The Protestant clerics, on the other hand, were by far more honest. They hardly tried to conceal the fact that they were motivated more by the profits to be accrued from slave labor than by their obligation to "save the souls" of the slaves. In fact, it was not until the second half of the eighteenth century when the Non-Conformist Churches appeared on the scene that the scramble for Amerindian and African souls began to occupy the energies of the several Christian denominations.

Protestantism
(Anglicanism -- The Church of England and Presbyterianism -- The Church of Scotland)

In England the struggle between Church and State over the question of supremacy, which took a leap in the seventeenth century, was finally resolved during the early decades of the eighteenth century in favor of the State. As a consequence, the State was successful, after 1717, in stripping the Church of its remaining administrative and judicial functions. In spite of these reverses, the Church of England still exercised considerable power both in England and in the colonies. Presbyterianism, the Church of Scotland, is a British denomination which played a subordinate role to the Church of England in the colonies, but was also instrumental in furthering the aims of British imperialism. As an established church, it enjoyed most of the colonial privileges and, like the Church of England, was a valuable ally of the plantocracy. The representatives of these two denominations in the Caribbean during the early period of colonization were practically nonfunctional; partly because of the lawlessness, riotousness, debauchery, revelry and brutality that prevailed, and partly because the clergy itself was a part of that general picture.

The moral distinction between governors, clergy, pirates and adventurers was, therefore, merely one of degree, inasmuch as the New World in general and the Caribbean in particular were the dumping ground for the secular and clerical riff-raff of the mother-countries. The clergy, even if it were so inclined, had virtually nothing to do because of the irreligious disposition of the colonists. Consequently, the State, like its Spanish and French counterparts, intervened with the aim of creating religious uniformity in the colonies. The Church of England and the Church of Scotland in the Caribbean became extensions of the Bishoprics of London and Edinburgh. Church attendance was made compulsory for all settlers; but the measure proved ill-advised and very unpopular, serving as a deterrent to prospective settlers – religious and non-religious alike – and was subsequently abolished. The attempt at uniformity was ultimately abandoned during the reign of Charles II. In 1689, the Toleration Act of William and Mary provided, *inter alia*:

> [That] penal laws were no longer to be enforced against the Protestant (i.e. Dissenting) subjects of the sovereigns providing that they took the oaths of allegiance and supremacy and denounced the Catholic doctrine of transubstantiation. Quakers were excused from taking the oaths because of their abhorrence of swearing. They were asked, however, solemnly to denounce the papacy.[29]

The religious freedom granted to Dissenters, therefore, specifically excluded Catholics.

In spite of its poor spiritual performance, the Church of England wielded tremendous power in the colonies. Blasphemy, for instance, remained a misdemeanor until the twentieth century. Further, all important secular functions took place in the churches. The legislative assemblies convened in the churches (especially during the seventeenth and early eighteenth centuries) and most of the ex-officio members of the colonial legislatures were clergymen. The official records of births, deaths, baptism and marriages were kept by the Church. Sunday was set aside by the Church as a day of rest, a rule that even the most exacting slavemasters had to obey. The Church was also provided with free land and exemption from taxation.

Nevertheless, the Church of England was greatly compromised by the lack of Convocation during the first two hundred years of existence in the Caribbean. Additionally, the fact that its priests were appointed and served at the pleasure of the Governor, and planters and merchants served in the vestry negated any sense of religious independence from secular practices. In this regard, Dale Bisnauth stated:

> Clergymen held office at the pleasure of the Governor. At the level of the parish, the vestry, which was composed of planters and which functioned as a civil as well as an ecclesiastical body, dictated the policy and the programme of the parish church. The fact that the Caribbean church before 1825 lacked any kind of Convocation and the fact that without bishops residing in the area it was bereft of local spiritual leadership did not help to reduce the influence which the plantocracy had on the Church. Further, the fact that many clergymen were deficient in both learning and piety did not help to make the Church a creative force or the clergy an imaginative body.[30]

It should be noted that the non-Anglicans and non-Presbyterians (Dissenters) in the British colonies, unlike the Jews and Quakers, were a motley group of fragmented individuals with no strong religious beliefs who were easily influenced to join the Church of England or the Church of Scotland and so share in the status and privileges that could be derived from such affiliation. This was especially the case if such Dissenters became successful planters and merchants.

> In England, where the Established Church of England became the Church of the squirearchy, and Nonconformity the religion of the poorer classes, it was not unknown for many an erstwhile Dissenter to join the Established Church once he became wealthy enough to be regarded as belonging to a higher social class. He would have had, of course, to acquire the graces of his new class.[31]

As with the Dutch Lutheran and Reformed Churches, the Anglican and Presbyterian Churches excluded the African slaves from their ministration. The Society for the Propagation of Christian Knowledge (SPCK) and the Society for the Propagation of the Gospel (SPG) were established by the Anglican Church in 1699 and 1701 respectively, but their spiritual efforts were restricted to the British laboring classes which they sought to convert into "upright", "honest", "industrious", "law-abiding" and "god-fearing" citizens.

The resistance of the British and Dutch Protestants to propagating the gospel amongst Africans was not solely because of laziness and indifference, but also because they were still trying to grapple with the enormous impact resulting from the suddenness of their contact with Africans south of the Sahara. Unlike other Europeans – Greeks, Italians, Turks, Spanish and Portuguese – who have had extensive contact with Asians and Africans for centuries, this was a relatively new experience for the British, French and Dutch. Jordan wrote:

> In this respect the English experience was markedly different from that of the Spanish and Portuguese who for centuries had been in close contact with North Africa and had actually been invaded and subjected by people both darker and more highly civilized than themselves. The impact of the Negro's color was the more powerful upon Englishmen, moreover, because England's principal contact with Africans came in West Africa and the Congo where men were not merely dark but almost literally black: one of the fairest-skinned nations suddenly came face to face with one of the darkest peoples on earth.[32]

Therefore, for years the Protestant Churches, with the full support of the plantocracy, excluded Africans from their missionary work. The Anglican Church became more organized when the Sunday School Movement was developed in London during the eighteenth century. Encouraged by its successes among the British working classes, it expanded the work of the SPCK and the SPG to include the Caribbean. However, in keeping with its policy of denying instruction to the African slaves, missionary work among the oppressed was restricted to poor whites in the colonies.

The failure of the Anglican Church to administer to the "spiritual needs" of the African slaves was the basis of Pere Labat's commentary:

> The clergymen do not instruct the slaves or baptize them, and the negroes are regarded more like the beasts to whom all license is permitted so long as they do their work properly. They are allowed to have several wives and to desert them as they please, and provided that they have plenty of children, work hard, and do not get ill, their masters are quite satisfied and ask no more of them.[33]

The Anglican and Presbyterian Churches, beneficiaries of British imperialism and the institution of slavery, regarded Africans as mere commodities with the capacity to procreate and produce new material wealth; not as humans with the ability to appreciate things spiritual. The Protestant Churches rationalized this attitude on the grounds that Africans were inherently incapable of grasping instructions of such philosophical and ideological complexity.

Therefore, for more than a century and a half Christian education to African slaves was forbidden in the colonies; partly because of the hostility of the plantocracy to any kind of instruction and partly because of the Protestant Churches' own negative attitude towards non-Whites. The result was that for centuries Africans in the Caribbean were born, grew up, were married and buried in accordance with what they remembered of their own customs in conjunction with what they had acquired from their new surroundings.

The Protestant Churches deeply believed in the incapacity

of Africans to understand religious instructions. They subscribed to the view propagated at the time that Africans were stupid, ignorant, and incapable of assimilating ideas. Indeed, even the proponents of conversion were themselves not entirely free of these views, in that the rationale underlying their support for religious instruction was that it would make the slaves more tractable and useful. What is also noteworthy is the fact that the Anglican and Presbyterian Churches, in denying religious instructions to Africans, were simultaneously repudiating the Slave Code which was enacted in England in 1696 providing for such religious instructions. The Slave Code provided, *inter alia*:

> All masters, mistresses, owners, and employers are to endeavor as much as possible the instruction of their slaves in the principles of the Christian religion; and to facilitate their conversion, and do their utmost to fit them for baptism; and as soon as convenient cause all such to be baptized as they can make sensible of a Deity and the Christian faith.[34]

The Slave Code did not recognize Africans as full members of humanity, but it did concede to them the capacity to be "god-fearing" as well as to be able to assimilate Christian principles. The Church of England and the Church of Scotland, however, did not share this view and they ignored the Slave Code for more than one hundred years.

The plantocracy expressed and the members of the clergy endorsed the view that human enslavement was incompatible with Christianity. The premises they employed to arrive at that correct formulation were that Christian religious instruction was intended for humans (which the Africans were not) and that if African slaves were to gain knowledge of the principles of Judaeo-Christianity they would be misled into believing in the social and spiritual equality between themselves and their white masters. The clergymen further compounded this absurd position by subscribing to the thesis that Africans were "savages, lacking in humanity, in spite of their physical appearance; and were in fact closer to the simians than to humans (whites)." Therefore, the question of rights, secular or religious, pertained exclusively to "humans", not the enslaved and colonized. This idea was alluded to by Edward Long, who wrote:

> What the Puritans thought of their rights towards the Red Indians, the West Indian Planters thought of theirs towards the Negroes, and such was and we believe still is the attitude of the Dutch farmers of South Africa towards the natives of the Cape and the Transvaal.[35]

Unlike the American mainland colonies where the opponents and proponents of the institution of slavery debated vigorously the issues of "liberty," "rights" and "capacity" in regards to Africans, opponents of slavery in the Caribbean were centered in the United Kingdom, Spain, France, the Netherlands and Denmark. In the American colonies and, after 1776, the United States, a considerable number of individuals and organizations, secular and religious, black and white, were actively engaged in the anti-slavery movement. For example, at the Philadelphia Yearly Meeting in 1758, the Quakers renounced all future involvement in the buying and purchasing of slaves and two of their leaders, Anthony Benezet and John Woolman, became internationally renowned for their passionate and eloquent anti-slavery advocacy. Quakerism in the Caribbean, however, disappeared in a relatively short period of time. Although Baptists and Methodists in the Caribbean had no slaves of their own, they did not actively oppose the institution. They fully complied with the instructions of not commenting, orally or in writing, on anything pertaining to the institution of slavery in the colonies. Anti-slavery activism, therefore, was carried on by their co-religionists in England.

Protestantism
(The Dutch Reformed Church and the Lutheran Church)

The Dutch Reformed and Lutheran Churches were as unproductive as the Anglican and Presbyterian Churches. Their respective clergy did precious little to promote the scriptures among Europeans, let alone Amerindians and Africans. The clergy, whose views and activities were barely distinguishable from those of the planters because of its greater preoccupation with temporal rather than spiritual pursuits, was only able to establish five churches in the huge colonies of Demerara-Essequibo and Berbice as late as 1800.

During the early years of colonization, only adherents of the Dutch Reformed and Lutheran Churches were permitted to become colonists. Jews were exempted from this prohibition. As a consequence, the Dutch West India Company, which then administered the affairs of the colonies, had to ensure that all of its officials were members of either of the two churches. Although they were forbidden to perform missionary work in the colonies, Roman Catholic priests settled in Aruba, Bonaire and Curacao when enforcement of the religious restrictions became lax. Some clandestinely, but diligently worked with the slaves and free Africans until they were officially permitted to engage in large-scale and overt missionary work in the nineteenth century.

The Reformed Church and the Lutheran Church, the Established Churches in Surinam, came immediately after that colony was ceded to the Netherlands at the Treaty of Breda in 1661 in exchange for New Amsterdam (New York). Like the Churches of England and Scotland, the Reformed and Lutheran Churches had a difficult time administering to the religious needs of the settlers.

It is true that all of these denominations were in many ways deficient to carry out any spiritual function. However, even if better equipped, they would still have been unsuccessful because religion ranked so very low on the scale of priorities of the early settlers. There were very few ministers available who would be willing to work for the measly salary that was offered to them. This was so even with the imposition of taxes on the settlers to obtain funds to enable the Church to carry out its functions.

The Lutheran Church, although reformist, was less radical than the Calvinist-oriented Reformed Church. Like Henry VIII, Martin Luther was not anti-Catholic. He was opposed to the Catholic Church's usage of indulgences to "wash away the sins" of the wealthy in exchange for financial contributions. He merely wanted a cessation of these ecclesiastical improprieties. For that reason, Lutheranism, like Anglicanism, operated as a *via media* between Roman Catholicism and radical Protestantism. In the colonies, the contradictions between the Lutheran and Reformed Churches were rendered non-antagonistic primarily because of the prevailing conditions – hostile Amerindians, difficult terrain, resentful and belligerent African slaves, and the threat of attack from rival Europeans. Although both churches received the protection of the Dutch government, the Lutheran Church supported itself financially.

In Saba, St. Eustatius and St. Maarten the Reformed Church and the Lutheran Church "operated" to the exclusion of all other denominations until the first half of the eighteenth century. Between 1667 and 1735 the Reformed Church "dominated" the scene in Surinam. It was later joined by the Lutheran Church, which had a more visible presence in the colonies of Curacao, Aruba and Bonaire; but there was hardly any real evangelistic Christian religious activity until the advent of the Non-Conformist Churches.

In 1743 the Lutherans established a church in the Dutch colony of Berbice and made attempts later to extend their influence into the colonies of Demerara and Essequibo. Twenty years later their efforts were put to naught by the mighty rebellion staged by the Africans in the colony of Berbice. In the second half of the eighteenth century the Anglicans came and were later joined by a number of Non-Conformist denominations. Although the missionaries of the Reformed Church and the Lutheran Church considered it a waste of time trying to proselytize the Amerindians and Africans, they were not prepared to give their blessings to the missionaries of any other denomination who were willing to test their fortunes at "saving heathen souls." Consequently, they enjoined, with the assistance of the Dutch government, all other denominational missionaries from conducting religious work in the colonies.

Non-Conformism and Its Struggle for Survival
The Society of Friends or Quakerism

The Society of Friends or Quakerism, as it later became known, developed in England during the years 1640-1660. Its period of greatest importance and influence was during the Protectorate of Oliver Cromwell (1649-1660). The Friends were hostile to the Church of England and they challenged its ecclesiastical authority at every opportunity. The Friends refused to take oaths; considered drama and sports an abomination; and did not believe in creeds, sacraments and organized religion.

> Their authority and source of truth was the inner light from God shining in the heart of the individual. The greater part of their meeting for worship was spent in silence as they waited upon God for illumination. The silence was broken only when someone duly illuminated felt led by the Spirit to speak or to offer prayer.[36]

The end of the Protectorate had implications not only to the monarchy in England but also to the New World in general and the Caribbean in particular. The restoration of the monarchy also meant the return to prominence of the Friends' nemesis, the Church of England, which used its prestige and authority to undermine the Society wherever it existed. The Quakers' aversion to war, (an inevitable occurrence during the seventeenth and eighteenth centuries), and their attitude towards the institution of slavery (ambivalence at first, and later opposition) rendered their religious platform unattractive to most Europeans in the colonies. As a consequence, they became marginal and gradually lost their influence in islands like Barbados, Jamaica and St. Kitts where they were once prominent.

The British Virgin Islands represents a good example of the

loss of influence of the Society of Friends in the Caribbean. In 1727 Quakerism was introduced to the islands by Joshua Fielding. Although many of its relatively small membership were slaveholders, the denomination was ambivalent about the institution of slavery. The fact that the Quakers were uneasy about human enslavement brought upon them the opposition of those who did not belong to their Society.

> John Pickering around whom revolved the future prosperity of Quakerism was removed from the influential position as Lieutenant-Governor of Tortola in June, 1742, and replaced by Captain John Hunt who was described as 'a very cruel enemy to Friends, a haughty, proud, austere man whose wife had suffered cruel persecutions on account of her being one.' In explanation of the decrease of numbers in 1743, it was claimed that some members were alarmed at the prospect of persecution, due to the change.[37]

The Quakers were among the first colonists in the Virgin Islands and the Society of Friends the first Christian denomination to be established there. The Friends held high offices and were among the most prominent in the colony. The first Anglican clergyman, John Latham, who was appointed by the non-Quaker inhabitants in 1745 to combat the growth of Quakerism, actually married one of the leading Quaker women, Dorcas Powell. She was, as a consequence, disowned by the Women's Monthly Meeting.[38]

Quakerism failed in the Virgin Islands for a number of reasons: Although the Friends had African slaves, their uneasiness about the institution was deemed undesirable by the non-Quaker slaveholders. The situation became worse when slavery was outlawed by the parent organization in Pennsylvania in the 1750s. At that time, the Caribbean in general and the Virgin Islands in particular were steeped in lawlessness, cruelty, violence, war and banditry. Every able-bodied white person was needed to defend the colony against enemy incursions and slave uprisings. Accordingly, the Friends' philosophy of peace, goodwill and honesty was an anomaly which made it quite difficult to attract new recruits. Indeed the discipline demanded by Quakerism was strict even for those who were already converts. Isaac Dookhan wrote:

> In 1746, was reported 'great declension from the Christian Plainness and humble deportment which our ancient worthies were exemplary in.' Members were admonished or disowned for breaches of discipline and meetings were unattended through indifference. In 1755 it was reported that 'Meetings for business are so much neglected from a supineness among Friends that nothing more remains at present than to nominate the date such meetings will be held on.' By 1762 Meetings for business had ceased though Meetings for worship continued a little longer, and in 1763 the last letter, signed by six Friends, was sent to London. Quakerism was in effect at an end. Those who had not been rejected for breaches of discipline were removed by death culminating with that of John Pickering in 1768.[39]

The Moravian Brethren, Methodism and the Baptist Society

In the eighteenth century the Roman Catholic, Anglican, Presbyterian, Lutheran, and Dutch Reformed Churches were faced with a formidable challenge from the Non-Conformist Churches – the Moravians, Methodists and Baptists. In 1732 the Moravian Brethren of Germany came to the Caribbean and established a mission in the island of St. Thomas, Danish Virgin Islands. The Moravians, a profoundly patriarchal sect, subscribed to and participated in African slavery, but, like the Spanish and French Catholics, believed that African slaves should be provided a "Christian" education.

Teaching the slaves to be obedient to their masters was the essence of this education. And obedience was premised on the thesis that "God had created kings and queens and masters and slaves." The Moravians expressed the view that Africans were slaves because they were Canaanites – Ham's (Canaan's) descendants – who were supposedly being punished for their father's sin.[5] The slave, therefore, should be satisfied with his lot in life and should not see it in a negative light because it was "the will of God." In a nutshell, the Moravians taught that African slavery was punishment ordained by God.

The early missionaries, Leonard Dober and David Nitschmann, had arrived penniless in St. Thomas, but by 1738 the Moravian Church was the proud owner of several missions and plantations. Alarmed by the economic and spiritual successes of the Moravians, the Dutch and Danish planters, in alliance with the Roman Catholic and Dutch Reformed Churches, secured the arrest and incarceration of the missionaries. Indeed they would have surely perished in prison had not their patron, Count Zinzendorf, intervened and arranged for their release. The Count later purchased an additional plantation for the Moravian Church. Within a few years the Moravians had established themselves throughout the Danish Caribbean, but they remained victims of harassment from the planters who feared that their teaching might be "misinterpreted" and thereby create a spirit of rebellion among the slaves.

Likewise, the Roman Catholics and Lutherans regarded Moravians as dangerous rivals. Opposition to the Moravians

---

[5] According to the Book of Genesis in the Old Testament, Ham, one of the three sons of Noah, had sinned by having carnal knowledge of his inebriated father. His enraged father allegedly sentenced him to eternal damnation and declared that his descendants *(Africans, according to the Moravians)* would become servants of his brothers' children *(Caucasians).*

gradually declined when a number of influential planters in the Danish Virgin Islands became convinced that the Christianized slaves were more tractable and trustworthy than their unconverted kinfolk. According to Bisnauth:

> The Moravians had demonstrated more unwittingly than had hoped that the Codrington experiment [in Barbados] would prove: that the Christian slave was more an asset than a liability on the sugar plantation. So well had they done this that their missionaries were actually invited by planters to go to Jamaica (1754), St. Kitts (1777) and Tobago (1790).[40]

The Moravians were less successful in Surinam, Berbice, and Demerara-Essequibo where they made several attempts to conduct missionary work among the Amerindians and Africans. In 1735 they established a mission on the left bank of the Berbice River.

> From this they made journeys to the Indian settlements around. One of the brethren, named Schuman, made good progress in the language of the Arawaks, and their labours amongst that tribe were fairly successful, three hundred people living at or near their station in 1756. A terrible epidemic, followed by scarcity of provisions, soon after thinned their numbers; and their Mission, reduced to twenty three members, was totally destroyed by the revolted Negroes during the insurrection of 1763.[41]

Thus, the Great Rebellion led by Cuffee and Atta, in conjunction with hostility from the Dutch planters and the Dutch Reformed and Lutheran Churches, and the general indifference of the Amerindians and Africans collectively put an end to Moravian missionary pursuits in Berbice, Demerara and Essequibo.

A few years later the missionaries Daehne and Fischer attempted to revive the Moravian presence in the territory, but their efforts also ended in failure. In 1812 the denomination resumed its missionary work and this time succeeded in establishing a lasting presence in the region. However, as early as 1754 the Moravian Church had already established its presence in the British Caribbean and, by the end of the century, it was joined by the Baptist Society and the Methodist Church. The evangelical work of the Moravians among the Africans was successful as compared to that of the Anglicans, Presbyterians and Lutherans. However, it was very modest when compared to the work of the Baptists and Methodists. This was so because the overwhelming majority of the Africans did not accept their thesis regarding the divine character of African slavery.

The Methodists and Baptists came to the Caribbean during the fourth quarter of the eighteenth century (*circa* 1782) and within a few years had gained a significant following. Methodism was introduced by one Nathaniel Gilbert, a planter and Speaker of the Antigua Legislature, who became a convert of the denomination while on a visit to England. The Methodists and Baptists in England, like the Quakers, were opposed to the institution of slavery. The advent of these new denominations to the Caribbean was seen by the planters, Roman Catholics, Anglicans, Presbyterians, Dutch Reformists, and Lutherans as a dangerous threat to the established secular and spiritual order.

The planters were uncomfortable with these new denominations partly because of their uncertainty about the type of impact the religious teachings of the new missionaries would have on the slaves; and partly because of the need to show solidarity with their allies in the Established Churches. The planters' suspicion about these Non-Conformist denominations, however, was more fanciful than real. The Moravians, for instance, were the proud owners of thousands of slaves and they rationalized the institution on the grounds that African enslavement was sound religious doctrine.

> The Moravian Church's acceptance of the *status quo,* its advocacy that slaves also accept it because it was of divine ordering, and its emphasis on industry on the part of slave children, were calculated to entrench slavery and thus provide the sugar industry with a reliable, highly manipulable and placid labor force.[42]

The anti-slavery advocacy of the Methodists and the Baptist Society was the work of the denominations' leaders in England, not in the colonies. The missionaries were instructed on their arrival in the colonies to let their focus be on the "salvation of the souls of the slaves" and not on their earthly beings. The condition of the slaves and the institution of slavery were forbidden subjects. Nor was it permissible to correspond with anyone in England or in the colonies about these subjects. The evangelical missionaries, including the Baptists and Methodists, dutifully obeyed these instructions. Bisnauth wrote:

> Evangelical missionaries were persecuted not because they actually advocated the abolition of the slave trade but because, as the counterparts of dissenters in England, they were suspected of being in sympathy with a cause advocated by some of their co-religionists there. The fact that blacks constituted the bulk of the membership of their chapels and meeting-houses lent weight to these suspicions. But the evangelical missionaries to a man observed the instructions given to them on their arrival in the colonies.[43]

The Baptist Society was inherently more problematic for the plantocracy and the Established Churches. George Liele, founder of the Baptist Mission in the British Caribbean, was an ex-slave from the Commonwealth of Virginia. After gaining his freedom from his master, who had served as a British officer in the

American War of Independence, Liele went to Jamaica in 1783 and established a church in Kingston. The fact that he and his aide, Moses Baker, a Mulatto, were non-Europeans, contributed greatly to making their pulpit more attractive to the slaves.

These non-European missionaries did not advocate the abolition of slavery, but their very existence was a source of anger and irritation to the planters and the Established Churches for many reasons. Their mere presence was a challenge to the very foundation of the plantocracy's existence – the system of slavery. Secondly, the organization and administration of a Christian denomination and the articulation of the scriptures by Africans served to shatter the myth perpetrated by the Established Churches and the plantocracy about the moral and intellectual inferiority of Africans, their inherent incapacity to comprehend and assimilate complex religious instructions," and the "divine character" of African slavery. Finally, an African-led Christian denomination in eighteenth century Caribbean society was not only an institutional anomaly but also an intolerable rival that undermined the authority and credibility of the Established Churches and the colonial state itself.

Planter reaction to these dissident missionaries ranged from polite aloofness in Antigua and Nevis to naked aggression in Jamaica and Barbados. Notwithstanding the secular and clerical hostility, the Non-Conformists were the first to make significant gains among the Africans in the British, Danish and Dutch Caribbean. And it was their successes that persuaded the Protestant Churches to address the question of slave religious instruction.

As a consequence, in 1794 the Church of England created what it called the "Society for the Conversion and Religious Instruction and Education of the Negro Slaves in the British West Indian Islands," which immediately commenced a period of unsuccessful work among the slaves. Central to the hostility to, and the persecution of, the Non-Conformists was the opposition of their pro-active co-religionists in England to the institution of slavery. As a result, when the struggle for supremacy between the industrial capitalists and the plantocracy heightened in the early nineteenth century, the persecution of the Non-Conformist missionaries in the Caribbean, whom the planters considered agents of the industrialists, also intensified.

The Christian Denominations and the Question of Slavery

In the Spanish and French colonies the policy of excluding non-Catholics remained in force. While there were individual priests who opposed the system of slavery, there was no Catholic Order, (except the Jesuits in France, whose Society was ultimately disbanded by the French monarchy shortly before the outbreak of the Bourgeois Revolution) that actively campaigned against it. The Roman Catholic Church was the most influential denomination in the Danish Caribbean colonies where it had begun its activities in 1701, but the clergy's attitude was one of cooperation with the plantocracy. This was so because the colonial administrators were its friends and associates and the Catholic Church was itself a slaveholder.

In France the Philosophy of Reason found sympathizers not only among the laity but also among the clergy. As a result, when the French Bourgeois Revolution exploded in 1789, the class contradictions within the Catholic Church itself came out in bold relief as the lower clergy supported the Third Estate[6] and the upper clergy, the aristocracy. Indeed the Revolution's watchword: "Liberty, Equality and Fraternity" was as liberating to the lower clergy as the Edict of Emancipation was to the African slaves.

The feudo-clerical reaction existing in Spain was even more pernicious in the colonies. The corruption and ineptness that characterized the colonial administrations were also manifest among the clergy whose leaders – the bishops – were the second most important officials in the colonies. By the nineteenth century,

---

[6] The First Estate comprised the royal family and the aristocracy; the Second Estate the upper echelons of the clergy; and the Third Estate the rest of the citizenry.

the Spanish colonial bureaucracy was but a mere shadow of its former might and glory. In Cuba, the contradictions existing between the Peninsulares (Spanish merchants and businessmen living in Cuba) and the Creoles (local Cuban capitalists, primarily planters) also found expression among the clergy. Franklin W. Knight wrote:

> Above all, the Church itself was having its own internal problems. For the clergy was bitterly divided between Spanish priests and Cuban priests, each group preaching the same religious doctrine, but hopelessly separated on matters of secular opinion. The Spanish priests, like the Peninsulares, actively identified themselves with Spain and supported Spanish power on the island. This did not necessarily weaken the organization of the Church, but made the insistence of the priests in delicate matters such as slavery less likely, or merely perfunctory.[44]

Attempts at amelioration or enlightenment of the people in the colonies were ruthlessly suppressed by both State and Church. The Haitian Revolution, for instance, was opposed not only by the French upper clergy, but also by the Spanish State and Church which used its colony of Santo Domingo as a base for counterrevolution. Spanish and French Catholic priests actively aided the counterrevolution and gave aid to both the French planters and the British interventionists whose aim was to restore slavery in the French colonies.

These conflicts within the Roman Catholic Church, between the upper and the lower clergy and between Spanish and local priests, were also manifest in the Latin American Independence Wars. In Chile, Mexico, Bolivia, Argentina, Colombia, Uruguay, and Paraguay, many of the revolutionary leaders were priests from the lower clergy who fought against both the Spanish colonialists and the upper clergy. This legacy, however, was not the case in Cuba and Puerto Rico. The clergy in Cuba was the most backward and reactionary in the Caribbean and perhaps in all of Latin America. It vigorously advocated the continuation of slavery as a legal institution,[7] opposed the Cuban War of Independence and sustained a harmonious relationship with the unpatriotic and oppressive regimes throughout the first half of the twentieth century.

A notable distinction between the Roman Catholic Church and the Protestant Churches was the theoretical equality in the sight of God that the former accorded the Africans and Indians since the second half of the sixteenth century when the question as to whether an African could have a soul was affirmatively settled. A plethora of laws and rules stipulated that within the organization of the Church there could be no overt racial segregation. Religious instruction for Indian and African slaves became a legal requirement.[45] This, however, did not obscure the fact that though the Roman Catholic Church might have theoretically considered the Africans and Amerindians the spiritual equals of the colonial masters, the Church itself was a part of the engine of oppression.

> The Church was a part of the system of slavery. It supported, reinforced, and reflected the status quo. It preached obedience to the white master among the slaves, and propagandized the then present inequality and suffering as preparation for an equitable afterlife. Even though the Church may have treated its own slaves with some measure of paternal gentleness, no one could ever precisely assess how great was its moral suasion among the slaveholding laymen.[46]

Between 1720 and 1815 Evangelism had gained large numbers of converts among Africans and poor Europeans in the United States and, by the third decade of the nineteenth century,

---

[7] The Papacy finally "outlawed" slavery in the late nineteenth century after it had already been abolished by civil law.

African Methodist and Baptist churches began to appear. However, with the exception of Liele's Baptists and small pockets of African-American Episcopalians in Haiti, these African-led denominations did not really blossom in the Caribbean until after Emancipation.

The White planters in the Caribbean opposed any religious activity which, in their minds, would tend to cultivate a sense of equality and a spirit of rebellion among the slaves. Therefore, only those missionaries with strong connections in the mother-countries could conduct work among the slaves with any degree of safety. The Anglican and Presbyterian Churches in the British colonies united with the planters to fight the growing influence of the Methodists and Baptists. George Liele's fate exemplifies this Church-State intolerance. He was arrested on numerous occasions, put in chains, and incarcerated for preaching. In 1791, (the year the Haitian Revolution began) the St. Vincent Assembly passed an ordinance forbidding Baptist and Methodist evangelicals from preaching to African slaves. On June 15, 1807 an ordinance aimed at suppressing the activities of the Non-Conformists was passed by the Jamaican Assembly to "prevent the profanation of religious rites and false worshipping of God, under the pretense of preaching and teaching, by illiterate, ignorant, and ill-disposed persons, and of the mischief consequent thereupon."[47]

The Methodists, who had commenced their missionary activities in Barbados in 1788, were systematically harassed by the planters and the Anglican and Presbyterian clergy. They were accused of complicity in the 1816 revolt in the colony and, with the acquiescence of the planters, merchants and the Established Churches, their meetings were disrupted and they themselves physically abused by mobs. In 1825, as the struggle between the industrialists and the agrarian capitalists intensified, the Methodist Mission in Barbados was burnt to the ground and its head, the

Reverend William Shrewsbury, arrested and subsequently expelled from the colony. In 1815 the plantocracy enacted a law which approved of Anglican missionary work among the slaves and an increase in the salaries of the clergy. In 1824 the British government provided the Anglican Church with an annual sum of 20,000 pounds for conducting its work in the colonies. The Presbyterian Church and the Roman Catholic Church of Trinidad were the only other denominational bodies to receive this aid.[8]

A decade earlier, Moses Baker, Liele's assistant, had applied to the British Baptist Society for financial aid. In return Baker and Liele were required to share leadership of their church with the Society which sent John Rowe, a White missionary, to Jamaica in 1814. Rowe died shortly after the commencement of his ministry. In 1824, the Reverend Thomas Burchell was sent by the Society to replace Rowe. This marked the beginning of the end of African leadership of the Baptist Church in the island for the next one and a half centuries. However, by 1815 disenchantment with the Baptist Society by its African membership had already set in. Monica Schuler wrote:

> At Baker's urging, most of his followers accepted Burchell's leadership, but many who joined the Baptist Church eventually left. Baptist orthodoxy obviously had little to offer them, and they preferred a religion that combined Baptist and Myal elements in a way that deserves to be called Myalist rather than Black Baptist.[48]

While the Anglican and Presbyterian Churches were enjoying these favorable conditions, persecution of the other denominational sects had reached a crescendo. Several laws

---

[8] Trinidad, a Spanish colony, was ceded to Britain in 1797 by a treaty which obligated the new government to respect the rights of the predominantly Roman Catholic population.

calculated to restrict the scope of Non-Conformist evangelical work among the slaves were passed by the colonial assemblies. Among these laws was the Consolidated Slave Law which provided for the whipping and imprisonment of slaves found preaching and for the closing down of meeting places between the hours of sunset and dawn. The purpose of this law was to make the slaves inaccessible to the missionaries since, besides Sundays (the days on which they cultivated their garden plots in order to make some money of their own), sunset to dawn was the only period in which they did not work for their masters.

The Jamaican Assembly also passed a resolution to investigate the "sinister activities" of the Baptists and Methodists. And the Anglican and Presbyterian clergy, many of whom were Justices of the Peace, councillors, and assemblymen who shared the prejudices of their plantocratic colleagues, were among the principal architects of this persecution. By the 1820s the voices of the Methodists and Baptists became stronger in England as the industrial bourgeoisie threw its support behind them. In fact the very survival of Methodism and the Baptist Society in the Caribbean in many ways hinged on the outcome of the struggle for African emancipation.

In 1823 Thomas Buxton, William Wilberforce, Zachary Macaulay and other abolitionist legislators proposed to the British government the introduction of an alternative system of serfdom for the African slaves as part of a gradual abolition process. This was countered by Lord Canning who advocated instead the adoption of measures to merely ameliorate the condition and treatment of the slaves. The British Parliament adopted Canning's proposal and sent a dispatch to the governors of the colonies for its implementation.

In the colony of British Guiana, it was rumored among the slaves that the British monarch had granted them their liberty and that the planters were involved in a conspiracy to deprive them of it. As a result, they decided to revolt. Some of the rebellious organizers were members of the congregation of the Reverend John Smith, a Baptist missionary and an advocate of non-violence. Over the objections of the more realistic slaves, the plan for an unprecedented bloodless revolt was adopted. The plan involved the apprehension and confinement of the plantation owners, managers and overseers in the stocks. After disarming them, they (the slaves) would then persuade them to "honor the 'King's decree' granting them their liberty."

The revolt was aborted as a result of the treachery of Joseph Packard, a house slave, who informed his master of it. The colonial administration and the planters reacted swiftly and ruthlessly. Hundreds of slaves -- Christian and non-Christian -- were butchered on the East Demerara Coast, their heads severed from their bodies and mounted on pikes. Scores were arrested, "tried", and executed, including one of the leaders, Jack Gladstone, who had persuasively argued in favor of non-violence. Many slaves who fled into the jungle, like Quamina, the pacifist deacon and father of Gladstone, were hunted down and shot to death by Carib bounty hunters.

It was a bloody massacre of a people whom the persecutors knew to be victims of a misunderstanding. The barbarism of the colonial administration and the planters becomes even more glaring in light of the fact that no harm of any kind was inflicted on either European life or property. Governor Murray also ordered the arrest and trial of Reverend Smith whom he falsely accused of complicity in the plot. During his trial Smith tried in vain to persuade his accusers that he had remained faithful to his promise of not criticizing the institution of slavery or counselling disobedience among the slaves. An account of his defense notes:

> He begins by insisting that throughout his years in the
> Colony he has kept to his instructions from the London

Missionary Society to have nothing to do with the temporal conditions of the slaves. He points out that he moved his chapel away from the plantation so that he might not have to see how his flock lived. One by one he denies the charges, only admitting his aversion to slavery, believing it unnecessary for him to justify himself in this.[49]

By this time (1823), the struggle for supremacy between the plantocracy and its religious allies on the one hand, and the industrialists and their religious allies on the other, had become very acute. Rev. Smith was seen as an ally of the industrialists and, consequently, his denials were to no avail. He was found guilty of treason and put in prison pending an appeal of his case. He was later granted a reprieve, but died in prison without knowing of it.

In Jamaica the slave rebellion of 1832 led by Sam Sharpe, a slave preacher, was blamed on the Baptists. In fact it was even characterized as the Baptist War. Prominent Baptist leaders like William Knibb and Thomas Burchell were arrested and incarcerated. Schuler indicated that the reference to the uprising as the Baptist War, though understandable, was a misnomer. The blend of African and European religious beliefs and practices of the so-called Native or Black Baptists who led it, was really Myalist, not Baptist.[50]

A formidable gang of hooligans – planters calling themselves the *Colonial Church Union* – vandalized Baptist missions resulting in damages in the hundreds of thousands of pounds. Slave houses and their small garden plots from which they obtained a negligible income and sustenance were destroyed. The irony of it all is that the Baptist missionaries were discredited in the eyes of the Africans because the freedom that they said "was a-coming" had not materialized, and they had failed to identify with the insurrection.

The Assembly then enacted a law providing for the imprisonment of any free person, not qualified by the laws of Jamaica or Great Britain, who should preach or teach in meetings of "Negroes or free persons of color."[51] The fact that the British Government, which also compensated the aggrieved missionaries for the losses they had sustained, struck down this law, testified to the waning influence of the plantocracy and the growing strength of the industrialists. The alliance between the plantocracy and the Established Churches, therefore, found its antithesis in the unity of the industrialists and the Non-Conformist Churches. Central to this contradiction was the institution of African slavery, the abolition of which would result in the preeminence of the industrial capitalists and the emancipation of the Non-Conformist Churches from ecclesiastical tyranny.

For a number of reasons the struggle between Roman Catholicism and Protestantism on the one hand, and Protestantism and Non-Conformism, on the other, did not exist in Belize. The peculiar development of that colony, the absence of a plantation system and the coarse, irreligious disposition of the early colonists (pirates and lumbermen) were most discouraging to missionary work. In fact missionary work commenced in the colony about the same time that the struggle elsewhere between the plantocracy and the industrialists was nearing its peak.

Baptist missionaries were the first to arrive in Belize, a somewhat unusual occurrence, inasmuch as the Established Church always followed in the wake of the colonizers. The Baptists came to Belize in 1822, the Methodists in 1825 and the Anglicans in 1827. The antagonism between Protestantism and Non-Conformism was absent because the institution of slavery was already at an end when the Anglicans arrived; there was no longstanding relationship between the Anglican clergy and the lumbermen; and the newly arrived clergy did not have the time to cultivate a vested interest in the institution of slavery in the colony. For these reasons, the Anglican and Presbyterian clergy in Belize had no basis for carrying out the type of persecution against the Non-Conformists as did their counterparts in the other colonies.

Therefore, Baptists and Methodists were able to provide instruction to the slaves and perform baptisms and funeral ceremonies, although they were still forbidden by the Anglican Church to perform marriage ceremonies. Indeed it was not until the Anglican and Presbyterian Churches were disendowed in 1866 and disestablished in 1872 that the Non-Conformist Churches were permitted to carry out all of their clerical functions.

The second occasion in which the Anglican Church was preceded by another denominational body was in the 1720's when the Quakers established a mission in the British Virgin Islands and for a number of decades remained the only denominational body. The Anglicans came in 1742 and the Methodists in 1789. Religion had never played a central role in the lives of the white settlers of the Virgin Islands. For that reason missionary work by the Christian denominations among them was very unrewarding. They did, however, encourage religious instruction among their slaves, so long as they were satisfied that it would make the slaves more tractable and consequently more useful and valuable.[52]

In the Virgin Islands, the antagonism and competition that characterized the relationship between Protestantism and Non-Conformism gave way to assistance and cooperation. Whites were largely disinterested and Anglicanism with its pro-slavery platform was not attractive to Africans. As a consequence, Methodism was able by the turn of the nineteenth century to make thousands of converts among Africans. The Methodists, however, had to agree to let their missionary focus be on proselytizing as opposed to education, which would be the domain of the Anglicans. Dookhan wrote:

> Education, as distinct from religious instruction, was more the undertaking of the Anglican clergyman. Admitting the pre-dominance of the Methodists in spreading the gospel, when he himself had failed to an appreciable extent to attract the negroes, the Rector abandoned his earlier antagonism towards the Methodist missionaries. Cooperation replaced competition. The activities of the two missions became complimentary, the Methodists concentrating on religion, and the Anglicans on education.[53]

The Post-Emancipation Scramble for Souls

The non-involvement of the Baptists and Methodists in the institution of slavery won them a significant number of African converts after Emancipation. The Baptist Church attracted the largest following among the ex-field slaves and later, working class; and the Methodist and Anglican Churches among the Mulattoes and free Blacks and later, middle class. The Moravian Church, because of its endorsement of, and participation in the institution of slavery, became and remained a marginal denomination among working class Africans. Most of the Europeans in the colonies retained membership in the Established Churches.

The Roman Catholic, Anglican, Presbyterian, Lutheran and Dutch Reformed Churches were principal subscribers to the institution of slavery. However, unlike the Moravian Church, they were the Established Churches, *de jure*, and later *de facto*. As such, they were extremely important vehicles for social mobility. Within the first decade after Emancipation, membership in the Baptist Church multiplied a hundredfold. It had become the fourth largest denomination in the Caribbean, preceded only by Roman Catholicism, Anglicanism and Methodism.

Even today the class and color contradictions that evolved in the colonies are also manifest in the Christian Churches. These cleavages are present even in small colonies like the Cayman Islands where most of the inhabitants are Africans. The overwhelming majority of the 7,000 people in the Turks and Caicos Islands are also Africans, but the economic and social life of the colony was and continues to be controlled by Europeans who constitute less than one per cent of the population. Most Europeans live on the island of Grand Turk, and the Church of England is strongest there. Most Africans live in the Caicos Islands, and the

Baptist and Wesleyan (Methodist) Churches are strongest there.

Between 1840 and 1900 the interdenominational competition for control of the minds and souls of the people – the scramble for souls – began in earnest. The former Dutch colonies of Demerara-Essequibo and Berbice, which became known as British Guiana, were transformed into a spiritual battleground by the several Christian denominations. Roman Catholic priests from neighboring Brazil were there several decades earlier competing with the Lutherans and Moravians. The field of competition was now enlarged to include the Presbyterians, Methodists and Baptists. In 1839 the Anglican missionaries, Rev. C. Carter and W.H. Brett, were sent out by the Society for the Propagation of the Gospel to begin the process of proselytizing the Arawak Amerindians.

Rev. Carter became ill and was obliged to abandon the project and Brett decided to proceed on his own. He would have perished from malaria and hunger had it not been for the kindness of an old African woman. "On the hospitality of this poor negress, the young Missionary was for many months totally dependent. She furnished his hut from her own, shared with him her food, and nursed him through the attacks of fever which, in those swampy districts, are inevitable to Europeans."[54] But for a long time he was shunned by the Amerindians because their bohitos (priests) threatened to bring down sickness and death on any Arawak who listened to his teaching.

Reverend Brett's luck began to change when he befriended a former bohito whom he baptized and had his name changed to Cornelius. With the help of Cornelius, the wall existing between the mission and the Arawak people was gradually removed; a school was built to instruct the children in the scriptures; and the mission thenceforth began to flourish. Cornelius also provided invaluable assistance to Dr. Austin (consecrated Anglican Bishop of Guiana in 1842) in the translation of the Christian Bible into the languages of the Arawaks and Caribs. The translations were printed by the SPCK in London and became the decisive factor in securing for the Anglicans the largest following among the Amerindians in the colony.

The Anglicans, greatly aided by their preferred status as the Established Church, next turned their attention to the Chinese and the Hindu and Muslim East Indians whose religions they arrogantly condemned as "paganism." They were of the opinion that for the East Indians, having been removed from their native environment – their shrines, mosques and temples, and from their holy places – the process of conversion would have been relatively easy. In one of its early reports, the Society for the Propagation of the Gospel wrote:

> The first organized effort made amongst them (the East Indians) was to attract and educate their children. But it was difficult at that time to get the little Hindoos to attend the Ordinary Creole schools, so separate schools were opened for their benefit. A lady in Berbice, Mrs. A. Winter, established five on the estates with which her husband was connected, and the work was taken up with the clergy and others with a fair prospect of eventual success.[55]

The Anglicans later discovered that the conversion of the East Indians, even with assistance from British-educated converts from India, was not the simple process they thought it would have been. It is also noteworthy that far less attention was paid to the conversion of adult East Indians. The central focus at all times was on the children. The wisdom underlying the emphasis on children was that conversion of the parents would be facilitated through their children's involvement in the schools.

The Presbyterians were competing with their Anglican allies

for African and Asian souls in Trinidad. At first they did not fare too well, but subsequent efforts proved quite rewarding. Rev. Harricharan gave this account:

> The United Presbyterian Church of the United States established a small mission in the southern village of Iere in Trinidad in 1843, but hardship, illness and death of its missionaries occasioned the abandonment of the mission in 1853. However, the small Negro congregation with a few elders, a church building and a manse would become the humble beginnings of the first Canadian Missionary, John Morton.[56]

The Rev. John Morton ultimately became one of the first successful missionaries among the East Indians in Trinidad. Under his leadership several schools were built for East Indian and African children and membership in the Presbyterian Church multiplied tenfold.

In the Dutch colonies of Saba, St. Eustatius and St. Maarten the Lutherans, Dutch Reformed missionaries, and Anglicans had an early start on their Non-Conformist rivals. During the wars of the eighteenth century, these colonies came under British control on a number of occasions and the Anglicans and Presbyterians, following the trail made by British canons, established themselves during those periods. In Aruba, Bonaire and Curacao, however, Roman Catholicism and the Dutch Reformed Church were fully entrenched. In the colony of British Guiana, the Established Churches – the Church of England and the Church of Scotland – were the largest and third largest denominations respectively. The Roman Catholic Church, whose missionaries had worked clandestinely for nearly two centuries with the Amerindians and Africans, enjoyed a membership that was almost as large as that of the Church of England. In the Danish Caribbean, the Roman Catholics, Lutherans and Moravians were faced with competition from the Anglicans, Presbyterians and Methodists.

In the former French colonies of Dominica, St. Lucia, Grenada and St. Vincent a fierce rivalry (which had its origin in 1762 at the end of the Seven Years' War) between the Anglican and Presbyterian Churches on the one hand, and the Roman Catholic Church on the other, prevailed. The struggle became even more intense when Methodists, Baptists and Moravians entered into the competition for African souls. In the final analysis, the British ruling class had won the battle for control of the natural and human resources of these colonies, but the Anglican and Presbyterian Churches suffered a resounding defeat in the struggle to win the souls of the people and, thereby, extend influence over public affairs.

The British Protestant Churches were rejected because of their naked plunder of Roman Catholic property in the colonies and their humiliation of Catholic priests. The Protestants denied Catholic priests the right to conduct legal marriages and to officiate at funeral ceremonies. However, most obnoxious of all was the promulgation of a law which provided that Roman Catholics had to make a declaration against transubstantiation (the belief that the bread and wine at Holy Communion are changed into the body and blood of Jesus) in order to participate in the political process in the colonies. The consequence of these policy measures was an unusual strengthening of Roman Catholic conviction among the populace.

During the same period, the Non-Conformist Churches were experiencing a steady decline among their African membership. The Baptist Church lost thousands of its African members between the years 1845 and 1860. There were a number of factors responsible for this drastic decline. In the first place, the Baptist Church was introduced into the Caribbean by Africans, who resented the fact that their representation among the leadership was steadily being diminished. The ordination of a number of African ministers and the establishment of the Calabar Theological College in Jamaica in 1843 to train Baptist ministers, including Africans, failed to heal the wound.

In the second place, there was a revival of African religions (especially Shango and Myalism) following the arrival of thousands of indentured servants from West Africa. In addition, Emancipation and the ensuing millennium that the leaders of the Baptist Church had promised Africans remained elusive, and Africans had merely become emancipated unequals. A fourth reason was that the European Baptist leaders had become an integral part of the colonial establishment and were not interested in the economic and political upliftment of Africans. Finally, and of equal significance, was the conviction of the African ministers that their European counterparts did not regard them as their equals.

The ex-slaves had a sound basis for their judgment. By the 1850's persecution of the Non-Conformists had become a thing of the past and the Methodist and Baptist Churches had gained not only official respectability, but had also become subscribers to and practitioners of racism, which was institutionalized after Emancipation. These racist attitudes and prejudices were evident even among the most eminent and distinguished Baptist and Methodist clergymen of the period. In his commentary on the class and color contradictions in Haiti, the Reverend Edward B. Underhill wrote:

> The long existing feud between the brown and the black in Hayti, unchecked by the energy and superior will of the white, has been the fruitful source of its anarchy and decrepitude. It is incumbent on every friend of the negro race to discourage, and in every proper way to repress, a similar strife in Jamaica. For years to come the predominance of the European will be necessary for this

purpose – to harmonize, by impartial and just regard to the rights of all, the conflicting social elements which differing color and race produce.[57]

Reverend Underhill identifies color differences as the basis of the social contradictions in Haiti. According to him, the resolution of these social conflicts could only be provided by white leadership. Haiti, the only country in the Western Hemisphere at the time which was not ruled by Europeans, was condemned by the good Reverend for its state of "anarchy and decrepitude." Not one single word was mentioned by him about the intrigues, conspiracies, and unrelenting economic and political seige of Haiti by the Western powers which kept the country in a state of instability and zero-growth. His deep-seated bigotry is laid bare by his appeal to those who were concerned about the welfare of the African people to *"discourage and even repress any striving on the part of Africans to create another Haiti,"* that is, to rule themselves.

The eminent theologian made it clear that without European leadership Africans would become victims of their own savagery and ineptitude and degenerate into a state of anarchy. These views, incidentally, were similar to those of the philosopher David Hume and President Jefferson of the United States, among others. Reverend Underhill's commentaries about Africans in Jamaica was equally reprehensible. He stated that the "people of Jamaica are great deceivers and liars," adding that it might be a remnant of slavery influences; but that it seemed in most cases, "inherent in their character, almost a natural peculiarity."[58] This opinion regarding the relationship between Africans and Europeans was universal among Europeans, secular and clerical, in Europe and the colonies. William Wilberforce, a champion for the abolition of slavery, stated:

[A]s far as the lower classes in general were concerned,'their more lowly path has been allotted to them by the hand of God,' and that it was 'their obligation faithfully to discharge their duties' in their given station in life and 'contentedly to bear its inconveniences.'[59]

Bermuda was one of the four British colonies (the others being Barbados, Jamaica and the Bahamas) to retain the old representative form of government without African participation after Emancipation. Indeed as late as 1960 racial segregation in Bermuda had legal sanction. Africans were prohibited from entering European restaurants, nightclubs, hotels, theaters, and so forth. Africans could not play cricket or soccer with or against Europeans. If an African was caught watching a game being played by Europeans, he or she was subject to arrest.[9] The churches and schools were segregated, notwithstanding the fact that these institutions were the province of the Christian denominational bodies.

This prejudicial attitude, common among the European Christian clergymen, transferred to the victimized the conquerors' characteristics of dishonesty, cruelty and treachery and brought out in bold relief the fact that these Non-Conformist Churches, in their struggle against the institution of slavery, were in fact merely fighting for their denominational interests, for respectability and recognition, but not really for Africans. The institution of slavery was the pillar on which the wealth and power of their adversaries rested. Thus, their alliance with Africans was a calculated political measure through which changes could be secured that were

---

[9] When cricket and soccer were legally desegregated, the European clubs discontinued the playing of these games and turned to yachting, rugby, and field hockey – sports which have failed to captivate the interest of Africans because of the cost involved in pursuing them.

beneficial to the denominations' leadership.

Emancipation produced great excitement among the African slaves in the British colonies. In the French colonies anger was more widespread than happiness. Some of the slaves fled from the smaller islands even before Emancipation was proclaimed. In May 1848, there were fires and looting in Desirade and Martinique. In June 1849, Europeans on the island of Marie Galante fled from their homes and businesses in response to a rumor that Africans intended to arm themselves and attack them from all sides. The rumor did not appear to have been an idle one, because the ex-slaves did attack and make bonfires of the properties of the Europeans.

There were many factors underlying this expression of rage by the ex-slaves: in the first instance, they were outraged by the fact that they received nothing from the French ruling class after suffering centuries of indignities and humiliation. They were also anxious to have their revenge on the Europeans for the nightmare to which they subjected them between the years 1802 to 1848. Furthermore, they resented the attempt of the French colonialists to prolong the period of servitude through what they called 'the Organization of Labor" – the French version of the apprenticeship system. In addition, many of the ex-slaves were being "emancipated" for a second time by the French ruling class, and they had no intention of being enslaved again. And, finally, having been told that they were citizens, they intended to exercise the same rights as their European counterparts.

The Africans were quite correct in their analysis because the revolutionary French Government, which had conceded to them the rights of citizens in 1848, was overthrown by Louis Bonaparte who proclaimed himself Emperor of France. The colonies were then stripped of representation in the French Assembly and the rights of citizens for the ex-slaves withdrawn. It is indeed ironic that the Edict of Emancipation, which was proclaimed in 1793 by Revolutionary France liberating the African slaves, was repudiated by Napoleon Bonaparte who overthrew the First French Republic, declared himself emperor, and restored slavery into the colonies. In 1851 Louis Bonaparte, Napoleon's nephew, overthrew the Second Republic, proclaimed himself emperor, and deprived the ex-slaves of citizenship and representation in the French Assembly.

The ex-slaves in the French colonies who remained on the plantations decided to work on their own terms. The planters rejected their wage demands and the once prosperous plantations, severely weakened by competition from European beet sugar and the opening-up of the French market to foreign products, became paralyzed.

In the British colonies, immediately after Emancipation, a considerable number of ex-slaves left the plantations, purchased land by pooling their savings or simply availed themselves of vacant land, especially in mountainous areas, and established themselves as independent small farmers. Within 25 years they were the proud owners of assets in property – livestock, cattle, pigs, goats, horses, donkeys, poultry, crops, carriages, houses and land – valued at several million pounds sterling.

> The Africans, who had been paid for their overtime work during the days of apprenticeship, had saved their money by the well-known African custom of 'throwing box'. With this money they now proceeded to purchase land, for they saw clearly that it was only by owning their own land on which they would build their own homes and establish farms which no one could destroy, that they would be free from the tyranny of the planters.[60]

The purchase of small estates and the creation of several towns and villages after Emancipation were accomplished by Africans in many parts of the Caribbean, especially in British Guiana and Jamaica. Morley Ayearst also notes this point:

> Where possible some bought small holdings of their own, often a bit of a subdivided estate. In British Guiana many cooperative purchases were made by associations of freedmen. In Jamaica with its wild mountainous country, the freedmen tended to become squatters in some high valley or in remote parts in the back lands of the estates. In any case they avoided working in the cane fields if they could manage to get away. Not even high wages would tempt them.[61]

Those Africans who remained on the plantations demanded better working conditions and higher wages. During the period of slavery, the slaveholders were responsible for feeding, clothing, and providing shelter and health care to the slaves. What the planters attempted to do shortly after Emancipation was to pay the ex-slaves next to nothing for their labor while depriving them of all the amenities they had enjoyed as slaves. In British Guiana, the Africans went on strike to register their opposition to these measures.

> In 1842 they reduced the wages of field and factory hands from 48 to 32 cents per day, they discontinued allowances of food and medicine and they refused to pay for work done after a certain hour in the morning. Hog-pens were destroyed, laborers not residing on the estates were not to reap what they planted, and there was to be no fishing in the estate trenches. The Negroes answered these moves with a six week strike -- the first in Guiana.[62]

The newly emancipated slaves, having over the centuries cultivated a deep revulsion for forced labor and the institution of slavery with which it was associated, everywhere tried to liberate themselves from plantation life. In the ensuing struggle to make real the freedom that the Emancipation Act had promised, the ex-slaves made a determined effort to become independent of former masters and to extend into the years of legal freedom the social, cultural, and economic values and institutions they had cultivated zealously during slavery.[63] The planters in the British and other colonies responded to these developments by the enactment of legislation like the Vagrancy Laws of the British Caribbean "for the punishment of idle and disorderly persons, rogues and vagabonds and incorrigible rogues." They also appealed to the home governments to correct the "labor deficit" with Asian immigration.

The Spanish colony of Cuba lagged behind the rest of the Caribbean in economic and social development. In 1850, at a time when sugar and production by slave labor were at their peak in Cuba, slavery had been abolished in the British and French colonies and the struggle for abolition in the Dutch colonies was intensifying. Emancipation in the British and French colonies had a negative impact on Cuba. This, coupled with the fact that Europeans, who had hitherto represented a majority of the population, were then a mere 40 percent, created uneasiness among the Spanish ruling class and the local plantocracy. To make matters worse, the African slaves were also showing signs of uneasiness.

The slave laws of 1842 ushered in an era of increased repression for the slave population.

> In the summer of 1841 there were a number of risings on the sugar estates and the coffee plantations and in the autumn, slaves building a mansion in Havana for the largest slave owner in the country rebelled. The rebels were crushed and a new slave code instituted a pass system for slaves leaving their own plantation and substantial rewards for informers. But in March 1843, in the heart of the sugar lands near Matánzas, rebellion broke out again; several plantations were involved and this outbreak was obviously better planned than the others. Further rebellions followed in November near Cárdenas.[64]

These rebellions were all defeated, but the Spanish ruling class remained uneasy. The struggle for the abolition of slavery in Cuba found support among some Cubans with pro-independence sentiments, pro-abolitionists in Jamaica, the United Kingdom, and the United States, and the British ruling class itself. The British Government demanded that Spain honor its treaty obligations and compelled the Spanish Government to permit the establishment of a Commission in Havana to monitor the trafficking of slaves in the colony and to liberate those slaves who had been imported in violation of the 1807 Treaty abolishing the Slave Trade. Franklin Knight noted:

> In the late eighteenth century, more than 60 per cent of the population were white. By 1842 the percentage had declined to a little more than 40 per cent, and events elsewhere in the Caribbean had further increased the uneasiness about the longevity of slavery in the area. Indeed, by 1842 the Cubans were forced to defend slavery in their land, as slaveholding societies became steadily more scarce in the western world. British opposition to the slave trade was powerful and persistent.[65]

The British Government appointed as consul to Havana David Turnbull, an efficient and ebullient man who had an abhorrence for the institution of slavery. He thoroughly exercised his authority to investigate and emancipate all slaves illegally brought into the colony and became a thorn in the sides of the plantocracy and the colonial administration. He was subsequently accused of exaggerating the facts in his reports to London; provoking the danger of a slave insurrection in 1841; encouraging "emancipados" to present their claims through the British consulate; inciting his creole friends to declare an abolitionist republic under British protection; and in general, abusing his lawful powers as consul.[66] The Spanish Government demanded and obtained his removal in June 1842, but he returned to the country four months later in the capacity of Superintendent of liberated Africans. Along with his African aides who accompanied him from Jamaica, Turnbull continued his work on behalf of the illegally imported Africans.

In January 1844, the Spanish authorities in the province of Matánzas claimed that it had unearthed an alleged conspiracy whose objective was to overthrow the government, emancipate the slaves, and create a republic of free citizens. The colonial administration launched a vicious assault against the non-European middle class, mostly free Africans, slaves, and white abolitionists. This alleged conspiracy, which was called *"La Escalera"* by the administration, served as an excuse to eradicate the anti-slavery movement and destroy the rising non-European middle-class. Approximately 500 persons were tortured to death, some executed, in an attempt to make them "confess"; 1,500 imprisoned; and several hundreds, mostly free Blacks and Mulattoes, banished from the island.

Captain-General O'Donnell was determined to "kill several birds with one stone." David Turnbull and José de la Luz y Caballero, a prominent educator and writer, were among the "suspects". Turnbull was thrown in prison and his Jamaican aides summarily executed. He was subsequently released and deported only because of his diplomatic status and his British citizenship. O'Donnell also implicated and executed the well-known poet, Gabriel de la Concepción Valdes ("El Placido"), Andres Dodge (a popular dentist), and musician José Miguel Roman. The authorities then carried out a reign of terror against abolitionists and other revolutionaries, Whites and non-Whites, in a vain effort to intimidate them and suppress their ideas. One year later people were still being arrested, tortured and murdered as suspects in the alleged conspiracy.[67]

O'Donnell's ruthless actions were supported by the Cuban planters who began to feel a greater sense of security. Nevertheless, they remained skeptical about Spanish ability to contain the growing abolitionist and revolutionary sentiments that were taking deep roots inside the country. A number of them began to look towards the United States for the protection of their investment in the institution of slavery. They began to advocate U.S. annexation of the colony because of the profits that could be realized from the strengthening of economic ties with that country, and because of the security that the United States, itself a major investor in African slavery, could provide for their investment in that institution. Mary Turner noted:

> The planters, however, soon recovered from the fears induced by the slave rebellions. The market prospects for sugar seemed very good; Britain passed the Equalization of Sugar Duties Act, European and North American sugar consumption was increasing. Cuba seemed ideally suited to supply the market and, it was hoped, destroy the prospects of the beet sugar producers if only sugar production could be increased.[68]

The Cuban planters, like their counterparts in the Dutch colonies, saw Asian indentureship as a means of supplementing slave labor, increasing production, and maximizing profits. The planters in the British and French colonies looked to Asian indentureship for countering the labor demands of the African ex-slaves. Consequently, between 1845 and 1917 approximately three quarters of a million Chinese, East Indians and Javanese (Indonesians) were brought to the British, French, Dutch, Spanish and Danish Caribbean as indentured laborers. The institution of slavery still prevailed in the Dutch and Spanish colonies in the

1850s and in the French the 1840s. The institution of slavery was not affected by the introduction of Asian indentureship because the two systems were substantively similar, although legalistically and formalistically different.

> Between 1853 and 1874 Cubans imported 124,835 Chinese coolies. ... The Chinese came in overcrowded vessels, lodged closely together as the Africans had been. Their long voyage across the Pacific and the Indian Ocean took a heavy toll of lives. Yet they came to satisfy the insatiable labor demand of sugar production in a faraway tropical island. And since the mold of sugar production had already been established, they became coinheritors with the Negroes of the lowliness of caste, the abuse, the ruthless exploitation, and the rigid derogation of all those workers on the ingenio. Chinese labor in Cuba in the nineteenth century was slavery in every social aspect except the name.[69]

The contradiction between master and slave was also sharpened as a result of the late blooming sugar revolution in Cuba. Large-scale sugar production in Cuba, as elsewhere, produced many casualties. The small farmers and ranchers, who originally came to Cuba from the poorer regions of Spain – Andalusia, Extremadura, Galicia – and the Canary Islands, were engaged in tobacco, coffee cultivation and animal husbandry.[70] In Cuba they were uprooted and transformed into *guajiros* (landless whites).

The Cuban small farmers and ranchers were systematically thrown off their land in order to make way for United States "investors". From the first half of the nineteenth century U.S. capital had begun to penetrate the Cuban economy; and by 1860 the amalgamation of the sugar factories and the introduction of the railway radically transformed the sugar industry in Cuba. Huge plantations and sugar-milling centers known as *centrales* were established by the Americans. The sugar processing facilities of the local planters were primitive in comparison to the complex, steam-driven machinery of the *centrales* which could process enormous quantities of cane.

Until the 1880's African slaves were the principal source of labor for the *centrales*, but dispossessed farmers were its main employees. As a result of these developments, Cuban output per factory increased from 30 tons in 1792 to 268 tons in 1859, 500 tons in 1870, and 1,330 tons in 1890. The average output per factory in 1894 was 2,635 tons.[71] Eric Williams noted:

> By 1893, the largest plantation, 'Soledad', owned by United States capital, comprising 12,000 acres, of which 5,000 were in cane, contained 23 miles of private railway and employed 1,200 men in harvest time. Another United States enterprise, 'Santa Teresa', of 9,000 acres, represented a capital investment of US$1,565,000. 'Central Constancia', the most important sugar factory in the world at that time, produced 19,500 tons of sugar. The Cuban crop of 1894 was valued at over US$62 million. Some US$30 million were invested in the Cuban sugar industry in 1896. The 1894 sugar production in Cuba was 1,054,214 tons compared to the 260,211 tons, the combined output of the British Caribbean.[72]

The U.S. capitalists had other interests in Cuba besides sugar. It owned several tobacco, coffee and cocoa plantations, manganese and iron mines, and a number of commercial enterprises. By the 1890's its investments in Cuba was in excess of US$100 million. Trade between the two countries also soared to the hundreds of millions of dollars.

The dispossession of the small white farmers and ranchers in Cuba, like those of the United States, created a deep-seated bitterness among them. However, their anger was not directed at their dispossessors – the American and Spanish capitalists – but at the African slaves. And over the years, this anger, albeit misplaced, developed into one of the most intense forms of racial prejudice in the hemisphere. It was the Cuban Revolution of 1959 that eradicated some of its worst expressions. Jorge Duany underscored this point:

> In nineteenth-century Cuba, as two centuries before in Barbados and the other West Indian islands, the sugar revolution uprooted many small farmers, ranchers, and gardeners. In Cuba, these were absorbed into the labor force of the ingenios, and even dockyard workers, foundry workers, and other small artisans of the urban areas like Bejucal and Santiago followed suit --- sometimes under pressure, sometimes attracted by the higher wages. The slaves suffered indirectly from the displacement of these small poor farmers: many of the *guajiros* (landless whites) developed a strong racial prejudice which they vented in severe punishments for simple misdemeanors, or brutal hunting excursions after runaways.[73]

Because of its diversified economy, sugar played a lesser role in Puerto Rico and the results were markedly different. Coffee and tobacco production and cattle-ranching continued, along with sugar, to play important roles in the economy. The *jibaros*, many of whom came from a similar Spanish background as the *guajiros*, were able to retain their status as small farmers and cattle-ranchers. As sharecroppers and peasants with a stake in landownership, mostly in the mountainous, isolated, and sparsely populated areas, they had no reason for cultivating hostility to the comparatively smaller slave population.[74]

The planters in the British and French colonies hoped that Asian indentureship would render ineffective the labor demands of the Africans, reduce production costs and increase profit margins.[10]

---

[10] The planters in the Dutch and Spanish colonies believed that Asian indentureship could become an appropriate alternative to African slavery

In his commentaries on the labor dispute between the planters and the newly freed Africans, Ayearst wrote:

> The embittered planters made matters worse by refusing to continue traditional gratuities and by adopting hard bargaining practices while they continued to treat their Negro laborers with the same rough arrogance they had employed in their dealings with the slaves. The freedmen deeply resented this treatment. Furthermore, slavery had been the worst possible training for free wage-work. Slaves might work hard in their own garden plots but estate work had always meant working in gangs at a prescribed pace under constant and often brutal discipline. Above all, emancipation meant to them freedom from this kind of work, whether wages were paid or not.[75]

The expectations of the planters did not materialize for a number of reasons. The Non-Conformist missionaries who found Asian conversion to Christianity a very tedious and unrewarding activity and a number of Mulatto assemblymen (in the case of Jamaica) objected to Asian immigration on the grounds that it would weaken the position of the African laborers by allowing the planters to reduce wages. The Mulatto members of the Legislative Council, in general, had their own agenda. Convinced that only men of color should govern Jamaica and aware that they needed an expanded black electorate with an expanded economic base, they were nevertheless not revolutionary thinkers, as their actions in acquiring agricultural land and working it with African immigrants so tellingly reveal.[76] The planters were unable to raise the necessary capital to develop central factories and an efficient transportation system – key prerequisites for a viable sugar industry.

Then came what seemed to the planters to be the final and catastrophic blow. In 1840 duties in Britain on

---

which at that time was receiving widespread condemnation.

sugar from India and Mauritius had been equalized with those on West Indian sugar. Free trade had triumphed completely by 1854. Meanwhile sugar prices had been falling. Only the most efficient producers with the best sugar lands could hope to survive and many West Indian planters were bankrupted at once or after a few additional crops.[77]

In 1857 there was a severe commercial crisis in Britain – the wealthiest and most powerful of the colonial powers – which resulted in the bankruptcy of several prominent West Indian merchants who had provided credit to the planters. This crisis also had a severe impact in Cuba whose modern factories and transportation system, among other things, had transformed it into a leading sugar producer in the world. Railroads were in service in all the major sugar producing areas of the island. The capital to found the enterprises came principally from England, raised under the auspices of the Cuban Junta de Fomento. The widespread depression of 1857 in Cuba hit the railroad companies very hard, and many suffered heavy operational losses for the first time.[78]

The banks in other areas of the Caribbean also failed. Many farmers were ruined and many estates abandoned. Wages were either drastically reduced or not paid at all, and there were strikes and disorders in many colonies which felt the severe impact of the crisis. Many planters in the Bahamas, St. Lucia, Grenada and Tobago opted for the sharecropping system or *Metayage*, as it is called. This system allowed the planters to pay wages in kind rather than in cash. 'The laborer, now in 'partnership' rather than on wages, 'shared' with the planter the risks, expenses and profits of sugar production. The laborer now supplied all the manual labor necessary for the cultivation, reaping and manufacture of the canes grown on a plot of land loaned to him by the planter: the planter supplied carts, stock and machinery for the manufacture of the sugar; and the sugar produced was [theoretically] shared between them.'[79] In practice, however, the planter's share was secured before that of the laborer.

In the colony of Jamaica the depressing economic condition was but an addendum to the island's woes. According to Sir Alan Burns:

> [The economic crisis in the island was but an addendum to] the cholera epidemic in 1850-1, which caused the death of over 40,000 persons, and was followed by an epidemic of smallpox in 1852. A severe drought added to the distress, many of the white planters had been ruined and could provide no employment, and the Civil War which broke out in the US in 1861 raised the price of food which had formerly been imported in large quantities. By the beginning of 1865 the position of most of the Negro population was desperate.[80]

Commenting on the conditions existing in the colony before and after 1865, Roy Augier stated that the 'society was marked by a certain restlessness. The religious revival had involved its devotees in a long march around the island. Their provision grounds untilled, they poured out their energies, physical and emotional, in repeated acts of devotion. Their unrestrained fervour indicated how sick the society was. The American civil war had brought to all an economic depression, worsened by a succession of floods and droughts on provision grounds.'[81]

Dr. Eric Williams underscored the severity of the economic crisis in Jamaica. He wrote:

> Where there were 859 sugar estates in 1804, 646 in 1834, and 644 in 1844, the number declined to 508 in 1848 and 330 in 1854. Jamaican sugar production fell from 68,198 tons in 1828 to 29,624 tons in 1850; Jamaica's share was 15% of the world total in 1828 and 2.5% in 1850.[82]

At the same time, the policy of Lord Howick, the erstwhile abolitionist, to increase the price of land so as to make it difficult for the ex-slaves to leave the plantations and establish their own farms was still in effect. A policy of high taxes and road tolls was designed to augment the difficulties of the ex-slaves. A costly license was imposed on the producers of small quantities of sugar and coffee – a class that was almost exclusively African.

Aside from the cost, the license had to be first approved by a majority of the justices and the vestry of the parish in which the farmer lived. The producers of 200 pounds of sugar and 50 pounds of coffee or more were not required to obtain licenses. The small farmers could not get around this formidable hurdle because the cooperative pooling of resources to satisfy the legal requirement was forbidden and the license was no good outside of the parish. If they sold their produce without a license, they were subject to heavy fines and imprisonment.

The ex-slaves were further traumatized by a well-organized network of white scoundrels who, taking advantage of institutionalized racism, laid claim to properties which the ex-slaves had bought with their hard-earned money and which they had laboriously cultivated and improved for more than two decades. The courts, working in collusion with these criminals, validated the fraud by providing them with titles to the properties of the ex-slaves and notices of eviction to the true owners.

When the Africans resisted this barefaced "legal" plunder of their property, many of them were brutalized, forcefully evicted from their property, and incarcerated on trumped-up charges. Warrants were issued for the arrest of those who had escaped apprehension. Meanwhile, in British Guiana, Africans (primarily Mulattoes) who had, after Emancipation, dominated the retail trade in provisions and dry goods, were systematically displaced by

Portuguese small businessmen who had been brought to the colony as indentured laborers. The wholesale merchants withdrew the credit they had previously provided the Mulattoes, and made it available to the Portuguese instead.

Thus, as African entrepreneurs and retailers were being displaced by Europeans in some colonies, African workers and small farmers were being hammered by the severe economic crisis; unemployment; competition from the system of Asian indentureship; unfair and burdensome taxation; vindictiveness of their former masters who, in their determination to make free labor cheaper than slave labor, destroyed the homes, garden plots and the produce of African workers; and the ultimate plunder of their property by private and official scoundrels.

What is most interesting is that in the face of all these outrages there was, for all practical purposes, the telling silence from the Protestant and European Non-Conformist Churches. In Jamaica, these churches did indeed speak out against Asian indentureship, but this was a comparatively minor issue that caused no major offense to the colonial establishment. In any event, the main reason for their opposition was the great difficulty they experienced in trying to proselytize the Asians. Thus, it was the Native Baptist Church and an outspoken Mulatto assemblyman, George William Gordon, who became the voice of the African ex-slaves.

George William Gordon reminded the Governor of his duty to work in the best interest of the colony, which meant the protection of the social and legal rights of all its inhabitants. He castigated the Anglican Church for its apostasy and he exposed its spiritual noncommitment. For his outspokenness he was singled out for attack by Governor Edward John Eyre who removed him from the magistracy for making what Eyre described as "wilful misrepresentations" against the clergy of the Church of England. Gordon was described as "a most mischievous person, and one likely to do a great deal of harm amongst uneducated and excitable persons, such as are the lower classes of this country."[83]

Gordon remained undaunted and continued to speak out against the unjust treatment of the African majority. On June 9, 1862, he wrote the following letter to the Governor's Secretary:

> It is my duty to bring to His Excellency's knowledge the intense suffering of a considerable portion of the inhabitants of this city, who are pining for want, and almost daily dying of 'starvation'. ... No signs of civilization or benign influences can be traced to the corporation of Kingston. It seems stricken, and is powerless for good, and a system of hard-heartedness disgraces its existence. Seeing that all this is true, and justly cannot be denied, it becomes necessary that the Government which has encouraged an expensive and profuse system of immigration of Asiatics and others to this island take some notice, and use some efforts in relief of the suffering inhabitants and strangers of Kingston.[84]

Gordon's letter was ignored by Governor Eyre. In the early months of 1865 Gordon and other sympathetic assemblymen brought the plight of the African population to the attention of Queen Victoria of England. The Queen's assistance was sought to alleviate the desperate circumstances of the ex-slaves, and she was specifically asked to permit them to cultivate on the Crown lands in order to feed their starving families. Acting on the advice of Governor Eyre and on the lack of compassion characteristic of her class, her response (which became known as the **"Queen's Letter"**) was cold, heartless, unsympathetic, outrageously insensitive, and cruel.

The Queen's response was that the ex-slaves should solve

their problem by working hard and continuously as wage laborers at such times when their labor is wanted, and for so long as it is wanted; and that it was from their own industry and prudence, and not from any such schemes as have been suggested to them, that they must look for an improvement in their position.[85] Copies of this letter were posted all over the island. Understandably, the Africans, who had lost both their real and personal property to official and unofficial swindlers, and their means of livelihood to avaricious profit-seekers, became very angry by this manifestation of royal dismissal of their well-documented desperate condition.

Gordon attempted to discuss the situation with the Colonial Officer, but was denied access to him. On July 29, 1865, he held a public meeting at Morant Bay in the parish of St. Thomas. Among other things, he said to the large gathering:

> Poor people! Starving people! Naked people! You who have no sugar estates to work on, nor can find any other employment, we call on you to come forth! Even if you be naked, come forth and protest against the unjust representations made against you by Mr. Governor Eyre and his band of custodes. You don't require custodes to tell your woes; but you want men free of Government influence – you want honest men.[86]

Honesty and a sense of justice were fundamental threats to the men and women who occupied positions of authority in Jamaica and Britain. The calculated omission in addressing the economic and social conditions in the colonies constituted an act of criminal negligence. Emboldened by this show of official support, white swindlers continued to dispossess the ex-slaves of their land with the aid of judicial, police and military violence. The well-documented entreaties of Paul Bogle, a Native Baptist minister, to the Governor, imploring him to intervene and bring an end to these outrageous and lawless acts, fell on deaf ears.

On October 9, 1865, the police attempted to arrest a number of dispossessed African farmers against whom warrants had been issued. A large number of Africans intervened and compelled the policemen to set the captives free. Two days later a crowd of demonstrators led by Bogle assembled at the Morant Bay Courthouse where a meeting of the Parish Council was in session. The demonstrators came to protest their state of unemployment, the systematic theft of their land, as well as other social abuses. The soldiers opened fire on them, killing several persons. The incident became an uprising when a number of unemployed Africans in the city of Morant Bay entered the fray and forced the soldiers to retreat into the courthouse. The courthouse was set on fire; 15 Europeans and an indeterminate number of Africans were killed at the courthouse; and, on their way home to the village of Stony Gut the Africans attacked a number of plantations, killing three more Europeans.

Governor Eyre's response was swift and brutal. Troops were sent from Kingston and Spanish Town to encircle Morant Bay; others came from Barbados and the Bahamas; Spanish warships arrived from Cuba; and a detachment of troops came from Halifax, Canada. This mighty juggernaut was assembled by Governor Eyre to crush the rebellion of a small group of oppressed and frustrated farmers from the small village of Stony Gut. The next few days were a nightmare for the African residents of the area as European soldiers and civilians went on a rampage. Several hundred houses belonging to Africans (whether or not they had participated in the uprising) were burnt to the ground; 439 men and women were executed or hanged; approximately 1,000 men and women were publicly flogged, receiving between 50 to 100 lashes; and Paul Bogle was hanged and his body unceremoniously displayed in the Morant Bay town square. Governor Eyre characterized his actions as "a prompt and terrible retribution that is never likely to be forgotten." But "since so many were innocent," Roy Augier argues, " the act of October 1865 was not retribution, it was murder."[87]

The Governor could not miss this golden opportunity to settle scores once and for all with his old nemesis George William Gordon. He accused Gordon of being the instigator and architect of the uprising. As a consequence, Gordon, who was in Kingston at the time of the uprising, was arrested and taken to Morant Bay on a charge of high treason. On October 21, he was "tried" by court martial, sentenced to death and hanged two days later.

In Jamaica, the planters, who had opposed Governor Eyre and had petitioned for his removal prior to the uprising, solidly supported what they referred to as his "skillful handling of the incident." The Jewish **Daily Gleaner** newspaper described Eyre as "heroic". In England, his actions created a stir within the ranks of the British ruling class. Although people like the "illustrious" Sir Thomas Carlyle, Lord Cardigan, Charles Kingsley and Lord Alfred Tennyson considered Eyre "just, humane, valiant and faithful to his trusts,"[88] the British ruling class as a whole was greatly embarrassed by Eyre's barbarism. Nevertheless, a Royal Commission set up to investigate the "incident" found Eyre's declaration of martial law justified and his skill and promptitude in putting a speedy end to the rebellion praiseworthy. However, it was of the view that the punishment of death was unnecessarily frequent; the floggings reckless and barbarous; and the burning of the houses wanton and cruel. Notwithstanding this finding, Eyre was thanked by the British government and then recalled to England.

In England a valiant struggle was waged against Eyre by the members of the Jamaica Committee, consisting of John Stuart Mill (Chairman), T.S. Huxley, Goldwin Smith, Sir Thomas Fowell

Buxton, John Bright and Herbert Spencer. The Committee took Eyre to court on a charge of murder, but the case was dismissed. Charges of murder were also brought against Lieutenant Brand, the naval officer who presided over Gordon's court-martial, and Sir Alexander Nelson who confirmed the court's findings, but the Grand Jury refused to act.

There was a general silence, and lack of sympathy by the European Churches – Protestant, Roman Catholic, and Non-Conformist alike. In fact the Anglican and Presbyterian Churches were solidly behind Eyre. In light of these realities, it was not at all surprising that the African ministers and their congregations continued to desert these churches and establish their own – the African Methodist Church and the Native Baptist Church. Some of the African ministers who remained within the European Churches were later expelled for their "apostasy" and "immorality" on account of their attempting to interpret Christianity in a manner that was sensitive to the cultural traditions of their congregations.

The Shouters of Trinidad and the Shakers of St. Vincent, respectively, were expelled by the Baptist Missionary Society of England at the turn of the century. The Shakers, distinguished by the shaking of their bodies during worship, were closely related to the Shouters. The Shouter Baptist Faith is an African-influenced branch of Protestant Christianity which developed in Trinidad during the nineteenth century. The members of the Faith claim lineage from the biblical figure John The Baptist. They believe in the inerrancy of the Bible, particularly The New Testament, as the revealed Word of God. They practice adult baptism by immersion, mourning as the means of spiritual purification and advancement in the Faith, bell-ringing, and recognition of the visitation of the Holy Spirit during worship. The shouting by believers gives the Faith its distinct character – hence the name, Shouters.[89] The fact that both groups experienced "possession" and "spoke in tongues" also contributed to their expulsion.

The intolerance of the Baptist Missionary Society was taken to another level when the colonial legislature in St. Vincent enacted the Shakerism Prohibition Ordinance in 1912 at the Society's promptings. In 1917, the Legislative Council of Trinidad and Tobago enacted the Shouters Prohibition Ordinance, which was modeled after the St. Vincent version. Both religious groups were described by the colonial administrators and the *de facto* Established Churches as public nuisances and, accordingly, their followers were treated as criminals. The nightmare that the Shouter and Shaker Baptists experienced at the hands of the colonial government and their fellow Christians has been well documented by the Caribbean Historical Society.

> There was one leader Roach, who acquired his nickname, "Braveboy", from his ignoring the fruit skins and rotten eggs hurled at him while he preached on street corners. Leader Smith of Tobago - also called Cold Poke, one of the Ancients, was set upon by the police, arrested and beaten while preparing to baptize converts to the Faith in a river at San Juan. While performing baptisms in a stream, Leader Patrick of Sangre Grande was arrested, along with members of her congregation. When the case was heard in court, she received a three-month sentence, but the members were released.[90]

Thus, the Shakers and Shouters were hunted down like common criminals, arrested, beaten, jailed, convicted and sentenced for propagating the gospel. It is ironic that the Non-Conformists, especially the Baptists, would have given their blessings to such actions, simultaneously manifesting amnesia about their own persecution by the colonial governments and the Established

Churches but a few decades earlier. The persecution of the Shakers and Shouters continued unabated until 1952 when opposition to the ordinances, spearheaded by Dr. Elton George Griffith, later consecrated Archbishop, had gained such widespread support and momentum that the colonial governments were ultimately obliged to repeal them.

Racism was also the principal factor underlying the rupture that took place within the Methodist and Baptist Churches in the United States. African ministers were treated with the utmost disrespect by their European counterparts. They could not conduct sermons nor administer to a mixed-race congregation. The African members of a congregation had specific places in the Church to sit and were subject to a host of other intolerable and humiliating conditions for the privilege of membership.

In 1787, Richard Allen, a free African American, was interrupted while praying at the altar in St. George Methodist Episcopal Church in Philadelphia and told that Africans were not permitted to pray at the altar. Nor were they allowed to sit at the front of the church. Allen left the church at the end of his prayer never to return. Along with other African members of the congregation, he rented a storeroom and established the African Methodist Episcopal Zion Church (A.M.E.). and the Christian Methodist Episcopal Church.

In the Caribbean, the Roman Catholics, Anglicans, Presbyterians, Lutherans and Moravians were the principal religious enslavers of Africans and, (except for the Roman Catholics) had never attracted a large following among the African masses. However, members of the black middle class and aspirants thereto did become members of these denominations primarily for the purpose of social mobility. In general, the struggle for souls among the Christian denominations during this period brought out the insincerity and class and racial prejudices of their respective leaderships.

Education: A Major Instrument
of Colonial Control

In the post-Emancipation period the struggle for souls by the various denominations became more organized, more systematized, and more consistent with the socioeconomic and political beliefs and policies of the European ruling classes. The Christian Churches were entrusted with the task of programming the minds of the colonized, of molding them into obedient servants and laborers. Just as the abolitionist, Lord Howick, had been appointed by the British government to develop a strategy to ensure continuance of the plantation system after Emancipation under the aegis of the apprenticeship system, so was his religious counterpart, the Reverend John Sterling, chosen to "investigate the status of education in the British Caribbean" and to make recommendations reflecting the new system's interests. The Reverend's report included the following:

> Although the negroes are now under a system of limited control which secures to a certain extent their orderly and industrious conduct, in the short space of five years from the 1st of next August their performance of the functions of a laboring class in a civilized community will depend entirely on the power over their minds of the same prudential and moral motives which govern more or less the mass of the people here. If they are not so disposed as to fill these functions, property will perish in the colonies for lack of human impulsion[91]

The Reverend's report was submitted in 1835 during the period of "apprenticeship" (Lord Howick's creation) in the British colonies when the slaves were compelled to work for six years (later reduced to four), without wages, in order to compensate their masters for the "losses" they incurred as a result of Emancipation. The report laid bare the fact that a similar strategy of victimization and economic, political and spiritual exploitation was employed by the rulers of Britain against the British working class.

Reverend Sterling's major preoccupation was with the preservation of capitalist property which he thought could only be guaranteed if the laboring classes were persuaded to obey without question their regular course of industry. Thus, the same "moral motives," – "Judaeo-Christian morality" – successfully employed to control the minds and behavior of the British working classes, were again being recommended by Reverend Sterling as the instrument to control the thoughts and conduct of the ex-slaves. Just as Lord Howick's recommendation of the apprenticeship system and the post-Emancipation economic and social policies were adopted by the French, Dutch and Danish ruling classes, so too were the religious recommendations of Reverend Sterling adopted and implemented in the French, Dutch and Danish Caribbean. It was the mission of the Christian Church to ensure the success of this strategy.

The Sunday School Program, first developed in England by the Anglican Church during the eighteenth century and successfully implemented among the British working classes, was introduced into the Caribbean for both adults and children. The ex-slaves were taught the cardinal virtues: honor, obedience, honesty, temperance, industriousness and Christian piety. The glaring contradiction, however, is that while the Church was insisting on the cultivation of these virtues by the colonized, its closest friends and associates (the colonial administrators, planters and merchants – "legal" thieves, hooligans and dishonorable recalcitrants) were publicly displaying their profound contempt for the maxim: "from the sweat of thy brow shalt thou eat!"

The leaders of the various Christian denominations were not acting out of ignorance. On the contrary, they were engaged in a conscious effort to ensure the maintenance of the master-servant relationship in the Caribbean for the benefit of the local and metropolitan ruling classes. In an environment in which the people are victims of economic, political, racial, juridical and cultural oppression, the insistence by the Christian denominations on the cultivation of these virtues amounted to a demand that the subjugated accept injustice as a way of life.

After enslaving the Africans for over three hundred years, the Europeans, at the end of that period, provided them with no resources, financial or otherwise, with which to cope with a society which had been and continued to be hostile to them. On the other hand, their immediate victimizers, the planters, were compensated for the "losses" they suffered as a result of Emancipation. As far as the ruling classes were concerned, the primary duty of the lower classes was to work, to be contented with their lot and to respect their social superiors.[92] Education was seen as a path to moral reformation rather than as a lever of upward social mobility. Accordingly, the 'useful skills of reading, writing and arithmetic, together with simple craft work and a tremendous amount of moral and religious instruction, with a strong emphasis on the virtue of obedience to social superiors, were the staple of the schools.'[93]

The schools existing in the region prior to Emancipation were run by religious institutions and were very few and exclusive. These colonial schools were largely for the children of those merchants and planters who, for one reason or another, did not send them to the "mother-countries" to pursue their primary and secondary education. There were also a small number of schools which were founded by philanthropists, such as Wolmer, Codrington, Manning, and Rousea, and by organizations like Mico Trust. These were initially limited to the white middle-class, but their doors were later opened to the children of free Mulattoes.

Government involvement and support of education in the colonies was very minimal. Between 1834 and 1845 the British government provided a total of £300,000 for the education of the former slaves in the British colonies. Roy Augier noted:

> Between 1834 and 1845 the Negro Education Grant largely supported primary schools in the West Indies. But the accountants in the Imperial Parliament persistently questioned the philosophy behind these activities until the Colonial Office and the Treasury understood that it would be very difficult to get the House of Commons to vote the money necessary to sustain that policy. When in 1841 he signalled the approaching end of the Negro Education Grant, Lord John Russell justified the decision on the grounds that the Negroes were much better able to pay for the education of their children than could English labourers.[94]

Education thus continued to be the exclusive domain of the religious denominations, philanthropic individuals, and private organizations. In Barbados, for instance, the Codrington family established a secondary school (Codrington College) in the early eighteenth century and it was not until 1733 that a second school was founded by one J. Harrison, a merchant residing in the colony. Five decades later, Sir John Alleyn, Speaker of the Barbadian Assembly, established another.

Despite the paucity of schools in the colony, an educational bequest made in 1721 remained unused for more than three-quarters of a century. Several other educational bequests in Barbados and elsewhere were lost forever because of a failure to administer them. In the **Journal of Assembly** of Jamaica, according to Mr. Caldecott, there was a list of 218 legacies between 1667 and 1736, and yet there were only three schools in existence.[95]

The colonial governments were at best indifferent to

education and a majority of the European settlers in the colonies had not yet cultivated an appreciation for it. The planters opposed it because they feared that it might serve to influence the Africans to eschew plantation work and reject the culture associated with that way of life. Carl Campbell wrote:

> What was more frightening to the planters, however, was the prospect that the next generation of negroes, undisciplined by the rigour of plantation slavery, might have their alleged distaste for agriculture sharpened by exposure to literacy. Since the curriculum of the denominated day schools was literary and not agricultural, there were widespread fears on the part of the white upper classes that book learning would stimulate the negro's ambition for white collar jobs and upward social mobility.[96]

Consistent with the recommendations of Rev. Sterling, the former slaves should be provided a moral education to ensure a continued abundance of cheap agricultural labor and a retention of the substance of the pre-Emancipation master-slave relationship. In his commentary on the education of the children of the merchants and planters, Caldecott wrote:

> Most boys of the upper class were sent home for their education. The few who remained were placed under private charge of the clergy. Fewer girls were sent, because of the expense; those remaining had to be content with brief periods of governesses, with itinerating masters for music and dancing.[97]

In colonies such as Curacao, St. Eustatius, Jamaica, Surinam, St. Kitts, and Trinidad, special schools were established and maintained by Jews as early as the seventeenth century. The poor Whites of Barbados, Jamaica, Bermuda, the Bahamas, Guadeloupe, Martinique and other colonies for the most part constituted a part of the illiteracy statistics. They had no access to the prestigious academic institutions, but they enjoyed other privileges that Africans (Blacks and Mulattoes) and even Jews, however wealthy, were denied. As far as pre-Emancipation schools for the African masses were concerned, this was a rarity. In fact the law prohibiting the teaching of Africans was rigorously enforced in some colonies.

> The solitary case of a school for Negroes was that on the Codrington Trust Estates, or rather there were two, one on each Estate; they are the only schools scheduled in a Government Report of 1812 in the whole region of Barbados, Antigua, Windward Islands and Trinidad; but there was a school in Antigua belonging to the Christian Faith Society, which somehow escaped mention.[98]

The two schools cited by Caldecott were established primarily for the benefit of Mulattoes and former house slaves. The former field slaves would have to await the introduction of primary schools between the 1840s and 1870s to get access to an "education".

In an environment in which non-Europeans were regarded as sub-humans, education for Africans was the exception. This class and racial policy, amended over the years to admit a greater number of the sons and daughters of the Mulatto, Asian and Black middle class to the prestigious institutions, remained in force until the 1950s and 1960s. In the British Caribbean (1840s), the French and Danish Caribbean (1860s) and the Dutch Caribbean (1870s), a number of primary schools were established by religious and philanthropic organizations specifically for the sons and daughters of the laboring classes. All major denominations in the Caribbean participated in the primary school program. Day schools were established for little children, evening schools for adolescents, and Sunday schools for all church-goers.

Day school curricula consisted of reading, writing, language (of the "mother-countries") and religious knowledge. Arithmetic, woodwork (for boys) and needlework (for girls) were later added. The more efficient and qualified teachers taught at the institutions catering to the White and Mulatto elite; the poorly-trained and ill-equipped, at those serving the poor non-Whites. Indeed, many of these latter teachers were themselves students from the upper grades who were appointed to teach students in the lower grades. A further contradiction existed between the urban and rural areas, with the former being better served than the latter or the latter having no service at all.

Secondary schools had history, literature, and language (of the "mother-countries"), arithmetic, Latin, bookkeeping, religious knowledge, geography (primarily of Europe"), and theological history as the curricula. What the colonial powers and the churches developed in the Caribbean was essentially two separate and profoundly unequal educational systems based on class and race -- the one designed to ensure that the sons and daughters of the working classes would continue in the footsteps of their parents as agricultural laborers, nannies, gardeners and domestic servants; the other to produce civil administrators, court functionaries, and professionals; and both were designed to further the aims of colonialism.

In the British Virgin Islands, a day school was established in Road Town in 1827 by the Anglicans. By 1835, four schools were in operation: one at Virgin Gorda, one at Kingstown and two in Road Town.[99] The local government, like its counterparts in other areas of the Caribbean, provided no financial assistance to education. It gave moral support to the Christian denominations, but restricted expenditure to the maintenance of a single clergyman of the Church of England.[100] A request by the Methodist Church for financial assistance to establish more schools was denied because of the government's own indifference towards education and because the Established Anglican Church was opposed to any action that would give an edge to its competitor.

The Canadian Presbyterian Church in Trinidad understood from an early date that missionary work with the Hindu and Muslim East Indians would be best rewarded by establishing schools for their children. In furtherance of this view, it established a number of schools in the Indian communities, gained a knowledge of their language and instructed them in their own tongue. This strategy was very successful among the Hindus and it made the Presbyterians the largest Christian denomination among East Indians in Trinidad. As Rev. Harricharan noted:

> The school was the right arm of Presbyterian Evangelism and was instrumental in opening the door of many homes to the Gospel... The curriculum provided for the usual secular subjects, but the emphasis was placed upon reading, writing and arithmetic. Gardening became necessary for the boys and sewing for the girls. Religious instruction was an important ingredient of the curriculum.[101]

By 1911 the Canadian Presbyterian Mission in Trinidad was administering a total of 61 schools, 56 of which were receiving assistance from the colonial government. A Presbyterian College was also established in 1892 with the Rev. Dr. John Morton as President. Its purpose was to train and prepare local preachers for denominational service. East Indian and African converts and graduates served as lecturers at the institution. Encouraged by their successes in Trinidad, the Canadian Presbyterians then went to Grenada in 1884, St. Lucia and British Guiana in 1885 and Jamaica in 1894.

The Anglican Church in Trinidad, acknowledging its failure to attract East Indians to the mixed schools for Africans and Indians, and learning from the example of the Presbyterians, established five schools specifically for Indians in predominantly Indian areas in 1888. And within a few years, hundreds of East Indians received an education through this process.[102]

The Roman Catholic Church, the largest Christian denomination in Trinidad and the second largest among East Indians, was able to gain East Indian converts not only through the school system but also through its work among Indian lepers and other destitute members of the Indian community discarded by a cruel, inhumane and insensitive plantocracy. The plight of the East Indians, who were lured to the West with rosy promises of a bright future, is described by Rev. Harricharan:

> Health conditions were abominable and the few hospitals had poor medical facilities. There was a high incidence of hookworms, bowel ailments, dysentery, malaria, and skin diseases among the East Indians. Leprosy was fairly prevalent too.... Afflicted with debilitating illness and in destitution, swarms of beggars took to the streets in the towns, where they slept in the parks, on business premises and under archways. Ragged, unkempt, under-fed they roamed the streets by day, constantly harassed and cursed by passers-by.[103]

The compassion demonstrated by the Roman Catholics in rendering assistance to the destitute East Indians won them a lot of converts. And they were the first denomination to open their primary schools to all, irrespective of class or color.

> The principle of non-exclusiveness in primary school education had been enunciated by the first Roman Catholic Archbishop, Patrick Smith, as early as 1852 and the Roman Schools accepted children of different races and creeds. However, for the first 20 years of the East Indians' arrival in the Colony, there were hardly any East Indian children in the 30 Ward Schools and the 13 unaided Roman Catholic primary schools which existed in 1869. The main reason for their absence was the expectation that all would return to India.[104]

In the Spanish and French Caribbean colonies, all schools – primary and secondary – were initially run by the Catholic Church. Spain's concern for the intellectual development of her subjects was next to nil. The only "education" that the slaves received was instruction in the catechism of Roman Catholicism. Free Africans, Mulattoes and poor Europeans were "educated" at primary schools where the curricula largely consisted of a heavy indoctrination of Roman Catholic teachings and the glories and majesty of Spain. The children of the planters, merchants, and middle class obtained their education in Spain and other European countries and, between the 1820s and 1850s, increasingly in the United States. In the 1850s, the growing movement to have Cuba annexed by the United States, spearheaded by Creoles, many of whom had studied in the United States, created such an alarm among the Spanish ruling class that it promulgated a decree forbidding all further studies in that country.

After the overthrow of Napoleon III in 1870 and the Paris Commune[11] in the following year, the French ruling class began to woo the subject peoples in the colonies. Between 1871-1946 successive French governments pursued a utilitarian policy of assimilation in an attempt to eschew the ugly image of imperialism or be branded imperialists by their detractors. It restored the voting franchise which had been withdrawn by Napoleon and, consistent with its policy of assimilationism, provided funds for the establishment of schools for the colonized, most of which were operated by the Roman Catholic Church. The dual school system

---

[11] The first attempt by an urban industrial working class to create a government under its leadership. It was successful in establishing a government in Paris that lasted from March 18 to May 28, 1871, when it was drowned in blood by the French bourgeoisie and the military.

was a key feature of an explicit French colonial educational strategy – one for the production of local functionaries; the other for laborers, gardeners, nannies and domestics.

In the Dutch Caribbean colonies there were special schools for creole Whites, and Mulattoes. Jews continued to maintain their own schools. No provisions were made for the "Bush Negroes" and Amerindians until 1876 when elementary education was made compulsory in the colonies. In Surinam, special emphasis was placed on the process of educating African children between the ages of seven and twelve in the Dutch language, as that strategy was thought to represent the only hope of the ruling class in "Dutchifying" the colony.

The East Indians and Javanese were permitted to have instructions in their own languages, but the usage of Sranantongo by Africans in school was prohibited. In furtherance of this "Dutchification" process, a law was enacted in 1874 making it an offense for Africans to practice their traditional religious ceremonies. The Mulatto middle class actively supported the suppression of African languages and religions, because these surviving relics of African culture – its own cultural heritage – reminded it of a past it desperately wanted to forget. Thus, the Mulattoes, like the Dutch government, felt that if the Dutch system, language, and culture were to survive in Surinam it was necessary to transform the Africans whom they believed to be the best guarantors of that process.

The East Indian and Javanese agricultural laborers, their hearts and souls still in their native countries, remained virtually isolated from the rest of the society until the 1930s when Governor Kielstra made their inclusion in the "Dutchification" process the cornerstone of his policies. Their isolation was the direct result of the Dutch policy of "divide and rule", as well as their own refusal to relinquish their languages and religions in favor of Dutch and Christianity. The Christian missionaries considered it a waste of time trying to convert them and, for a while, the churches excluded them from their programs.

The conditions that were used as justification for the rigid implementation of the "Dutchification" program in Surinam were, however, virtually non-existent in the Antilles. There the ruling class was, to a measurable degree, able to adopt a system of education comparable to that of the British and French colonies. The financial contribution of the colonial governments to this dual educational system was insignificant. The planters and merchants who controlled the legislatures considered it wasteful and dangerous to educate a laboring and "inferior" class of people. They saw it as a threat to the organization of labor in the colonies. Thus, government contribution to the educational system remained negligible until the 1950s. Even when the local governments did assume a greater involvement, it was primarily in the area of administration.

In the Bahamas the first government high school was established in 1926. Of the 14 high schools in the colony in 1960, eight were run by denominational bodies, one was independent, four were grant-aided, and one was run by the government. Indeed it was not until 1946 that a Director of Education was first appointed. In 1950 a teachers' training college was founded and a technical institute was established in 1962. Even then, approximately 30 percent of the primary schools were still being operated by the churches. As late as 1959, of the 327 primary schools in British Guiana, 298 were run by Christian denominational bodies with the aid of governmental funds for equipment, maintenance of buildings, and payment of teachers' salaries. Only 21 of those schools were directly operated by the government.

In the Dominican Republic, education, hitherto the exclusive domain of the Roman Catholic Church, became the responsibility of the state after the country won its independence from Haiti in 1844. Henceforth, every cabinet had its minister of education, but the extent of government concern was exemplified by the national budget of 1857, which provided for no more than five schools in the whole country.[105] It was not until the 1880s that some semblance of an organized school system was introduced under the guidance of the Puerto Rican-born educator, Eugenio de Maria Hostos. Even then, governmental leadership remained modest.

> Hostos envisaged teacher-training schools as part of a plan to establish a centrally controlled nationwide system on the French model. In 1884 he drafted a law placing, as a first step, local authorities under an obligation to provide and finance primary schools and the *normales* for training their teachers and making the central government responsible for secondary education. Hostos' progressive liberalism, however, coupled with his free masonry brought him into conflict first with the Church and then with Heureaux, [the President - PH] who in 1895 enacted his own legislation that provided for a Higher Council of Education to be responsible for secondary education and for provincial councils local committees to look after primary schools.[106]

Hostos' attempt to centralize education in the country was unsuccessful and, as a consequence, individual municipalities and the Catholic Church continued to provide leadership in this area. It was, ironically, the dictator Rafael Trujillo, (whose political regime would most certainly have been opposed by Hostos) who effectuated Hostos' centralization process – the system existing in the country at the present time. He enacted the Organic Law of Education in 1951 which made education free and compulsory for children throughout the country between the ages of seven and fifteen. State education at all levels through secondary was placed under the control of the Secretary for Education and Fine Arts. The same textbooks and curriculum had to be used in both public and private primary schools, and all diplomas at the secondary level had to be certified by competent authorities and otherwise conform to state standards.[107] Thus, Trujillo essentially brought the system of education in the Dominican Republic into conformity with that of the British, French and Dutch colonies.

The victory of the Independence Movement in the Indian subcontinent in 1947 and the subsequent establishment of the independent countries of India and Pakistan had a tremendous impact on East Indians in the Caribbean. It imbued them with a new sense of pride and self-importance. It gave new energy to the fledgling Hindu and Islamic movements such as the orthodox Sanatan Dharm Maha Sabha (SDMS), with representatives in British Guiana, Trinidad, Cayenne, Martinique and Surinam; the Arya Samaj, a Hindu reformist movement; the Sunnatival Jamaat, an orthodox Sunni Islamic movement; the Anjuman Sunatul Jamaat Asssociation (ASJA), the principal Islamic organization in Trinidad; and the United Sadr Islamic Anjuman, the largest Islamic organization in Guyana. In the 1940s organizations like the SDMS and the ASJA established schools to provide secular and religious instructions to their children and to resist any further erosion of their religion, languages and culture from Christian and Western influences.

> In this period, the SDMS saw itself as the vanguard of liberation for the East Indian community. It was actively involved in the building of East Indian schools and in the promotion of East Indian cultural festivals and overall way of life. These actions on the part of the SDMS sustained and increased an intense feeling of unity among East Indians and also had political implications.[108]

The foregoing are examples of the attempts by the colonial authorities, in collaboration with Christianity, to protect their economic, political and ideological interests by using education in a manner ensuring the intellectual isolation and underdevelopment of the Caribbean people. The mission of the Christian Churches eventually met with some successes, but for several decades it encountered the most stubborn resistance from the Africans, Amerindians and Asians. The churches also committed a number of errors during the initial stages, thereby compounding their difficulties.

One grave error was the decision to charge a fee for attendance at the primary schools. Most of the colonized had suspicions about the educational system and were not about to inconvenience themselves financially to send their children to school. Further, there were many parents who would have liked to send their children to the schools, but could not afford it. Others needed the services of their children either on their own little plots or on the large sugar estates in order to supplement the family's meagre income. Some saw it as a costly waste of time, mainly because even the "educated" had few opportunities other than working side by side with their uneducated counterparts in the fields. Others – a large percentage – rejected the school system as just "another of the white man's evil schemes."

Among the Asians, the Chinese were most receptive to the educational program, largely because of the relatively small population of Buddhists, Taoists and Confucianists in the colonies (Cuba excepted). The receptiveness of the Chinese was partly due to their desire to take advantage of the preferential treatment subsequently accorded them by the colonial rulers at the termination of Asian indentureship. The Muslims and Hindus refused to send their children to the Christian denominational schools, most of them entertaining the view that the school system would rob them of their religion, language, and culture.

The attempt to Christianize East Indians via the medium of education was largely a failure, although modest successes were achieved by the Presbyterians, Roman Catholics and Methodists in Trinidad, by the Baptists in British Guiana, by the Baptists and Roman Catholics in Belize, and by the Roman Catholics in Cayenne, Martinique and Guadeloupe. However, the general feeling among the various denominations that missionary work among East Indians was a very unrewarding exercise remained throughout the colonial period.

In the last quarter of the nineteenth century, the element of force was introduced. Primary education was made compulsory for all children irrespective of parental sentiments and the wall of resistance was shattered. It is significant that during this period the principal flouters of the law were the avaricious planters who inveigled many parents to keep their children out of school so that they (the planters) would continue to have a source of cheap labor.

The early failures of the Church were blamed on what the clerics called "paganism," "immorality" and "backwardness." However, the Reverend Underhill, in his commentary on official clerical attitudes towards African emancipation in the British Caribbean colonies, came closest to some of the real reasons when he wrote:

> It must not be overlooked that a very large proportion of the present population was born and bred in slavery; and that there is, therefore, a keen remembrance of the events of those days of sorrow. Black men in Kingston, do not forget that a minister of one of the leading denominations, now holding an important position in the city, preached, at the time of the insurrection (1831-32), a vigorous sermon in defense of the Divine institution of

slavery; a sermon which, since emancipation, no little pains have been taken to suppress. Black men do not forget that when the period of emancipation for domestic slaves approached great efforts were made to register them as agricultural slaves, in order to retain them two years more in bondage.[109]

To overcome some of the obstacles that impeded the work of the Christian Churches, the old laws against Obeah, Myalism, and Shango were revived and strictly enforced. This too was an error, because persecution generally tends to give strength, veracity, and authenticity to the prohibited practice. Indeed, the power of Obeah and Shango became so strong that even Africans who had long ago become converts of Christianity reverted to their former religious practices. Fearful of the wrath of Olorun, Obatala, Ogun, and Shango, many converts fled from the Christian missions, while others deemed it more discrete to keep "one foot" inside the Christian Churches and the other inside their traditional religious institutions.

In Haiti the growth and development of Roman Catholicism had been disrupted by the Revolution in 1791. In the 1840s, Christian missions were established at Jacmel, Port-au-Prince, Cap Haitién, Jeremie, Cayes and Gonaives. The denominations included British Baptists, African-American Free Mission Baptists and African Methodist Episcopalians. At the close of the administration of Jean-Pierre Boyer in 1844, it was estimated that there were only about 1,200 Protestants in the country, mostly Methodists and Baptists, and these primarily African-Americans who had fled from racial oppression in the United States to settle in the republic.[110]

The Episcopal Church came to Haiti in 1861 when a group of 110 African-Americans decided to emigrate to an all-Black country. One-third died, another third returned to the United States to escape the tropical diseases, but among the third that remained was the Rev. James Theodore Holly of Detroit, Michigan, who proposed to improve "corrupting influences of society here where neither the public morality nor religion have yet firmly taken root." He founded the Holy Trinity Parish in Port-au-Prince and established several branches of the Church in other areas of the country.

Holly's work was continued by the Rev. Harry Roberts Carson, the first ordained Missionary Bishop of Haiti. He completed the construction of the St. Trinité Cathedral in 1928 and by the time of his retirement in 1943 the Church had 62 missions, 13 schools, and 18 members of the clergy in Haiti.[111] His successor, Bishop C. Alfred Voegeli, a native of Morristown, New Jersey, was consecrated the same year, and under his vigorous regime the number of organized missions grew to 79, and the number of active clergy to 31, all of whom (excepting the Bishop and the Dean of the Seminary) are native Haitians.[112] Their successes among the populace, however, remained relatively modest because an overwhelming majority of the masses adhered to Vodun (a syncretization of Dahomean Vodu and Roman Catholicism) and the Mulatto ruling class to Roman Catholicism.

In 1860 President Geffrard made a Concordat with the Papacy which provided for the appointment of an Archbishop of Haiti by the Pope. A consequence of this agreement was the reemergence of Roman Catholicism as the official religion of Haiti. Subsequently, the Roman Catholic clergy, mostly French, came to the country, established missions and expanded the school system which had first been implemented by Alexandre Petión and Henri Christophe. By the 1950s the Catholic Church had established the most prestigious schools and was at the helm of the educational system in the country.

Five teaching and charitable institutions exercise their ministry in Haiti with government support. The Fathers of the Holy Ghost conduct the important institution of secondary education known as the College of St. Martial. The Brothers of Christian Instruction established the seminary of higher learning known as St. Louis de Gonzague, which includes the best library in Haiti; many government elementary schools are also under their jurisdiction. The Nuns of St. Joseph de Cluny have a large high school for girls and are in charge of many public schools. The Daughters of Wisdom conduct hospitals as well as schools in the provinces. The Belgian Sisters of Mercy manage several vocational schools for young women, including the Ecole Professionelle Elie Dubois in the capital.[113]

This is by no means exhaustive of the institutions operating within the educational arena in Haiti. It does, however, give an insight into the degree to which the hearts and minds of the Haitian people are influenced by the French Catholic clergy. In 1930 there were only eight Haitians among the 205 Catholic priests in the country. In 1955 there were 300, eighty of whom were Haitians. Few of the 220 French priests were able to speak Creole. At the same time the Haitian government sets aside the sum of $230,923.00 annually for the Church's ministration.[114] By way of contrast, the Haitian government provides no funding to the Protestant Episcopal Church which operates on a total annual budget of less than $100,000. Of this amount, $10,000 is devoted to the educational work of such institutions as the Grace Merritt Stewart School for Girls and the Seminary at Mont Rouis, where all the clergy receive their four-year training, and where a Boy Scout camp is maintained. Another $10,000 goes to the St. Vincent School for Handicapped Children, the only school in Haiti taking care of and training blind, deaf and crippled children. The Church's budget is made up mostly of funds contributed in the United States.[115]

Although a school for the preparation of a native clergy was established in 1918, almost all of the French priests are Bretons, graduates of the St. Jacques Seminary maintained by the Haitian government at Finisterre, France. The first Negro Bishop, Monseigneur Augustin, assistant to Archbishop Le Gouaze, was consecrated in 1953, at which time the Pope is said to have promised informally that the first native Haitian to become Archbishop would be made a Cardinal.[116]

That the Haitian government has continued to maintain the largely French Catholic clergy from its less than meagre resources simply in the hope that one of its sons would one day be ordained a Cardinal does severe violence to one's credulity. What is evident is that there was very little effort in the area of localizing the Catholic clergy, the nature of whose political activities was not necessarily in keeping with the national interests of Haiti. Harold Courlander wrote:

> The clergy which was soon to become a political force was entrusted with a secret mission: to create a climate of opinion favorable to a voluntary association of Haiti with France. ... In order to carry out the scheme, the French clerics concentrated on the education of the upper class. They opened excellent secondary schools where Haitian students were fully indoctrinated in the grandeur of France and exposed to insinuations about the backwardness of their country and its incapacity for self-rule. The plan failed and was given up in the late 1890's. ... By 1960 the clergy of Haiti openly took the side of the bourgeoisie. This led the opponent (in this case the government) to take stern measures against the alliance of the bourgeoisie and the clergy, and in the name of nationalism, to look for support from the masses and Vodoun.[117]

The intrigues of the resident French clergy, which had come to Haiti in the 1860s and had openly taken the side of the Mulatto ruling class against the black majority and in the 1950s against the government of Francois ("Papa Doc") Duvalier, greatly contributed to the reign of terror that for decades engulfed the country. The Duvalier regime routed the democratic forces that opposed its tyranny and humiliated the French clergy that treated it with contempt. A large number of priests, bishops, and an archbishop were deported. Those priests who remained were cowed into silence. The democratic section of the ruling class and a large number of the middle-class – the intelligentsia, professionals, and technicians fled for their lives. The dictatorship of the most backward section of the ruling class was in place. In 1964 a "plebiscite" made Duvalier president-for-life.

The tragic history of the French Catholic clerics in Haiti, like that of their Christian counterparts in the British, Dutch, Danish, French and Spanish Caribbean colonies, suggests that they were motivated neither by Christian charity, conscience, human fellowship, morality, nor the worthy mission of uplifting the oppressed and downtrodden. They sought to deprive the Haitian people of their national independence for the benefit of the French ruling class. Their not-so-secret aim was to succeed where the military might of France had failed – in the restoration of French colonial rule in Haiti. Indeed the economic and political backwardness of Haiti today is more a legacy of imperialist and clerical intrigues, coercion and extortion rather than of the internal class and color contradictions.

By the turn of the twentieth century the Christian Churches had partially succeeded in their mission of controlling the education of the colonized masses; of creating a semi-literate and unskilled population to serve as an everlasting source of cheap labor for the plantations. They created an educational system that was designed to ensure an unrelenting intellectual, cultural and aesthetic dependency on the metropolitan countries. Tertiary education had to be obtained in the "mother-countries." And even when universities were established in the colonies during the 1930s and 1940s, their curricula did not incorporate those areas of study which were vital to the economic and social development of the colonies and their inhabitants. Thus, training in specialized medicine, chemistry, engineering, agriculture, agronomy, dentistry, pharmacology, mechanics, and so forth, had to be obtained in the metropolitan countries.

Indeed the school system introduced into the Caribbean in the nineteenth century has remained virtually unchanged in most of the territories – the colonies, as well as the independent countries. For this reason, in spite of the existence of local universities today, the Caribbean is still deficient in the number of scientists and technicians indispensable to its economic and social development. At the same time, Caribbean students who acquire these very skills in the metropolitan countries are offered few opportunities in the region, and, enticed by the far greater remuneration offered in the metropoles, remain there indefinitely. Dr. Moya Pons underscored this point:

> Since in former days inter-island and intra-regional trade was not permitted in order to protect metropolitan interests, capital and loans always came from the mother country, and benefits and profits accumulated in London, or in Seville, or in Amsterdam, or in Le Havre, rather than in the islands, and since this capital was not invested in the region but in Europe, the result was the underdevelopment of the local economies many years before independence came about. This produced as a result the inability of the region to sustain its population, and the appearance of strong migratory movements which have accelerated since the mid 20th century.[118]

Those professionals who do return to the Caribbean, motivated by communal ties, patriotism and a commitment to the development of their country, quickly become frustrated by the absence of any mechanisms to absorb their skills. Their frustration is further compounded by a moribund bureaucracy – an institution designed to protect metropolitan interests – which stubbornly resists any innovation of a national character and views with suspicion anyone advocating a nationalistic development policy. Consequently, about 90 percent of the most skilled technicians, professionals and scientists from the Caribbean live and work in the United States, the United Kingdom, France, Canada, the Netherlands, Germany, Spain and other Western countries, while their own countries continue to depend on and pay higher costs to the metropoles for these very skills. Moya Pons further stated:

> At the top of these societies were always the colonial elites, for whom cultural excellency and economic betterment lay in the metropolis. No matter that the independence took place in 1804 or in 1844 or in 1903 or in 1962 or in 1966, these elites have always remained attached to the metropolitan cultural outlook and associated with extraregional economic interests through their participation in banking business, mining and manufacturing industries, sugar estates, oil companies and real estate development projects. Meanwhile, with the exception of Cuba, of course, the educational systems still perpetuate the continuation of old colonial values and attitudes.[119]

It was the Christian missionaries who created the foundation for this dependency. Their work manifested itself in the creation of a dual school system for promoting the principles of colonialism and Christianity, training children in obedience and cheerful industry, forbearance and goodwill. They taught them to respect private property, and made available to them lesson books which would teach them the identity of interests of the "mother-countries" and dependencies, the rational basis of their connection, and, above all, the domestic and social duties of the colored races.[120]

The New Scramble for Souls

The twentieth century saw the advent of large numbers of Pentecostal sects to the Caribbean. The newcomers included the Seventh Day Adventists, the Salvation Army, Jehovah's Witnesses, the Church of God, the Church of Jesus Christ of Latter Day Saints (the Mormons), the Plymouth Brethren and a multitude of lesser known denominations. The overwhelming majority of these sects, which continue to appear in the Caribbean to the present day, originated in the United States, which had virtually replaced the former colonial powers as the main investor and beneficiary of the region since the turn of the century.

In the British, French and Dutch Caribbean territories, American Protestantism accompanied U.S. capital. In the Danish Caribbean colonies the number of its adherents multiplied after the 1917 purchase of the islands by the United States. In Haiti and the Dominican Republic, it was preceded by US arms and capital in 1915 when those countries were invaded and occupied by the United States. In the wake of the "Spanish-American War," there was a mad scramble by the American Protestant Churches for the "salvation of the souls" of the Cuban and Puerto Rican people. Julius Pratt wrote:

> Religious groups that had favored the war as a humanitarian crusade regarded the quick and easy victory as a sure sign of divine approval and as a divine command to continue the good work in islands freed from Spanish tyranny. Although there were some dissenting voices, in general Methodists, Baptists, Presbyterians, Congregationalists, and Episcopalians, together with several of the minor sects, united in urging that the United States accept the civilizing and Christianizing mission that Providence had placed before it; and just as businessmen prepared to take advantage of the opportunities for trade and investment

in the former possessions of Spain, so the churches began laying plans for new missionary enterprises. If the new career upon which the United States was about to enter was to be tinged with economic imperialism, it was also to be, as one religious writer remarked, "the imperialism of righteousness."[121]

Thus, the American Protestant Churches, the abettors and beneficiaries of U.S. aggression and imperial arrogance, surged into the Caribbean to stake their claim much like gold-hunters are wont to do. In conformity with the prevailing bigotry of Anglo-Saxonism and Teutonism, the U.S. ruling class and its Protestant allies regarded the Cubans and Puerto Ricans with no less contempt than they did the Amerindians, Africans and Asians.

It mattered not that Spain, a European country, was the colonizer of the two islands; that Europeans represented nearly one-half of the population; and that Roman Catholicism, a Christian religion, was the faith of the overwhelming majority. According to these American clerics, Providence had placed before them the "mission of civilizing and Christianizing the people of the former Spanish colonies." In other words, Providence had commanded President McKinley (who claimed to be a devout Christian) and his Protestant countrymen to embark on the "imperialism of righteousness."

Today the Caribbean continues to be inundated with an endless stream of religious sects and organizations whose general obscurity contrasts with their financial assets. Their activities tend to be concentrated in areas where the intellectual life of the populace is at its lowest level. Among the new denominations the Church of God, the Seventh Day Adventist and the Jehovah's Witness were the most successful. Denominations like the Plymouth Brethren, unapologetically male-chauvinistic, profoundly puritanical and intolerant to most cultural expressions (drumming, singing, dancing, drama and so forth), continue to exist in obscurity. The Salvation Army, although less evangelistic than its Pentecostal counterparts, has been able to establish a very strong foothold throughout the Caribbean.

The successes of the Pentecostal Churches have been largely due to their dedication, perseverance, ubiquitousness and relatively close relationship with their congregations. Pentecostalism, especially the Church of God, gained many converts among the African people because of its capacity to accommodate many of their customs -- drumming, dancing, singing, possession (getting in the spirit), and glossolalia (speaking in tongues). Since the 1930s their membership has increased tenfold and they are to be found in virtually all areas of the Caribbean. Even the Church of Jesus Christ of Latter Day Saints (Mormon Tabernacle), which has historically regarded Africans as the "scums of the earth" and as being unworthy of salvation, now has missionaries in many areas of the Caribbean. Today the Mormons have amended their philosophy and have established a noticeable presence in the region, especially Jamaica, competing for souls with their Christian denominational rivals.

Overt discrimination and violence were no longer the methods used by the major Christian denominations to combat the influence of rivals. *De jure* establishmentarianism was abolished, but the major denominations -- Anglicanism, Roman Catholicism, Methodism, the Baptist Society, Presbyterianism, Lutheranism, the Reformed Church and the Moravian Church -- the *de facto* Established Churches -- have employed more subtle methods to combat Pentecostalism and the quasi-Christian and non-Christian denominations. Such methods included the enactment of legislation such as the Night Noises Prevention Law of Jamaica and other territories and the earlier enacted Obeah Law calculated to frustrate Pentecostalists, African traditionalists, Hindus, Muslims, Revivalists, and Spiritualists and indirectly coerce them into joining the *de facto* Established Churches.

Among the coercive methods was the legal requirement that religious marriages be performed by none but *"qualified"* ministers [a *qualified* minister belonged to one of the major denominations]. Procurement of the lowliest government job required a letter of recommendation from a qualified religious minister, and applications for jobs, passports, licenses, and so forth, provided for disclosure of the applicants' religious affiliation. In regards to the effects of these practices on East Indians, Glasgow wrote:

> A few of the direct effects (of statutory laws on the East Indian culture) were the refusal to allow for the cremation of the dead, the non-recognition of any but civil marriages, and the placing of low caste drivers over high caste workers. The extent to which East Indians accepted the beliefs and values of the system determined their status in creole society.[122]

In short, membership within the recognized Christian denominations became a prerequisite for any kind of social mobility. This type of coercion not only created severe difficulties for the minor Christian, quasi-Christian and non-Christian denominations, but also encouraged the deceptive but justifiable practice of maintaining nominal membership in the recognized churches for business and formal purposes, and active membership in the unrecognized churches for spiritual and social purposes.

Liberation Theology

From the foregoing, it becomes clear that in spite of their rivalry the major Christian denominations in the Caribbean manifested, to a greater or lesser degree, a shared adherence to colonialism, imperialism, racism and human exploitation. In short, they acquiesced in the material deprivation of the people whose minds and souls they sought to win. To cover up their involvement in the unholy alliance between the Church and the imperial powers, the Christian clerics established a rigid, albeit contrived, separation between the secular and the religious, between the material and the spiritual. Ministers and priests who failed to adhere to this convenient separation were disciplined, ostracized, persecuted or denounced for delving into matters that were "outside the pale of the Church."

For a very long time the Church was able to contain its internal contradictions and maintain its so-called policy of secular and spiritual separation. However, by the 1930s and 40s (especially after the Second World War), the struggles of the world's colonial peoples for self-determination and independence intensified. A shift in the balance of forces then began to take place within the Church. The entire colonial order was weakened after the War, and so was the power of its secular and religious standard-bearers.

At the same time, the voices of the opponents of "vulgar theology" had gained greater strength and could no longer be silenced. As a result, the younger leaders, especially those who were born and raised in the colonies, gradually began to appreciate the fact that the souls they sought to save represented an inseparable unity with the physical being of living humans, not phantoms. Nor could they tolerate any longer the deceitful pattern and practice of attempting to reconcile the principles of Christianity with racial oppression, exploitation and human degradation.

Members of the Roman Catholic clergy in the Dutch Caribbean, Puerto Rico and Cuba were among the first in the region to throw down the gauntlet against oppression and commence the process of saving the "soul" of the Christian Church from apostasy. In Puerto Rico, Roman Catholic clerics joined the patriotic forces in condemnation of the economic and political hooliganism perpetrated by the US ruling class in the island and openly supported the independence movement. In Aruba and Bonaire the Catholic Church formed the colonies' first political party to challenge the supremacy of the Dutch and Jewish ruling class. The Catholic Trade Union Movement of Curacao, which was founded in the 1950s by Father Amado Romer, emphasized the significance of the laborers' work in the society and advanced the idea that it was their right to share in the rewards of the society rather than a privilege to be granted at will by some higher authority.[123]

The Catholic Trade Union Movement was merely one of many operating within the Curacao Christian Confederation of Trade Unions. The Confederation criticized the larger trade unions, which operated under the umbrella of the General Conference of Trade Unions, because of their abnormal friendliness with the employers and the colonial administration. They were critical of the political parties because they allied themselves with the Dutch and Jewish ruling class and erected barriers against the full participation of Africans in the economic and political life of the Antilles.[124] The Confederation has established links with progressive Latin American labor unions and gives support to Caribbean patriots struggling against political repression.

In Surinam, Father Weidmann formed the Progressive Surinamese People's Party which advocated universal suffrage for men and women and a limitation on imports in favor of local production. The 1960s and 70s found the Roman Catholic Church in the French Caribbean heightening its struggle for a just and peaceful region. In Cayenne, the National Front which is struggling for the country's independence from France has considerable Catholic support. The announcement of the French Government in 1975 to send French citizens to resettle Cayenne created a mighty uproar in the colony. The people, led by their several organizations, including the Federation des Etudiants Catholiques des Antilles-Guyane (GAGEC), mounted an intense opposition. The National Front, in which the patriotic organizations, including GAGEC, have membership, opposed the announcement on the grounds that France was attempting to use its own nationals to obtain consensus for the permanent colonization of Cayenne. This would serve to frustrate and ultimately negate the independence movement. And the fact that the French government was obliged to abandon the idea is an eloquent testimony to the effectiveness of the national opposition.

In Cuba, a significant number of Roman Catholic parish priests abandoned the centuries-old policy of reaction and supported the patriotic movement which was crystallized in the 1930s and consummated in 1959. At the 1976 Convention of the Caribbean Conference of Churches (CCC, formed in 1973) held in Kingston, Jamaica, a Protestant minister spoke passionately about the "lack of freedom", religious and otherwise, in Cuba. A Cuban Catholic delegate rebuked the minister by saying that the Church experienced no restrictions in its activities; that the revolutionary process in Cuba, of which it is a part, is consistent with the Christian principles of human fellowship and the social and spiritual upliftment of the poor; and, that it would be heresy for the Church to be in opposition to the moral imperative to do justice.

In the British Caribbean the Christian Churches began a

modest struggle against oppression in the 1970s. In Guyana and Grenada secular struggles against the undemocratic practices of the regimes of Forbes Burnham and Eric Gairy, respectively, were strengthened as a result of the contribution made by the Christian Churches. The CCC became the unifying body for the major denominations throughout the region, and because of its new positive role in the struggle for peace and social justice in the region, the Christian Churches, in a general sense, are now seen in a different light by most people in the Caribbean.

Theologians, like the Reverends Alan Kirton, Leslie Lett, Ernle Gordon, Roy Neehall, Jimmy Tucker, Bishop Parilla Bonilla, Fr. Jean Bertrand Aristide, Fr. Antoine Adrien, Bishop Willy Romelus and many others, are today respected for their leadership and other contribution to the movement for progressive change in the Caribbean. Liberation theology, adopted and articulated by Father Romer in the 1950s, has become a major ideological trend within the CCC. Its essence was eloquently described by Reverend Lett in one of his sermons:

> "We need to be constantly reminded that we should never separate theology from action (praxis). This separation is possibly the supreme heresy of modern Christianity. Faith without liberating praxis is not only dead, it is murderous! .. Third World theology is not impressed with those who call on the name of God while denying his reality in the struggles of the poor; but it is impressed with those who, while denying the name of God affirm his reality as the moral imperative to do justice. And it warns afresh that not all who say "Lord Lord" will be saved. There is need to examine carefully the historical nature of "atheism" if the Church is to be saved from apostasy."

The profound involvement of liberation theology in the secular and spiritual affairs of the Caribbean and within the CCC itself represents a turning point in the policies of the Christian Churches. Ironically, it represents a continuum in the struggles of Amerindian Shamanism, the African religions, and early Christianity itself, against oppression. It vindicates the martyrdom of the early adherents who had advocated the unity of the material and the spiritual, and who had challenged the Christian Church to denounce exploitation and other forms of injustice. Finally, and importantly, it associates itself with the efforts of all religious and secular forces whose goals reflect the Christian objective of the international fraternity of humanity.

Indeed, the ongoing struggle to combat with a view to eradicating the contempt and snobbery extended to the non-Christian religious expressions and to have Christianity cultivate a measure of sensitivity to the cultural, social, and religious practices of the African, Amerindian and Asian masses have gained new converts, especially among parish priests and the younger ministers within the Caribbean Conference of Churches, as well as the African-American Christian Churches. According to Josiah Young:

> Contemporary Afro-American theologians and religionists, however, seek greater insight into the significance of African traditional religion for black theology. Thus, they have already suggested the need for indigenization of Black theology. As I have noted, their interest promises that African theologians might be instructive in the task of relating Black theology to the image of Africa and the vestiges of Africanisms within the United States, and those in relation to their prototypes in Africa and the Caribbean.[125]

The CCC's monthly organ, *Caribbean Contact*, became one of the most informative sources of Caribbean news. The CCC has a well-reasoned position in support of the Cuban Revolution and it had sympathized with the aims of the People's Revolutionary Government of Grenada. For its stance on the questions of social justice and peace, the CCC became a target of reproach from certain leaders in the region, especially Jean Claude Duvalier of Haiti, Joaquin Balaguer of the Dominican Republic and the late Tom Adams of Barbados in whose country the newspaper had its base. For its condemnation of the U.S. invasion of Grenada and the complicity of several Caribbean leaders, including Adams, the Caribbean Contact's editor Ricky Singh and a number of other journalists associated with the newspaper were expelled from Barbados.

Like the World Council of Churches (WCC), in which it has membership, the CCC was labelled "communist" by the Reagan and Bush administrations of the United States which used the communist bogey to discredit expressions of human decency and social justice throughout the world. In Puerto Rico, the secular and clerical leaders of the independence movement have been systematically harassed by the United States Government. Among them are Roman Catholic Bishop, Antulio Parilla Bonilla, who, along with Juan Mari Bras, General Secretary of the Puerto Rican Socialist Party, had taken the struggle of the Puerto Rican people for independence to the floors of the United Nations. Dozens of organizations such as the Puerto Rican Federation of Teachers, the Women's Federation, the independent labor unions, the Puerto Rico Bar Association, and various Christian and student organizations have been subject to abuses by the police and the military forces. Bishop Bonilla himself and several other clerics have been victims of systematic harassment by the U.S. authorities because of their outspoken demand for their country's right to self-determination.[12]

---

[12] Numerous Puerto Rican patriots have been incarcerated and killed by the U.S. authorities because they dared to demand their inalienable right to control their own destiny. Nationalist Party leader, Pedro Albizu-Campos, spent several years in prison during World War II, and another 14 years

In the Dominican Republic a large section of the lower Catholic clergy opposed the U.S. invasion of their country in 1965 and supported Juan Bosch and the national democratic movement. Accordingly, they were victimized by the U.S. and its local surrogates. Priests and nuns were among the dead when U.S. marines invaded the country and General Elias Wessin y Wessin bombed the city of Santo Domingo bringing death and destruction to thousands of civilians. Today the Roman Catholic Church in the Dominican Republic is a member of the CCC and a growing number of its clergy contributes to the democratic movement in the country.

In Haiti, the Roman Catholic Church, whose activities had contributed to the rise of Duvalierism, later became divided into essentially two main factions: the upper echelons who remained in alliance with the privileged section of the society and the military, and the lower clergy, mainly local Haitian priests, who became an important part of the leadership in the fight for democracy in the country. The lower clergy's outspoken criticisms of the fascist policies of Jean Claude Duvalier in the pulpits, on the radios, and in the newspapers helped to exhort the Haitian masses and strengthen their will to cast off the yoke of the dictatorship. The role of these clerics was not restricted to criticizing the regime. They were in the forefront of the popular movement that forced Duvalier and his family to flee Haiti in 1986. However, the flight

---

between 1950 and 1964. His only "crime" was the raising of the issue of Puerto Rican independence with the nations of Europe and Latin America. In 1950, Oscar Collazo and Griselio Torresola received prison sentences of 25 and 29 years, respectively, for taking actions calculated to call the attention of the world to the oppression of the Puerto Rican nation. In 1954, similar actions were carried out by Nationalist Party members, Lolita Lebrón, Rafael Cancel Miranda, Irvin Flores Rodriguez, and Andres Figueroa Cordero, who all received sentences of 25 years in prison.

of Duvalier did not result in the establishment of democracy in Haiti. A military junta, the National Council of Government (CNG), backed by the United States, assumed control of the government and its leader, General Henri Namphy, declared himself president.

Thousands of people, including priests, were murdered by agents of the new government and by the former secret police of the Duvalier regime, the Tonton Macoutes. The "*dechoukaj*," or uprooting, as the Haitians called the popular movement that ousted Duvalier on February 7, 1986, had become their nightmare. On January 29, 1987, Namphy, in an attempt to conceal his fascist intentions and his opposition to democratic reforms, orchestrated an election in which only his supporters participated. It was "won" by Leslie Manigat, one of his protégés. Six months later Manigat was "ousted" by Namphy who by then had dropped all democratic pretenses.

Namphy then adopted a policy aimed at systematically eliminating the leaders of the democratic movement. This same policy, aided and abetted by the United States, was also carried out in such countries as Chile, El Salvador, Honduras, and Guatemala. Random killings and human rights abuses continued unabated. The idea was to create so much terror that community organizers would take fright or simply abandon the democratic movement. The leaders and members of Haiti's largest peasant organization, the Peansant Movement du Papaye (MPP), were systematically eliminated and terrorized by the army and the Tonton Macoutes. On September 11, 1988, the church of Father Jean Bertrand Aristide was attacked during religious services by the Tonton Macoutes who hacked and gored 17 parishioners to death, wounded 77 others and then put the church to the torch.

On September 17, 1988, General Namphy was himself

overthrown in a coup d'etat by General Prosper Avril who declared himself president. The change in leadership, however, did not result in a change in policy. The repression against the democratic movement continued. The U.S.-trained army officers and the Haitian elite were determined to destroy the Constitution written by the people's representatives and ratified by them in a national referendum held on March 29, 1987. Among other things, the new constitution provided, as a matter of right, free education, decent housing, wage increases, safe working conditions, and safeguards against dictatorships. Notwithstanding Avril's maneuvering, the Independent Electoral Council, which was created by the people to lay the groundwork for a fair and free election, continued its work and called an election on November 29, 1988.

On election day, the Haitian people and the world were treated to the horrifying spectacle of voters being gunned down as they waited in line to cast their ballots. A wave of police and military terror followed as the regime sought to destroy everything which it conceived as a threat to its rule. The farmers' organizations, labor unions, human rights groups, and others which had sprung up in 1986 were all disbanded. Indeed, even the *Misyon Alfa*, a Church-sponsored literacy program, was not spared the regime's assault.

The Haitian regime, however, was unable to destroy the spirit of resistance among the people or to shake the commitment of their leaders. Bishop Willy Romelus and a number of Roman Catholic parish priests such as Fr. Antoine Adrien, Fr. Gerard Jeane Juste and Fr. Jean Bertrand Aristide played a critical role during this period. Father Aristide, who had to go into hiding following the burning of his church and the massacre of his congregation, continued the democratic and constitutionalist struggle. His courage, honesty, humility, and, above all, deep and abiding love for his people, transformed him almost overnight into the very symbol of the democratic movement and the hope for a constitutional order in Haiti.

The alienation of the Haitian ruling class from, and its contempt for the masses of the people deceived it into believing that its candidate in the election scheduled for December 16, 1990, Marc Bazin, a former World Bank official and leader of the Movement for the Institution of Democracy in Haiti (MIDH), would emerge the winner. The Bush Administration in the United States, partly because of its own wishful thinking, partly because of unreliable data from its Central Intelligence Agency (CIA) and other informants, anticipated a similar electoral result. Father Aristide, the candidate of the National Front for Change and Democracy (FNCD) – the people's candidate – was not taken seriously. But on election day the people went to the polls and elected him President with 67 percent of the vote.

Father Aristide's astonishing victory momentarily stunned the Haitian ruling class and its military and their official supporters in the United States. Even before the new government assumed office on February 7, 1991, its enemies had begun to conspire to derail and destroy this first genuine expression of democracy in the country's history. On September 30, 1991, the Haitian army, openly supported by the ruling class and its international allies, overthrew the Aristide government in a bloody coup d'etat which left at least 5,000 men, women and children dead.

The Christian Church, as exemplified in the work of Father Aristide, has, in most areas of the Caribbean, taken on a new image. The forces representing the old ideas, namely, the representatives of "vulgar theology", still remain a very strong faction. However, the enlightened and humanistic section – the advocates of liberation theology – who struggle to improve the material and spiritual life of the people here on earth occupies an influential position. The work of these theologians in many communities throughout the Caribbean; their outspoken criticisms of the backward and unpatriotic policies of many of the political regimes in the region; and their advocacy of Caribbean unity, peace and social justice have been a source of inspiration to Caribbean patriots, religious and non-religious alike.

The liberation theologians of the CCC represent but one expression of the newly progressive orientation of the Christian Church in the Western Hemisphere. In South and Central America the lower Catholic clergy played a vital role in the revolutionary Wars of Independence in the early nineteenth century. After independence was achieved in the several territories, the Church, in general, became comatose and its leadership allied itself with the new rulers. In short, it continued to be an abettor in the exploitation of the poor. Even when the violence and inhumanity of the political and military leaders became too shocking to the sensitivities of the clergy, it was unable to act because it had lost the moral authority to do so.

By the beginning of the twentieth century the revolutionary ideas that had guided the Wars of Independence had been completely repudiated and the alliance between the local latifundistas and U.S. corporate interests had become cemented. The political outrages and social abuses perpetrated by the local rulers and the U.S. multinational corporations, especially the United Fruit Company, against the people served to rekindle a sense of patriotism and Christian mission among the lower clergy whose members were themselves frequently victims of those abuses.

Consequently, the patriotic movements led by Augusto Sandino in Nicaragua and Farabundo Martí in El Salvador received strong support from the lower clergy. This was also true for the democratic movements in Brazil, Paraguay, Uruguay, Argentina, Colombia, and Venezuela. By the 1970s, even members of the upper clergy had begun to raise their voices in support of democracy and human dignity. Archbishop Oscar Romero of El Salvador was a member of the upper clergy who spoke out against the government's excesses, corruption, and cruelty. The corporate and military hooligans demonstrated their contempt for all opponents, secular and religious, by brutally murdering the Archbishop during a religious service and raping and severely beating and disfiguring his sister.

The world expressed horror and disdain for the cowardly murder of an Archbishop. However, the continued series of murders of parish priests, nuns, and other members of the lower clergy by regimes in South and Central America largely pass unnoticed. Today the Roman Catholic Church represents a very important sector of the democratic movements in Latin America and, in a number of countries, constitutes the leadership. Nicaragua provided an excellent example of religious and secular leaders united by years of struggle against oppression and sharing the common goal of creating a just society, improving the material and spiritual life of the people, and defending their country from aggression by its local and international enemies.

In the United States it was the African-led Christian Churches that spearheaded the struggle against oppression -- a logical consequence of their being amongst the most oppressed in the society. The emancipation struggles of the African Christian community had deep historical roots. In 1800 Gabriel Prosser, an African slave preacher, led an uprising in Virginia in defense of human dignity. In 1822 this courageous act was repeated in the State of South Carolina by African Christian slaves under the leadership of Denmark Vesey, a freedman from the colony of St.

Thomas in the Danish Virgin Islands . Nine years later, yet another Christian preacher, Nat Turner, born a slave in the year of Prosser's uprising, rallied the African slaves in the state of Virginia under the slogan: "The first shall be the last and the last shall be the first!"

Their vision of freedom and justice was pursued in the battlefield for minds by leaders like Frederick Douglas, David Walker, Robert Alexander Young, Henry Highland Garnett, and others. Their numbers include brave martyrs – Christian and non-Christian alike – who were lynched during the period of Jim Crowism. They include leaders like Booker T. Washington and W.E.B. DuBois; the legal titans of the National Association for the Advancement of Colored People (NAACP), Wiley Branton, Charles Houston, Thurgood Marshall, and William Hastie; as well as Marcus Garvey and the Universal Negro Improvement Association (UNIA).

The same fire for justice and freedom that burned in the heart of Harriett Tubman consumed the passions of Sojourner Truth, Father Devine, Medgar Evers and Claudia Jones. The spectrum encompasses Langston Hughes, Claude McKay, Arthur Schomburg, and other giants of the Harlem Renaissance Movement; Paul Robeson, the Reverend Adam Clayton Powell, the Honorable Elijah Muhammad, Malcolm X, and the Nation of Islam. In the ranks of the torchbearers are the Reverend Martin Luther King and the Southern Christian Leadership Conference (SCLC), Kwame Touré (Stokely Carmichael) and the Student Non-Violent Coordinating Committee (SNCC), and the Black Panther Party. Today's Reverend Jesse Jackson, Minister Louis Farrakan, Congressman Charles Rangel and other prominent voices represent a continuum in the struggle for freedom, social justice and human dignity.

The above fighters and martyrs espoused many different

philosophies – secular, religious, and a mish-mash of both. However, the main object of all of these struggles was and remains Anglo-Saxonism and Teutonism – white supremacism – which fosters the economic, political, social, cultural, and juridical domination by the Europeans over all others. All, notwithstanding the disparateness of their respective philosophies, fought and continue to fight against racial oppression and for the right of all people to be treated as equal humans. And this is so because Africans, in our struggle for freedom, walk through many gates.

The European-American Christian Churches, on the other hand, made a significant contribution to the Abolition Movement. They were instrumental in establishing Liberia as a home for contraband slaves. But the overwhelming majority of these churches and their leaders (the Quakers, John Brown and some others are worthy exceptions) did not affirm the equality of Africans and Europeans. Consequently, when slavery was formally abolished in the United States in 1865, the struggles of the European-American Christian Churches for "human rights" virtually ceased. Between 1875 and 1960, thousands of Africans and other non-Europeans were victims of lynch mobs and other violence, their victimizers committing these outrages with impunity. Racial segregation, in which most of the European Christian Churches participated, prevailed throughout the country. Amerindians, Africans, Asians, Jews, Latin Americans, and other ethnic groups were subjected to official and unofficial outrages and abuses. Yet, there was a telling silence from the European-American Churches.

Unlike their European-American counterparts, the African-American Christian Churches did not and still do not have the luxury of retiring from the arena of struggle, because their leaders and congregations continue to be primary victims of class and racial oppression. In the 1950s and '60s, some European-American Churches became mindful of their Christian mission and participated in the Civil Rights Movement and the Anti-Vietnam War Protest. At the same time, a significant number of the European ethnic Christian Churches in the South and Midwest, which had supported the institution of slavery and the system of racial segregation, became the backbone of Christian Fundamentalism and, in the name of Christianity, continue not only their hostility to equal human rights in the United States and the world, but to the social gospel of liberation theology as well.

Since the 1950s, a gulf, which continues to grow wider and wider dividing them into opposite camps, has existed within the European-American Christian Churches. The rift, which began around the questions of African enslavement and the persecution of Amerindians and Latin-Americans, now encompasses civil rights for all people, equal rights for women, education, care for the elderly, equal employment, and health care. Today this rift has become a chasm between Fundamentalism – many of whose adherents have historical links to African enslavement, the Confederacy, Jim Crowism, the Ku Klux Klan, and the system of racial segregation and who hold on tenaciously, albeit in a different form, to the racist, theological and laissez-faire dogmas[13] of yesteryear – and liberation theology, which seeks to contemporize the democratic teachings and practices of early Christianity.

---

[13] Many of the fundamentalists advocate such things as the burning of all literature that is not in keeping with their understanding and literal interpretation of the Christian Bible; the termination of employment of all teachers, doctors, and other professionals who advocate the free flow of ideas and the right of women to choose whether or not they want to consummate their pregnancy. The extremists among them bomb and burn abortion clinics and family planning centers, fire-bomb the homes of, and terrorize and murder doctors who perform abortions. All of this intolerance, murder, cruelty, and viciousness are carried out in the name of Jesus Christ.

References

1. Amos Kidder Fiske, *The West Indies,* G. P. Putnam's Sons, New York-London (1899) p. 25

2. Dale Bisnauth, *History of Religions in the Caribbean,* Africa World Press, Inc., Trenton, N.J. (1996), p. 41

3. Ibid. p. 13

4. Id., (also cited in Lewis Hanke, *The Spanish Struggle for Justice in the Conquest of America*, p. 32)

5. Captain James Southey, *Chronological History of the West Indies*, Frank Cass and Company, Limited, London (1968), p. 91

6. Selden Rodman, *Haiti: The Black Republic,* the Devin-Adair Company, New York (1954), p. 4

7. Selden Rodman, *Quisqueya: A History of the Dominican Republic*, University of Washington Press, Seattle (1964), p. 17

8. Cornelis Goslinga, *A Short History of the Netherlands Antilles and Surinam*, Martinus Nijhoff, the Hague (1970), p. 18

9. Rodman, *Quisqueya,* p. 17

10. Arturo Morales-Carrión, *Puerto Rico and the Non-Hispanic Caribbean,* University of Puerto Rico (1971), p. 4

11. Philip S. Foner, *A History of Cuba and its Relations with the United States,* vol. 1, International Publishers, New York (1962), pp. 35-36

12.   Eric Williams, *Race Relations in Caribbean Society*, Caribbean Studies: A Symposium, Institute of Social and Economic Research, University of the West Indies (1957), p. 55.

13.   Sherburne F. Cook and Woodrow Borah, *Essays in Population History: Mexico and the Caribbean,* Volume 1, University of California Press, Berkeley (1971), p. 386

14.   Adalberto Lopez, *The Puerto Ricans: Their History, Culture, and Society,* Schenkman Publishing Company, Inc., Cambridge, Massachusetts (1980), p. 17

15.   John Eaden, *Memoirs of Pere Labat,* Frank Cass and Company, Limited, London (1931),   p. 33

16.   Ibid. p. 79

17.   Ibid. pp. 33-34

18.   Thomas Coke, *A History of the West Indies,* Vol. II, Frank Cass and Company Limited, London (1808-1811), reprinted 1971, p. 49

19.   Eaden, p. 148

20.   James G. Leyburn, *The Haitian People*, Yale University Press, New Haven and London (1966), p. 116

21.   Eaden, pp. 33-34

22.   Rodman, *Haiti: The Black Republic*, p.62

23.   Eaden, p. 36

24.   Leyburn, p. 118

25.   Ibid. pp. 118-119

26.   Id.

27.   Ibid. 123

28.   Id.

29.   Bisnauth, p. 53

30.   Ibid. p. 61

31.   Ibid. p. 24

32.   Winthrop D. Jordan, *White Over Black*, Penguin Books, Inc., Baltimore, Maryland (1969), p. 6

33.   Eaden, p. 126

34.   A. Caldecott, *The Church in the West Indies*, Frank Cass and Company, Limited, London (1970), p. 65

35.   Edward Long, *The History of Jamaica*, Vol. II, Frank Cass and Company, Limited, London (1970, First Edition 1774), p. 68

36.   Bisnauth, p. 63

37.   Isaac Dookhan, *A History of the British Virgin Islands*, Caribbean Universities Press, in Association with Booker Publishing Company, Essex, England (1975), p. 88

38.   Id.

39.   Ibid. p. 89

40.   Bisnauth, p. 109

41.   Society for the Propagation of the Gospel in Foreign Parts, *Historical Sketches*, No. IV - Guiana, Westminster (1900), p. 4

42. Bisnauth, p. 124

43. Ibid. p. 129

44. Franklin W. Knight, *Slave Society in Cuba During the Nineteenth Century*, the University of Wisconsin Press, Madison, Milwaukee and London (1980), p. 107

45. Ibid. p. 106

46. Ibid. pp. 106-107

47. Coke, Vol. II, p. 15

48. Monica Schuler, *Alas, Alas, Kongo*, Johns Hopkins University Press, Baltimore and London (1980), p. 36

49. Michael Swan, *British Guyana, The Land of Six Peoples*, Her Majesty's Stationery Office, London (1957), p. 42

50. Schuler, p. 34

51. William Gardner, *A History of Jamaica*, E. Stock, London (1873), p. 347

52. Dookhan, p. 89

53. Ibid. p. 91

54. Society for the Propagation of the Gospel, No. IV, p. 7

55. Ibid. p. 15

56. Rev. J. T. Harricharan, *The Work of the Christian Churches Among the East Indians in Trinidad During the Period of Indentureship, 1845-1917*, Tunapuna, Trinidad (1975), p. 15

57. Edward B. Underhill, *The West Indies: Their Social and Religious Condition*, Jackson, Walford and Holden,

London (1862), p. 227

58. Ibid. p. 423

59. M. K. Bacchus, *Consensus and Conflict Over the Provision of Elementary Education,* ("Caribbean Freedom: Economy and Society from Emancipation to the Present"), edited by Hilary Beckles and Verene Shepherd, Markus Weiner, James Currey, Ian Randle, Princeton, London, Kingston (Jamaica), 1993, p. 297

60. Vere T. Daly, *The Making of Guyana,* Macmillan Education Limited, London (1974), p. 141

61. Morley Ayearst, *The British West Indies,* New York University Press, United Kingdom (1960), p. 24

62. Daly, p. 142

63. Schuler, pp. 30-31

64. Mary Turner, *Chinese Contract Labour in Cuba, 1847-1874,* ("Caribbean Freedom: Economy and Society from Emancipation to the Present"), edited by Hilary Beckles and Verene Shepherd, Markus Weiner, James Currey, Ian Randle, Princeton, London, Kingston (1993), p. 132

65. Knight, p. 132

66. Arthur P. Corwin, *Spain and the Abolition of Slavery in Cuba, 1817-1886,* Institute of Latin American Studies, University of Texas Press, Austin (1967), p. 12

67. Ibid. p. 14

68. Turner, p. 133

69. Knight, p. 119

70. Jorge Duany, *Ethnicity in the Spanish Caribbean: Notes on the Consolidation of Creole Identity in Cuba and Puerto Rico, 1762-1868,* (Stephen Glazer, "Caribbean Ethnicity Revisited"), Gordon and Breach Science Publishers, New York, London Paris, Montreux, Tokyo (1985), p. 24

71. Williams, *History of the People of Trinidad and Tobago,* p. 151

72. Ibid. 151-152

73. Knight, p. 70

74. Duany, p. 109

75. Ayearst, p. 25

76. Schuler, p. 30

77. Ayearst, p. 25

78. Knight, p. 33

79. W.K. Marshall, *Metayage in the Sugar Industry of the British Windward Islands, 1838-1865,* ("Caribbean Freedom: Economy and Society from Emancipation to the Present"), edited by Hilary Beckles and Verene Shepherd, Markus Weiner, James Currey, Ian Randle, Princeton, London, Kingston (1993), p. 64

80. Sir Alan Burns, *History of the British West Indies,* George Allen and Unwin Limited, London (1965), p. 670

81. Roy Augier, *Before and After 1865,* ("Caribbean Freedom: Economy and Society from Emancipation to the Present"), edited by Hilary Beckles and Verene Shepherd, Markus Weiner, James Currey, Ian Randle, Princeton, London, Kingston (1993), p. 174

82. Eric Williams, *British Historians and the West Indies*, Andre Deutsch Limited, London (1972), p. 88

83. Burns, pp. 670-671

84. Id.

85. Ibid. p. 671

86. Ibid. p. 673

87. Augier, p. 174

88. Burns, p. 673

89. C. M. Jacob, *Joy Comes in the Morning*, Caribbean Historical Society, Port-of-Spain, Trinidad (1996), p. 7

90. Ibid. p. 151

91. Board of Education of Great Britain, *Educational Systems of the Chief Colonies of the British Empire: Special Reports on Educational Subjects*, Vol. IV, Her Majesty's Stationery Office, London (1901), p. 577

92. Carl Campbell, *Social and Economic Obstacles to the Development of Popular Education in Post-Emancipation Jamaica 1834-1865*, ("Caribbean Freedom: Economy and Society from Emancipation to the Present"), edited by Hilary Beckles and Verene Shepherd, Markus Weiner, James Currey, Ian Randle, Princeton, London, Kingston, Jamaica (1993), p. 263

93. Id.

94. Augier, p. 173

95. Caldecott, p. 62

96. Carl Campbell, p. 264

97. Caldecott, p. 62

98. Id.

99. Dookhan, p. 91

100. Ibid. p. 170

101. Harricharan, pp. 25-26

102. Ibid. p. 22

103. Ibid. p. 10

104. Ibid. p. 17

105. Ian Bell, *The Dominican Republic,* Westview Press, Boulder, Colorado, (Ernest Bell London) (1981), p. 165

106. Id.

107. Ibid. p. 166

108. Mahin Gosine, *East Indians and Black Power in the Caribbean*, African Research Publications, New York (1986), p. 48

109. Underhill, pp. 192-193

110. Leyburn, p. 125

111. Rodman, Haiti: The Black Republic, p. 76

112. Id.

113. Ibid. p. 63

114. Id.

115. Ibid. p. 76

116. Ibid. p. 63

117. Harold Courlander and Remy Bastién, *Religion and Politics in Haiti,* Institute for Cross-Cultural Research, Washington, D.C. (1966), p. 45

118. Frank Moya Pons, *Caribbean Consciousness: What the Caribbean is Not,* Vol. 5, No. 3, San Jose, Puerto Rico (Sept. 1978), p. 43

119. Id.

120. Vere T. Daly, *A History of the Guyanese People,* Macmillan Education Limited London (1975), p. 236

121. Julius W. Pratt, *A History of United States Foreign Policy,* Prentice-Hall, Inc., New Jersey (1965), p. 215

122. Roy Arthur Glasgow, *Guyana: Race and Politics Among Africans and East Indians,* Martinus Nijhoff, the Hague, Netherlands (1970), p. 77

123. William A. Anderson and Russell R. Dynes, *Social Movements, Violence and Change,* Ohio State University Press, Columbus (1975), p. 61

124. Ibid. p. 60

125. Josiah U. Young, *Black and African Theologies,* Orbis Books, Maryknoll, New York (1990), p. 112

SECTION TWO

THE NON-CHRISTIAN RELIGIONS

The Western Europeans, especially the English, regarded non-Christian religions with the same disdain as they did the non-European peoples. European Christians denied that non-Europeans had any cosmological capacity and characterized non-Christian religious beliefs as "witchcraft", "black magic", "paganism","heathenism", and "idolatry". Having been thus stripped of any theological legitimacy and transformed into the antithesis of spirituality, these religions were then relegated to the realm of "folk psychology", sociology, and anthropology to be studied by those with a penchant for quaint or exotic phenomena.

Unlike the Southern Europeans, English experience with Africans was relatively abrupt. In fact, even before the meeting of the English and the African, black had been used by the former to describe negative cultural concepts. White and black were antithetical. They connoted purity and filthiness, virginity and sin, virtue and baseness, beauty and ugliness, beneficence and evil, God and the devil[1]. Africans, therefore, became the anthropomorphic expressions of what had hitherto been mere concepts to the English. They were ultimately transformed into baseness, vileness, filthiness, ugliness, and evil incarnate.

About the same time that the meeting of Africans and Englishmen occurred, the latter were in the process of perfecting an aristocratic concept of "beauty" which was largely associated with the rosy, red cheeks and pale skin of their "virgin" queen, Elizabeth. The Africans not only failed to fit this ideal concept of beauty, but seemed the very picture of perverse negation[2]. The English, especially since the time of Elizabeth I, regarded themselves not only as the vanguard of Christianity, but also of civilization. The African heathens, therefore, were uncivilized because they were not Christians. Jordan stated:

> ......Christianity militated against the unity of man. Because Englishmen were Christians, heathenism in Negroes was a fundamental defect which set them distinctly apart. However much Englishmen disapproved of Popery and Mahometanism, they were accustomed to these perversions. Yet they were not accustomed to dealing face to face with people who appeared, so far as many travelers could tell, to have no religion at all. Steeped in the legacy and trappings of their own religion, Englishmen were ill-prepared to see any legitimacy in African religious practices. Judged by Christian cosmology, Negroes stood in a separate category of men.[3]

The Englishmen's regard for the African became even more negative when they learned that Africans depicted their god as being black and the devil as being white. From then on various theses, including geography and climate, innateness, polygenesis, and divine prophesy and punishment, were invented to explain not merely the color of the African's skin but his very essence.

It must be noted, however, that Africans (or Ethiopians as they were called in antiquity) were not unknown to the Greeks, Romans or early Christians. Homer made numerous references to the "long-lived Ethiopians" in *The Odyssey*. He also identified Ethiopia as the place where the gods retired to have nectar and ambrosia. Memnon, the Ethiopian king and a hero of the Trojan War who was killed by Achilles and made immortal by Zeus, was accorded the utmost respect and reverence by Homer in *The Iliad*. In his chronicling of the Punic Wars between Rome and Carthage, the Roman historian, Titus Livius, gave an equal, if not greater, respect to the Carthaginian (African) General, Hannibal Barca, than to the Roman General, Publius Cornelius Scipio. The same is true of the respect accorded the Numidians (ancient Algerians) by the Romans. In antiquity human enslavement was generally the result of conquest. It was never based on race.

The absence of racism as a determining factor in shaping the economic, social, and political policies of the ancients enabled imperial Rome in the fourth century A.D. to adopt Christianity, the religion principally of a non-European people, as the official religion of the empire. Many of the prominent Christian pioneers such as Saint Augustine, Bishop of Hippo Regius (Algeria), and Tertullian of Carthage (Tunisia) were Africans. In fact it was not until several centuries later that a deliberate and systematic attempt to Europeanize Christianity and Jesus Christ himself began to take place. The political and military ascendancy of the Western Europeans on the world stage and their own belief in the inherent inferiority of the colored races could no longer be reconciled with the worshipping of a god who was not in their own image and likeness.

Central to Christian theology is the belief that Jesus is the Son of God and the Saviour of all humanity. All Christians, including Western Europeans, believe this, thereby rendering Jesus' ethnicity or genealogy immaterial and irrelevant. Further, because all humans are equal in the sight of God, the logical inference is that one's color or ethnic background is of no importance. The European conquerors, despite their professed adherence to Christianity, thought otherwise. They not only made Jesus, the ancient Hebrews, and the early Christian leaders into their own image and likeness, but also complimented that transformation by designing "portraits of them" manifesting European phenotypical characteristics. Indeed, so complete has been the transformation that today Christians of all races and ethnicities not only believe that the founders of Christianity were Europeans but also regard as "heretics", "heathens", "blasphemers" and "anti-Christs" those who express a contrary belief[1]. What is an indisputable fact, however, is that whereas Christianity was itself an adopted religion to the Europeans, the religions of the conquered people constituted an integral part of their cosmological outlook.

---

[1] If the biblical scriptures are to be believed (and Christians, including Western Europeans, profess a belief therein), the story of Moses in the Book of Genesis in the Christian Bible is not only instructive but should also render unnecessary any ethnohistorical or anthropological data in order to shed light on Jesus' and the Hebrews' ethnic origins. The Hebrew Moses was brought up by Pharaoh's sister as a prince in the royal house of Egypt and no one – Hebrew or Egyptian – knew his real identity. If the story is true, this could only have been possible if both peoples were of the same pigment. Few today would peddle the badly discredited thesis that the North African people of antiquity, in general, and the Egyptians in particular were Caucasians. Accordingly, the Bible is in accord that Jesus Christ, a Hebrew, a descendant of Moses, was a man of color. But while it is apparent that he was a man of color, he could not have had the pigmentation of a sub-Saharan African, as is the claim of some Africans. Rather, he would have had a resemblance to his kinfolk of the Arabian peninsula and the Amharas of Ethiopia. The Western European conquerors could not reconcile the contradiction between the divine acclamation of Jesus by Christians universally, and their own belief in the inherent inferiority of the colored races. To resolve this patent absurdity, it became necessary to transform Jesus, his disciples, the ancient Hebrews, and the non-European Christian saints into the image and likeness of the conquerors. They were so transformed.

Amerindian Shamanism

Information regarding the people who inhabited the Caribbean at the time of the Spanish invasion is very sparse. This could not have been otherwise, because information was passed on from one generation to the next and, within a period of sixty years, the people who numbered in the millions when Columbus came were almost completely annihilated. Entombed with them were their mores, customs, laws, arts, crafts, religion, and so forth. As the Reverend Thomas Coke noted:

> A nation living in a state of nature, without any written records, must generally be the recorders of their own histories through traditionary reports; and in their extermination we must naturally expect to find that their persons and their registers will meet with one common grave.[4]

Knowledge about them, therefore, has largely been obtained from the chronicles of their conquerors and annihilators and, to a lesser extent, the reports of divers individuals who did not have the incentive to distort the truth. More recently, archaeological and ethnohistorical studies have helped to unearth some of the myths and to shed new light on the history of the Caribbean's first known citizens.

The popular but largely mythical historical rendition is that the Caribbean in 1492 was inhabited by three groups of people: the Tainos (Arawaks), a gentle, peace-loving, and "effeminate" people who inhabited the Greater Antilles, Trinidad, and a few of the smaller islands; the Callinagoes (Caribs), a fierce, warlike, and cannibalistic people who inhabited the Lesser Antilles and were in the process of driving the Tainos from the Bahamas and Puerto

Rico at the time of the Spanish conquest; and the Ciboneys (Guanahatabeys), a primitive people who occupied the western portion of Cuba.

Studies have been conducted which question whether the Ciboneys, a society of hunter-gatherers, ever existed. William F. Keegan expresses the view that their inclusion among the aboriginal peoples of the Caribbean was more fictional than real. He wrote:

> We presently lack sufficient evidence to support the belief that such a population survived in western Cuba until Spanish contact. The weight of the evidence suggests that the Guanahatabey was a creation of the Spanish or the Taino imagination, or both, that has been given life by modern investigators eager to add substance to a prehistoric material culture. In sum we must dispense with the Guanahatabey until more conclusive archaeological evidence for their existence is uncovered, and we must explain the aceramic remains found throughout the Antilles solely on the basis of material evidence.[5]

The Tainos (Arawaks)

Available evidence indicates that the Tainos were an agricultural people who originated in the Orinoco Basin in South America. By A.D. 600 they had colonized southern Quisqueya (Hispaniola), Xaymaca (Jamaica) and eastern Cuba. By A.D. 1200 they were settled in the Greater Antilles proper. Their main crops included yucca (from which they made cassava bread), yams, sweet potatoes, maize, chilis, fruit and vegetables. They knew the art of irrigation and used it to protect their crops, especially during periods of drought. They also produced cotton which they wove into cloth of an excellent quality. It furnished them with beds and served other domestic purposes. To utility they also added elegance, and tinged their cloths with a variety of dyes[6]. Their diet included large quantities of fish and shellfish, lobsters, crabs, turtles, and manatees (sea cows). For fishing they used dugout canoes and wooden spears.[7] Of their pottery skill, this is what Bell had to say:

> They were good potters. Their bowls and ewers were serviceable and aesthetically pleasing. Although nothing has been found that bears comparison to the ceramics of Central America, their decorated pottery, which may have served some religious purpose, indicates a common heritage. In short, the Taino culture was late Neolithic.[8]

In spite of his characterization of the Tainos as savages, Reverend Coke gave high marks to Taino pottery. He wrote:

> Their domestic utensils were elegant and various, surpassing in number, and excelling in beauty, what might reasonably be expected from men in a savage state, inhabiting abodes unfrequented by strangers. When Bartholomew Columbus paid a formal visit to the unfortunate princess Anacaona, who then held considerable dominions on the island [of Quisqueya], he was surprised at the magnificence and value of the utensils which her house afforded. Nor was he less astonished at her generosity, than dazzled with the workmanship which many articles displayed.[9]

They made good use of the calabash tree that abounded in the islands. They used the barks to make hammocks, cords, ropes and portable baskets; and the leaves as covering for the roofs of their houses which were made from hard wood. They also used fine grass to cover the roofs of their houses because grass kept the interior of the houses cool[10]. Their hammocks, 6 to 8 feet long, were made from cotton cloth which they wove on their looms. This clearly illustrates that their nudity or semi-nude attire had nothing to do with an inability on their part to fabricate clothing.

The Tainos traced descent through the female line to a common ancestress. They spoke several languages, but there was one language that was used for political and commercial purposes. While there was some evidence of "private property", it was not reported as an important item of inheritance[11]. Although the wife resided patrilocally by moving to her husband's village, the husband resided avunculocally (with his mother's brother) in the village of his lineage[12]. Tainos in the Lucayans (the Bahamas) were matrilineal and matrilocal.

They lived in villages consisting of 3,000 or more residents. The society had a three-tiered structure. The first tier consisted of the village which was presided over by a headman or chief whom the Spanish called "cacique". The second tier consisted of the district which in turn comprised a number of villages and was headed by a district chief who occupied a position of higher authority than the village chief. The third tier consisted of the region which was headed by a paramount chief to whom the district and village chiefs were subordinate.

For diversions they held public dances in which the musical instruments were conch shells and the drum. Like the Africans, they composed songs about significant events and in honor of their fallen heroes. These songs, which were sung by all, in time became a part of the Taino lore. They played a game that was somewhat similar to cricket and they delighted in competing with each other in wrestling, foot and canoe racing, and other activities that demonstrated their physical prowess. Their relationship with their fellow men was characterized by honesty and integrity. Their word was their bond. In conformity with the climatic conditions, they wore very little or no clothes at all. Yet there was no word in their language for "rape" or "sexual abuse." Columbus and the Spaniards violently introduced these practices to them.

The aboriginal peoples of the Caribbean, like most of the Africans, had a philosophy of the world that corresponded to their way of life. They were a god-fearing people who saw a oneness between themselves and other natural phenomena and who believed in an omnipotent supreme deity. This pantheistic-type deity was manifested through the phenomena of nature. They believed in a life after death, the quality of which would be judged by a system of rewards and punishments at the end of one's earthly life. This philosophy of nature and the world, peculiar to the peoples of Southeast Asia, North and South America, and West, Central and other parts of Africa, is called Shamanism. The same Shamanist beliefs were once prevalent among Celtic, Germanic, Slavic and other European peoples. The Shinto religion in Japan, Lamaism in Tibet, Taoism in Chinese communities, and animism in Mongolia have Shamanist foundations.

The religions of the Amerindians have been largely misrepresented by people who failed to understand the connection they made between humans and god and who, because of racialist and ethnocentric sentiments, were unwilling to thoroughly investigate with a view to understanding these religions, or to concede any type of sophisticated, philosophical capacity to a non-European people whom they regarded as "savages". Thus, they ignored the fact that the fetishes (natural phenomena), allegedly worshipped as "deities", were mere tokens of the deity which is revealed and symbolized through such things as birds, lightning, thunder, and so forth.

The Tainos believed in a supreme being who was creator of

the world. He was the creator in the sense that it was he who, like Hurakan and Gucumatz of Guatemalan mythology, in the beginning when everything was under water, said "Earth!" and earth appeared. Mountains rose out of the water and the earth became covered with vegetation. Animals appeared on the earth and, at a later time, so did man.[13] The creator, whom they called Jocahuna, did not interfere in the daily lives of humans, but instead delegated this task to Zemis (servants) who in turn interfaced with humans through the bohitos (priests). It was the bohitos – the pharmacologists and village doctors – who conveyed the prayers of the Tainos to the deity. According to Reverend Coke, the Tainos' religion, notwithstanding their belief in a supreme being, was idolatrous and superstitious. He wrote:

> But though they allowed of a supreme God, to whose goodness they gave the fullest credit, they imagined, like most other savage nations, that he was utterly regardless of the world and its inhabitants. They conceived that, highest in felicity as well as power, he had committed the government of the world, and of all sublunary things, to the management of inferior agents or genii, which they called zemi, who by their power produced the various changes of moral and physical evil, which are seen here below. These subordinate beings to whom the Almighty had committed the government and direction of the world, they considered as of a malignant nature, aiming at the subversion of the original and grand design of God.[14]

It is extremely difficult to fathom how the relationship between the supreme being, the zemi and the bohito differed from that of Jehovah, the angels and the priest or minister. However, Reverend Coke characterized this as a perversion designed to fill the minds of the devotees with "frightful conceptions and horrid apprehensions." As far as he was concerned, a fraud calculated to control the people economically and politically was being perpetrated by the cacique and the bohito, both of whom worked together in concert. He believed that "the religion of these natives was idolatry, but it answered the end for which it was cherished. It was the tool of the cacique, the trade of the bohito, and the bugbear of the affrighted crowd."[15]

It is clear from Reverend Coke's political commentary that he chose to ignore not only the religious philosophy of the Tainos, but also their social organization, both of which constituted a cohesive whole. In a society that was governed by the force of customs, in which the communal form of ownership prevailed, the cacique and bohito could not have had the consciousness nor the aspirations attributed to them by Reverend Coke.

Greed, individualism, and the craving for wealth and power are historically determined phenomena that find expression in societies which are divided into social classes, and in which private property assumes a position of prominence. Indeed, even if one should argue, albeit metaphysically, that these characteristics could be cultivated independent of the historical conditions, the cacique and the bohito would have been like thieves who have stolen money which they cannot spend.

The essence of this "idolatrous" religion was revealed with the utmost clarity on July 7, 1494 by a venerable cacique in the island of Cuba. After extending the customary hospitality to Columbus and his men, he addressed them, through an interpreter, in these words:

> Whether you are divinities, or mortal men, we know not. You are come into these countries with a force, against which, were we inclined to resist it, resistance would be folly. We are all therefore at your mercy. But if you are

men subject to mortality like ourselves, you cannot be unapprized, that after this life there is another, wherein a very different portion is allotted to good and bad men. If therefore you expect to die; and believe with us that everyone is to be rewarded in a future state according to his conduct in the present, you will do no hurt to those who do none to you.[16]

Unable to show in what way this philosophy of life after death differed from that of Christianity, Reverend Coke expressed the view that this cacique represented an exception, a gem sparkling in the midst of surrounding rubbish, and that the Lord who works in mysterious ways had, through this cacique, revealed his greatness even unto savages.

Their belief in the hereafter, heaven and hell, bore a lot of similarity to that of Christianity and the African religions. The Tainos regarded heaven, Coyaba, as a fertile region with plants that never lost their verdant lustre, the abode for only those who were good during their lifetime. It was a region abounding with flowers, fruits, and gently flowing streams and rivers. It was a paradise of peacefulness and tranquility. Here, the spirits of those gone by, the ancestors, enjoyed the pleasantness, tranquility, and delicious fruit, free from worries and anxieties. In this place they would interface with other good people and be reunited with their ancestors. Those whose lives were characterized by evil would be denied access to Coyaba. They would be sentenced to a region that was bereft of fertility, a gloomy and desolate place consisting of evil and degenerate souls like themselves. Instead of the soothing music and laughter of Coyaba, there would be the incessant violence of the hurricane, the roar of thunder, and the blasts of lightning, in a climate at once hostile to their natures, and inconceivably terrible to their apprehensions[17].

The Callinagoes (Caribs)

The Callinagoes referred to the earth as "Mother" and treated "her" with the utmost reverence in appreciation of the gifts – food, amenities and life itself – she bestowed on them. In this regard, Bisnauth wrote:

> Of much more importance to the Caribs was the earth. To them, the earth was a bountiful parent who provided them with all the good things of life; but it is to be doubted that the earth assumed the status of a deity among the Caribs in the way it did among other peoples.[18]

They have been depicted as cannibals who continuously preyed on the peace-loving Arawaks. It was not explained, however, how the Tainos were able to withstand the incursions and voraciousness of the Callinagoes, more adept in the art of warfare than themselves, for so many years. In fact they were more advanced than the Tainos in the area of warfare because their weapons included the bow and arrow which the Tainos did not have.

Like the Tainos, the Callinagoes were tillers of the soil. They planted maize, manioc, yams and a variety of fruits and vegetables. They supplemented their diet with fish and shellfish. Like the Tainos, they fished for lobster, crabs, turtles and manatees. As Walters stated, the Callinagoes, as a people, did not eat human flesh, because they had an abundance of food at all times. From all accounts, the sea and the rivers were teeming with fish; agricultural yields were exceedingly high and there was an abundance of edible wild fruits[19].

If they were cannibals, they would have eaten the Taino women they captured rather than marrying them. In fact the ambition of many a young Callinago warrior was to marry a Taino woman, because such a marriage was at the same time a testimony to his military prowess. If they were cannibals, they would have eaten their European and Taino male captives rather than making them their servants. If they were cannibals, they would have eaten the aged members of their community rather than caring for them and terminating their lives only as an act of mercy. If they were cannibals, they would have eaten their dead and their fallen heroes, rather than burying them and mourning their deaths. If they were cannibals, the French priests who lived with them in Dominica for over twenty years in their attempt to proselytize them would long ago have sated the appetites of divers voracious Callinagoes. Keegan noted:

> The so-called cannibals are a legacy of the Spanish. On the one hand the Tainos were easily subjugated by the Spanish because they often attempted compromise and accommodation rather than warfare; they were thus considered peaceful. On the other, native peoples in the lesser Antilles adopted more aggressive postures toward the Spanish, French, English, Dutch, and anyone else who threatened their sovereignty. It is interesting to note that the Island Caribs' response proved the more successful since they survived unconquered into the eighteenth century.[20]

The Callinagoes also produced cotton and distinguished themselves in the art of weaving. The cotton cloth which they dyed to produce an array of colors were used to make their clothing and hammocks. They felled trees which they dug out and made canoes that could accommodate more than fifty (50) persons. Their pottery was of an exquisite quality, exacting from their detractors a grudging admiration. In spite of his arrogance and impudence, Reverend Coke gave high marks to their pottery skill. He wrote:

> In addition to this circumstance, they had established

among them a species of pottery, which supplied their domestic conveniences. These kitchen utensils they formed from the native clay of the islands. They gave them their form while in a malleable state, and burnt them in kilns, not unlike the potters of more refined nations, where arts and manufactures are carried to such degree of perfection as to raise such articles to a rank of national importance. Nor were these utensils of a rude and unseemly nature. Like the weapons of their warriors, they were finished with exactness and precision; and would have conferred no disgrace on the professed artists of England. Their materials, it is true, were adapted to these purposes; but still, nothing less than ingenuity, not often to be found among men who possessed hardly anything human but the shape, could have brought to perfection such articles as required a tedious though simple process.[21]

The Callinagoes also believed in a supreme being and an evil spirit which they called Hurakane,[2] each respectively personifying the concepts of good and evil. It was their belief that the supreme being, for whom they had no name, continuously battled with Hurakane to protect them from evil, but did not directly interface with them. Like the Tainos, they believed that the Supreme Will was communicated to humans through spiritual intermediaries who interacted with the boyez (priest). They also shared the view that at death the brave and worthy would be assured a place in heaven and the cowardly and despicable a place in hell. Drumming and dancing featured very heavily in the festivities, rituals and ceremonies of both peoples; and the boyez and bohitos

---

[2] Hurakane was in some ways analogous to Shango, the Yoruba god of Thunder. Yoruba culture and religion had a significant impact on the growth and development of Santería in what were the strongholds of Taino culture in Cuba and Puerto Rico.

– the philosophers, doctors and pharmacologists – administered to their medical and spiritual needs.

These are the same people whom the French Capuchin priests in Grenada described as being "indifferent to things spiritual." The confrontation between the Europeans and Amerindians was not simply the convergence of two different races. It was a clash of two different socioeconomic systems, cultures, values and ethics. In a word, a clash of two different worlds. In the Greater Antilles, the Tainos greeted the Spanish with the utmost hospitality, having no idea that their benefactors were capable of such evil. With the brutality characteristic of most colonizers, the Spanish invaders imposed on the Indians the iniquitous and painful condition of being strangers on their own soil.[22] The barbarity and genocidal acts of the Spanish are aptly described by Reverend Coke:

> Though capable of generous actions towards strangers in distress, though exercising the rights of hospitality with all ardour of disinterested friendship towards their invaders; they have been the unhappy victims of perfidy, and the whole race has long since been extinct. They were robbed of their native lands by strangers; they were plundered of their property; and their complaints, under such acts of injustice, only exposed them to the insults of their inhuman pillagers; and were made the pretext for new scenes of depredation. Their persons, as well as lands, were seized; and they were doomed either to expire under those burdens which the merciless Spaniards imposed, or to find a release from their calamities through instant death, though attended with circumstances of barbarity which scarcely anything short of the infernal demons could be able to inflict.[23]

By the time that the Tainos realized that their Christian "guests" were unmoved by their show of generosity and friendliness, and that fighting for their survival was an imperative, it was too late. Some of the Tainos, believing that loyalty to the Spaniards would be rewarded with gratitude, formed alliances with the invaders to crush the resistance of their fellow Tainos. Guacanagari of Quisqueya is exemplary of this treachery. Alonso de Hojeda was able to defeat the hosts of Guatiguana, using the loyal Guacanagari as an ally, and then lure the fierce Caonabo himself into ambush with false promises, and handcuff him to the wall of Isabella's crowded jail.[24] In the Lesser Antilles, the Callinagoes did not have to be told what the intentions of the Europeans were. They had been apprized of the fate of the Tainos and were prepared to defend themselves and their territory against the inhumanity of the invaders. They were able to defend themselves against the Spanish, French, English, and Dutch for at least two centuries. Some were massacred, like those in St. Kitts by the English and those in Grenada, Martinique, and Guadeloupe by the French. They continued their resistance until their final strongholds in Dominica and St. Vincent were overrun in the eighteenth century by superior arms.

The Black Caribs, the offsprings of miscegenation between African slaves and Callinago women, have survived in St. Vincent, Belize, and other countries. Bastide noted that in 1635 two Spanish vessels carrying Africans sank off the coast of St. Vincent, and the slaves, after massacring the European crew, made good their escape. In 1672, a similar fate befell an English slave ship. In both cases the Caribs reduced the Africans to slavery, but the slaves formed a part of the family, and miscegenation between the two races very soon began. This, he said, is the origin of the half-breed group known as 'Black Caribs'[25].

In 1795, the Black Caribs and the Callinagoes of Dominica

and St. Vincent, under the leadership of Chatoyer and his brother Devalle, joined forces with the Africans and the revolutionary French leader, Victor Hugue, against the British who were fighting to restore African slavery in the Caribbean territories. They were defeated and many of the survivors banished to the Yucatan Peninsula. The descendants of the Black Caribs are to be found in Honduras, Belize, Mexico and Nicaragua, and a small number in St. Vincent. A very small Callinago community still exists in the island of Dominica. The larger Taino and Callinago communities are to be found in Guyana, Surinam and Cayenne.

The Tainos and Callinagoes in the Caribbean islands who numbered between 5 to 10 million in 1492 were exterminated by the Spanish in less than seventy-five years. This carnage, the elimination of an entire people from the face of the earth, is unparallelled in human history. The self-acknowledged perpetrators of the genocide of the Tainos were the Spanish conquistadores, with the Roman Catholic Church of Spain a willing abettor. In like manner, the Roman Catholic Church of France, the Church of England, the Church of Scotland, the Lutheran Church and the Dutch Reformed Church were accomplices in the extermination of the Callinagoes.

The food of the Amerindians remains even today a central part of the diets of the populace in the islands of the Greater Antilles and Lesser Antilles, as well as the Guianas. Their methods of cultivation are also still being utilized; and, especially in Cuba and the Dominican Republic, Taino words constitute a part of the local vocabulary. In the Guianas the people and culture have survived but have not grown. They serve as a source of attraction to American, French, British, German, Dutch, and other tourists who visit the Guianas each year. They lead an isolated existence and the society continues to treat them as a part of its general fauna and flora. They have so far failed to meet the challenges of the 21st century, or to reconcile the contradiction between their material and spiritual condition and that of the rest of the society of which they constitute an integral part.

The African Religions

Most of the Africans who came to the Caribbean and the New World had a religious outlook that was essentially similar to Shamanism. Each ethnic group had its own religion, but the differences between them were more formal than substantive. Their religious and social practices varied according to region, climate, environment, and other factors. Young stated:

> Among the Sudanic Nuer, twins have traditionally been revered, whereas among the West African Igbo, tradition dictated that twins be destroyed at birth. Other examples of variance abound, revealing that African traditional religion varies considerably from place to place. Rain doctors, for example, are more prominent in areas susceptible to drought than in those in which the climate is more temperate.[26]

In spite of the differences among the several ethnic religious expressions, Africans, like Amerindians, had a certain unanimity in their philosophy. The essence of this unanimity lies in the belief in a supreme deity or deities with the qualities of omnipotence, omniscience, omnipresence and sanctimoniousness; the existence of intermediaries (lesser gods) which interacted with the priesthood; the existence of good and evil spirits; the close nexus between the living and the dead and the need to appease and retain a strong relationship with the ancestors; a system of punishment and reward after death; the inseparable connection between humans and their environment; and the sanctity of certain fetishes as attributes of the supreme deity. So striking are the similarities between the African and Amerindian religious expressions, that in the Black Carib religion – a fusion of the two cultures – it is difficult to distinguish the African from the Amerindian elements. Of the African belief in the supreme deity, Bisnauth wrote:

> Given the massive difficulties which the practice of
> African religion faced in the Caribbean, it must surely
> be one of the most remarkable things in the region's
> history that so many aspects of that religion survived.
> One such aspect was the African belief in the existence
> of an almighty god. The people of West Africa from
> among whom the slaves were recruited knew this deity
> by several names. The Akan-speaking Ashanti, Fanti
> and Brong peoples knew him as 'Nyame or Nyankopon;
> the Yorubas of the lower Niger, central Dahomey and
> Togo-land called him Oludumare or Olurun; the Ewe-
> speaking Fon of Abomey, Allada of Porto Novo, Ge of
> Togo and Ga of the Gold Coast called him Mawu. To
> the Igbos he was Chukwu.[27]

Africans believed themselves to be regents over nature and
attempted to manipulate their natural milieu by knowledge of its
properties and by appeals to the invisible, that is, divinities, spirits,
and ancestors[28]. They regarded themselves as integral parts of their
environment and of the universe. No wall existed between the
visible and the invisible, between the animate and inanimate, and
between the living and the dead. According to Young:

> Spiritual energy permeates the invisible and the visible.
> By way of that energy, humans interact with the
> invisible, manipulating the cosmos in order to promote
> fortune or misfortune. ..... That the ancestors are a
> prominent part of most traditional societies also bears
> repeating. Seen as a part of families, they reveal how
> intensely Africans believe themselves a part of the
> invisible. When ancestors, however, are no longer
> remembered by name, they become dangerous,
> unpredictable spirits inhabiting the bush or forest.[29]

African traditional society, therefore, was structured as a
cohesive social, political, and religious entity. Any breach of the

approved communal standard disturbs the balance in society and the unity between humans and god. As such, the violator will become subject to the wrath of the invisible, the gods. "More specifically, sin is incurred in the violation of taboos, the neglect of ancestors, and asocial behavior."[30]

When the African religions came to the Caribbean they lost many of their original features, an inevitable consequence of their being uprooted from the environment which represented an integral and vital element in their theological and cosmological outlook. Roger Bastide underscores this point when he wrote:

> A man's birthplace was not simply a fortuitous concatenation of mountains, lakes, or rivers, but a socio-geographic entity in which the local myths, the distribution of tribes over the territory, the established meeting places of the secret societies, etc., were but parts of a single whole. The African does not see the hillside just as a hillside, but as the abode of a certain spirit or the traditional center of a certain ceremony.[31]

Torn from their old habits, environment and customary way of life, it was impossible for the Africans to keep these religions intact. African religious beliefs, therefore, underwent considerable changes in the effort to adapt to the new and difficult environment. The problem of religious retention was further compounded by the deliberate policy of the colonizers to separate members of the same ethnic group in order to reduce the incidence of revolts. Bastide argues:

> While the slaves' minds might remain African, their actions were gradually being Americanized. Nevertheless, in the long run, and especially after the abolition of the slave trade, such memories were bound to lose their original clarity. They were out of place in this new environment; slowly but inevitably they became blurred, and at last faded into total oblivion.

This, at least, is what happened in the great majority of cases. If these memories were to survive, they had to attach themselves to some existing custom; establish a foothold in the here-and-now, find some sort of niche or hiding-place.[32]

Hiding-places were found in the mountains of Jamaica, Santo Domingo and Haiti, in the woods of St. Lucia, and in the jungles of Surinam, Cayenne and Brazil. These memories were refreshed in Cuba, Trinidad, Grenada, Brazil and Jamaica by the introduction of thousands of West Africans – slaves and indentured laborers. In the United States, the French and Dutch Antilles, Barbados, the Bahamas and the smaller islands of the British Caribbean, these religions have ceased to exist as cohesive theological expressions, but have survived as folklore.

The religions that have survived such as Winti of Surinam and Cayenne; Vodun of Haiti and the Dominican Republic; Santería of Cuba and Puerto Rico; Shango of Trinidad and Grenada; Big Drum of Grenada and Carriacou; Kumina and Convince (Bongoism) of Jamaica; Goombay of Belize; Kumfa of Guyana; Kele of St. Lucia; and Xango, Candomble and Macoumba of Brazil are all syncretizations of African religions (which have perished in their pure forms) and Roman Catholicism or Protestantism. And while the deities, rituals, ceremonies and religious objects are decidedly African, they relate to the Africa of yesteryear.

The attempt to separate members of the same ethnic group was unsuccessful, mainly because each European power acquired most of its slaves from its own hunting-ground in Africa; and because the slave traders were more concerned about profits than ethnic selection. As a result, Yoruba culture predominates in Cuba, Trinidad, St. Lucia and Brazil, which explains the close similarity between Santería, Shango, Kele and Candomble. The Yoruba "gods", Oshun, Ogun, Shango, Eshu, Obatala and others are also common to these religions. Like Vodun in Haiti and the Dominican Republic, they identify many of the "gods" with Roman Catholic saints and incorporate elements of Roman Catholicism. Kele, for instance, is essentially a form of Shango, having basically the same ceremonies and rituals. It is a highly syncretistic religion, but the dominant elements are unmistakably Yoruba.

The "Bush Negroes" of Surinam and Cayenne are largely descended from the Fanti-Ashanti people. Their culture, virtually free from European influence, is the "most African" of all in the New World. Their religion, Winti, has many of the religious characteristics of the Fanti-Ashanti people who have strong surviving roots in many islands of the British Caribbean, especially Jamaica. It contains features that are similar to Vodu of Dahomey and the religions of many of the West African ethnic groupings.

The Fanti-Ashanti culture is also the most dominant in Guyana and Jamaica, and the surviving religions – Kumfa, Kumina and Convince (Bongoism), respectively – reflect features that are common not only to Winti but also to Vodun, Santería, Candomble and Shango. The Yoruba gods Obatala, Oshun and Shango are also common to Kumfa, Kumina and Convince. The culture of the Ewe-speaking people of Dahomey is most dominant in Haiti, and their religion, Vodu, has survived as Vodun or Vodoun – a combination of Vodu and elements of Roman Catholicism. In the Dominican Republic, Vodun has a number of Amerindian deities, which suggests an early fusion of African Vodu and Amerindian Shamanism. Bisnauth underscores the fact that African religious practices have survived notwithstanding the deliberate attempt by the European conquerors to eradicate them.

In Guyana, "komfo" (i.e. akomfo) dancing with its emphasis on spirit possession has had a long tradition. In Trinidad, the worship of Shango, Ogun, Eshu and other recognizably African spirits survived. In St. Domingue, slaves worshipped Damballa, Legba, Shango and other gods of identifiably Dahomean origin. In both Trinidad and St. Domingue (Haiti), the worship of African divinities was to combine with that of Roman Catholic saints. ....The Bush Negroes of Surinam worshipped gods whom they associated with the woods and the rivers in the manner of their African forefathers. The *kele* ceremony as well as the *katumba* dance which survived in St. Lucia undoubtedly had its origin in the worship of African divinities. In the French islands in the eighteenth century, the belief in the 'water mother' existed, as it did in the Dutch colony of Surinam.[33]

The concept of the 'river-mother', which will be further discussed, is also peculiar to the religious beliefs of the Kongos and the Kromantins (Fanti-Ashanti).

Central to all these religions is a system of ethical norms and conduct; the arts and crafts of healing and folk medicine; the involvement of deities in the moral, social, and emotional affairs of humans; the existence of spirits which can be utilized for good or evil purposes; the practices of divination, conjuring, and exorcism; a profound belief in life after death; and the ability to communicate with the ancestors. The religion of the Black Caribs also reflect these features and, like the Jamaican Kumina and Convince, Guyanese Kumfa and the Big Drum of Grenada and Carriacou, a heavy accent is placed on the ancestral spirits; on the need to respect and appease them; and on the ritual which is always conducted in familiar settings.

In Brazil, the Candomble of Bahia embraces the belief in one god, Olurun, who is responsible for the creation of the universe, and whose agents, Orishas, (same as in Santería and Kele) act as intermediaries between him and mortals, provide advice, redress wrongs, cure illnesses, and so forth. The Xango in Recife, the Batuque in Belem, the Umbanda in Rio de Janeiro, the Macoumba in Espirito Santo, and the neo-African religious expressions in Porto Alegre reflect features that are similar to Candomble, Santería and others.

An examination of these surviving religions reveals that the process of syncretization was already taking place in Africa prior to the development of the Slave Trade. In the New World a further syncretization of the religions of the various African ethnic groups and of Amerindian Shamanism took place, producing religions dominated by the group with the most representatives and influence. Elements of Roman Catholicism and Protestantism were later added to produce a religion which was not African, but which contained elements that were substantially African. Hence, the distinction between these religious expressions is merely one of syncretistic degree.

What is also true is that although the African religions have perished in many of the Caribbean territories, many practices and beliefs associated with the traditional ceremonies and rituals have survived. In Barbados, for example, a deceased person is still honored with the traditional "nine-night" festivities. In the Bahamas people still appease the spirits by spilling some of their drink before imbibing. And in St. Kitts the practice of killing roosters and draining the blood on the foundations of a new house is still observed.

One of the religions which has not survived, but which played a significant role in the struggle against slavery and colonialism is Myalism. Bastide asserts that it was the religion of the Kromantin – Fanti-Ashanti – people. Its chief god was Nyame whose will was communicated to the myal-men (priests) by lesser deities. The river also played an important role in the lives of the Kromantins because many ceremonies were held in honor of the "River-Mother". Myalism disappeared as a religion, but it has survived in at least two forms – Revivalism and Convince. According to Bastide:

> Jamaica ... enables us to observe the decline and break-up of a genuine African religion into two separate fragments. One of these -- the ecstatic trance -- can be accepted by Christianity, and reinterpreted in Christian terms. The other, being too remote from white religious attitudes, declines into magic. The term signifying magic, obeah, is quite certainly derived from the Ashanti word obayifo, which bears the same meaning. The 'obeah-men' are generally male, but there do exist a few 'obeah-women' too. Their business is to prepare objects that are meant to kill, or cure, or procure someone's love. Such objects are called obi (we should not forget that the Ashanti priest in Africa is known as Obi O Komfo). The general beliefs concerning the powers of these sorcerers, male or female, are very much in line with the African picture. They can fly through the air, suck the blood of their victims, radiate light from their anus, and turn themselves into animals. They have a special connection with Sasabonsan,[3] so much so that sasa has come to be used as a synonym for obeah-man.[34]

Bastide's statement that Myalism was a "genuine African religion" is accurate only if it means that Myalism was developed by the African slaves in Jamaica; because from its inception Myalism was a syncretism of Christianity and the African religions. The Akan-speaking people of Ghana – Fanti-Ashanti – had the

---

[3] Word for "Satan", "Devil

greatest influence in Myalism because they represented a significant proportion of the slave population in Jamaica. However, it is not quite accurate to state that "Obeah represents one of the fragments of Myalism" because Obeah also existed in Surinam, Guyana, and other territories in which the Akan-speaking people had a significant presence and Myalism was absent. Obeah, therefore, existed side by side with Myalism as an African retention. Bisnauth's commentary on the *obayifo* underscores this point:

> A significant change came over the role of the priest. This is best illustrated by contrasting the Akan *okomfo* (priest) with the *obayifo* (wizard). In West Africa, the priest mediated between the tribe and its gods. His role was a social one and the worship services at which he officiated were public affairs. One of his functions was to challenge and condemn the operations of the obayifo. The obayifo (from whose name the word obeah is derived) was regarded as a disciple of Sasabonsam. Possessed of supernatural powers, this functionary used his gifts to injure or kill people, usually for a price. The obayifo worked clandestinely at nights. He was regarded as evil, and his functions were regarded as disruptive of the welfare of the tribe or village. .....The general disfavor with which the plantocracy in the Caribbean regarded slave religious practices, and the official ban that was put on those practices in some territories, forced the okomfo to perform his office clandestinely in much the same way that the obayifo did in West Africa.[35]

From all accounts Obeah had existed prior to African enslavement. What the institution of slavery and the ban on African religious practices did were to transform the hitherto respected akomfo, houngans and babalawos (priests) into outlaws and, in so doing, placed them in the same category as the obayifos or sorcerers. Because of the important role of the priest in the affairs of the family and the community, this served to further shatter the cohesiveness that was once a characteristic feature of the African village. Eventually, the distinction between priest and sorcerer became blurred even to Africans, who ultimately began to identify them both as *obeah men or sorcerers*.

It is important to point out that the failure of Europeans to openly embrace Obeah had little, if anything, to do with its "being too remote from white religious attitudes." In fact, many Europeans, including those who are overtly Christians, are as superstitious as Africans and other non-European peoples. In fact, obeah men, palm readers, astrologers and other fortune-tellers become wealthy at their expense. It must also not be forgotten that magic, witchcraft, sorcery, and exorcism remain the lucrative subjects of the Western entertainment industry and popular literature. A more accurate statement is the fact that while Europeans could openly embrace Revivalism because it was quasi-Christian, more easily rationalized, and more capable of being controlled by them, Obeah represented a highly developed system that was strictly under the control of the African. This meant that Europeans, at least in the initial stages, would have had to become followers rather than leaders – a proposition that was socially, politically, and culturally unacceptable at that time.

Schuler is of the view that Myalism is a religion that was indigenous to Jamaica and that it was heterogeneous and not restricted to one ethnic group. She wrote:

> Myalism was the first Jamaican religion known to have addressed itself to the affairs of the entire heterogeneous slave society rather than to the narrower concerns of separate ethnic groups. It thus reflected, and perhaps contributed to, a new and important spirit of cooperation among enslaved Africans.[36]

Myalism absorbed two central elements of the Baptist version of Christianity – the inspiration of the Holy Spirit, and Baptism, in the manner of John the Baptist, by immersion – because they seemed to correspond with beliefs or symbols already familiar to them.[37] They recognized a similarity between the Holy Spirit and their concept of the Supreme Deity and, ritual immersion by water, as Bastide argues, is associated with the River-Mother of the Kromantin people's religion. However, Myalism was not spearheaded by the Central African ethnic groups as Schuler suggests. It emerged as the first religious organization of Africans in Jamaica. But the most predominant elements were undoubtedly Fanti-Ashanti. Its characteristics, as Alleyne suggests, are those of the typical West African "secret cult societies".[38] It was an organization, a society, or a "movement", and as such added a new dimension to the already existing belief system.[39]

The fact that Myalism lasted for nearly two hundred years is a testimony to its pervasiveness and general acceptance by and among the African slaves and later ex-slaves. Unlike the Baptist Society, it associated such things as slavery, poverty, racism, injustice and oppression with the conscious acts of evil men. The Myalists, therefore, offered a remedy against the "spirits" or "sorcerers" identified with these evils. Schuler, therefore, concludes that Myalism is a useful instrument for examining how Africans and their Jamaican descendants dealt with such problems as achieving unity and harmony in a heterogeneous slave population, confronting and overcoming the colonial system, preserving their mental and physical health, adjusting to emancipation, and even coping with the arrival of African immigrants.[40]

The loose nineteenth century-type myal organization survives in the form of Convince. The advent of the Kongos in the nineteenth century helped to strengthen the African elements in Myalism and ultimately to produce what became known as Kumina. Elsewhere Myalism became tighter and more structured, especially when it took over Baptist churches, for it not only converted these churches to Myalism but incorporated Christian elements into its own organization.[41] This fusion of Myalism and Christianity gradually brought into being, as Bastide indicated, Revivalism – Pukkumina and Revival Zion.

The ultimate disappearance of Myalism in Jamaica was not merely the result of a change in environment and condition of existence. It was singled out for persecution because of its militancy, effective rivalry with the Christian churches, strong appeal and attractiveness to Africans, and the uncompromising disposition of its adherents to the institution of slavery and other injustices. Its influence is still present in Kumina, Convince, Revivalism, and Rastafarianism, all of which, in one form or another, continued that legacy of militancy.[4]

The Role of the African Religions

The religions of the African slaves served both a social and a political function. They became the organizers and the cohesive units, which coordinated struggles against colonialism and the institution of slavery. In the British and Dutch colonies they served

---

[4] An in-depth study of the African religions in the Caribbean and the New World can be obtained from the writings of Melville Herskovits, Roger Bastide, George Eaton Simpson, Harold Courlander, Remy Bastién, Fernando Ortiz and others, all of whom have done a considerable amount of work on the subject.

a particularly important function, inasmuch as the Anglican, Presbyterian, Lutheran, and Dutch Reformed Churches had adopted the policy of denying religious instructions to the African slaves. It was one of the tasks of the Myalists, wisi-men, babalawos, houngans, and others to help reconstruct the lives of the Africans in the new environment through the preservation of the rites and ceremonies associated with birth, marriage, accomplishments, and death, notwithstanding the harshness of their new existence.

They made every attempt to maintain the identity and legacies of their respective ethnic groupings, regions and customs, in furtherance of which they established various forms of social organizations – "nations", "societies" and "governments" as they were loosely called. These organizations were instrumental in bringing members of the same ethnic group together; encouraging members of different ethnicities to communicate with, and provide mutual aid to each other; and offering some measure of dignity to all. They elected leaders to whom they gave such titles as "kings", "queens", "governors" and "chiefs" and invested them with authority that extended over designated areas and ethnic groupings. In this way they were able to preserve the culture for two centuries, albeit in different and altered forms.

At the same time, however, these organizations contained their own antithesis. The slavemasters and colonial administrators regarded them with amusement and quickly perceived them as instrumentalities to be used to foster rivalries and divisions among the different "nations" – Ewes, Kongos, Angolas, Hausas, Yorubas, and so forth. The *cabildos* of Cuba are a case in point. These were associations for mutual help, usually composed of slaves and their descendants from the same geographic or ethnic area in Africa.[42] The *cabildos* were sponsored by the Spanish colonial government for nearly two hundred years. Consequently, while they were able to preserve significant aspects of the culture of the various ethnic groups, especially the most dominant, the Yorubas, this type of sponsorship and control served to greatly stymie any effective resistance against the institution of slavery.

The slavemasters manipulated these organizations into competing with each other, gave preferential treatment to one or two of them, and used them as a buffer between themselves and the slaves. Thus, by placing under the supervision of the African "officials" such matters as trials for runaways, punishment for disobedience, whippings, and so forth, the slavemasters cleverly deflected from themselves the anger and hatred of the slaves. In so doing, the principle of *divide and rule* was put into practice, as Africans were pitted against each other. Among these organizations, however, there were always significant factions that refused to be used as tools in the furtherance of their own oppression, and severe measures were taken by the colonial administrations to suppress them. The religious societies, initially tolerated by the slavemasters as a source of derision, were ultimately outlawed when it was discovered that the singing and dancing accompanying the ceremonies and rituals were often planned rehearsals for slave revolts.

African religious ceremonies were, as a consequence, banned in most of the colonies and the religious societies had to operate as secret organizations. These secret religious societies became the sentinels and guardians of the African cultural remains and the organizers and leaders of slave revolts. Indeed there was hardly a revolt that was not planned and led by their members. These militant organizations demanded the most stringent demonstration of loyalty and secrecy from adherents and initiates.

Myalism, Vodun and Winti were among the most militant of these religious societies, adopting a position of consistent opposition to the perpetrators of the institution of slavery.

The Great Rebellion in Jamaica in 1760 was spearheaded by Kromantins (some of whom were adherents of Myalism) and led by Tacky, an okomfo (myal-man). African priests or akomfo were represented among the leadership of the 1763 Berbice (Guyana) Rebellion led by Cuffee and Atta. Boukman and several other leaders of the revolt that culminated in the Haitian Revolution, were houngans (priests) of Vodun. On the night of August 14, 1791, the Haitian Revolt commenced with a ceremony in the woods presided over by Boukman in the midst of a thunderstorm. The flashing of lightning and the rolling of thunder strengthened the belief of the participants that Shango, Yoruba god of Thunder, was in favor of the revolt. These leaders, however, whose activities were profoundly political, religious and social, and who were highly respected among their fellow Africans, were classified by the European conquerors as obeah men and sorcerers, in furtherance of their policy to discredit and treat as common criminals those among the victimized who challenge their own criminal practices.

Armed revolt, however, was not the only form of resistance engaged in by these religious societies. The priests – houngans, myal-men, akomfo, and babalawos – like the mayomberos, obayifos, and other sorcerers – made use of their vast knowledge of herbs and, with the aid of specially selected house slaves, poisoned an appreciable number of white overseers and countless uncooperative slaves. Both the priest and the sorcerer used herbs and plants which were believed to have medicinal or magical qualities – the one to heal and the other to harm. During the second half of the eighteenth century, death by poisoning had reached such alarming proportions, particularly in the French and British colonies, that stringent measures were taken to eradicate the secret religious societies which the Europeans called "witchcraft," "Obeah" and "black magic." Hesketh Bell wrote:

> Fifty or sixty years ago, the practice of Obeah being the cause of so much loss of slave property by poisoning, it was found necessary to enact the most stringent laws for its repression, and an important ordinance was passed in all the West Indian colonies imposing heavy penalties on any person found guilty of dealing in Obeah. Unfortunately, through the knowledge possessed by some of the old negroes of numerous poisonous bushes and plants, unknown to medicine, but found in every tropical wood, it is to be feared that numerous deaths might still be traced to the agency of these Obeah men. The secret and insidious manner in which this crime is generally perpetrated makes detection exceedingly difficult.[43]

In the aftermath of the Haitian Revolution, an ordinance was passed in Belize providing for the punishment of death to anyone found practicing Obeah or influencing the slaves to rebel; anyone claiming to have the ability to communicate with the devil; and anyone pretending to possess supernatural powers, aiding and abetting runaway slaves or in any way counselling disobedience to the institution of slavery. Although many of these laws have remained on the books in most of the Caribbean territories, very little was achieved by their enactment because there was hardly an African – free person or slave – who had the courage to testify against an African priest or a sorcerer.

In Cuba, the harsh conditions of slavery failed to destroy the secret societies and the Yoruba culture was strengthened by new arrivals from Africa as late as 1880, thereby facilitating the growth and development of Santería. In the French Antilles, the secret societies of the Ewe-Fon people and Vodu were suppressed. What remains of Vodu in these territories is magic, with conjuring and divination as its main features. In the United States the severe persecution that was triggered by Gabriel Prosser's revolt in 1800 was heightened after Nat Turner's in 1831. Although Prosser, Denmark Vesey, and Turner were professed Christians, their Christianity was essentially a fusion of Vodu and Protestantism. The secret societies in Louisiana and Missouri also fell victims to persecution and assimilation and, as in the French colonies, what remains is folklore, sorcery, conjuring and divination. In most of the English-speaking Caribbean territories Obeah, conjuring and fragmented ceremonial and ritual practices are all that remain of the African religions.

The African cultural heritage in Trinidad was greatly enhanced by the advent of thousands of indentured West Africans in the 1840s and 1850s who remained in the colony after the expiration of their indentureship. The Yorubas, the dominant group, were responsible for the development of Shango and for the preservation of various African cultural features, including music and dance. The "prevalence" of Obeah in Trinidad would superficially suggest an earlier Fanti-Ashanti or Kromantin presence, but this is most unlikely. What is true is that until 1797 Trinidad was a Spanish colony in which the French constituted a majority of the European population. Most of the slaves in the colony were brought there by French planters from Grenada, St. Lucia, Martinique and other colonies. Very few, if any, of the French slaves came from Ghana – home of the obayifo. Additionally, Britain abolished the Slave Trade in 1807 and this

Santera, priestess of Santeria. Courtesy of the Government of Cuba.

A "Santero", priest of Santeria. Courtesy of the Government of Cuba.

served to greatly reduce further shipments of slaves from West Africa to the British colonies.

The British inter-colonial slave trade was subsequently developed to provide slaves to the relatively new Trinidadian and Guyanese markets and to make up for the "loss" caused by the abolition of the African Slave Trade. While it is possible that Kromantins might have come to Trinidad through this medium, it is unlikely to have had any significant impact. The argument pertaining to the "prevalence of Obeah" in Trinidad may be more plausibly explained by the many similarities among the African religions and by the tendency of the colonizers to characterize as "Obeah" or "Voodoo" all forms of African religious expressions. Commenting on the prevalence of Obeah in Trinidad during the 1860s, Donald Wood wrote:

> Not only the uneducated Creoles resorted to the 'obeah' man or woman; Lord Harris (Governor during that period) hinted that members of the upper classes made use of them as well. Obeah was seen as a tenacious and superstitious rival to Christianity; but it was possible to believe in both simultaneously. An ordinance was passed in 1868 to forbid its practice and fourteen persons were convicted in the first four years; a legal enactment was nevertheless useless against the deeply engrained desire to intervene in the future and to sway the course of events.[44]

As if Christianity, or any religion for that matter, is free of superstition, Wood ethnocentrically relegates the religious beliefs of the colonized to the realm of idolatry. It is quite true, however, that superstition transcends class and race in the Caribbean as it does throughout the rest of the world. Indeed, even today in many Caribbean countries it is by no means unusual to see a "Mercedes Benz", "BMW" or "Thunderbird" parked on some remote hillside, its owner, a member of the upper class, clandestinely consulting with an obeah man or woman, babalawo, houngan or sorcerer inside the crude nearby dwelling.

Haitian Vodun

Throughout the Caribbean, the intense persecution of all African secular and religious organizations (especially the secret societies) that followed in the wake of the Haitian Revolution forced Myalism and other secret religious organizations to make a retreat. In Haiti the Revolution and Vodun had triumphed and the houngans could now operate without the intense persecution of the European State and the competition of the Roman Catholic Church. As a result, Vodun – a syncretization of what was remembered of Vodu, the religion in their own country of Dahomey, and of Roman Catholicism – developed as the religion of the ex-slaves.

The victory of the African slaves over the Europeans in Haiti and the ultimate establishment of the Haitian Republic in 1804 were electrifying and epochal. Although the significance of this victory has been dismissed by the European chroniclers of history, the event was, nonetheless, treated as one of monumental proportions by slavemasters. It was a defeat of the system of slavery that must be ranked among the most astounding of all times. It was the victory of an army of slaves, desperate to live as free humans, against the imperial armies of France, Britain and Spain – three of the most powerful nations of the world at the time. The Europeans were fully aware of the political and social implications of that victory. Yet they took great pains over the years to belittle and discredit it and make insinuations about the people's incapacity for self-rule. What is true is that for Africans throughout the Western Hemisphere, Haiti was like a ray of light at the end of a long tunnel. It was a citadel of freedom and hope to which Africans

– slaves and free persons – took refuge from the cruelty, dehumanization and indignities inflicted upon them by Europeans.

Toussaint L'Ouverture and other leaders of the Revolution were aware that France and the other European powers would attempt a reconquest of, and restoration of slavery in Haiti. Mats Lundahl wrote:

> That the French aimed to restore slavery is evident from official correspondence. Thus, the First Consul [Napoleon Bonaparte-PH] in a letter to the Minister of Marine, Decrès, on 7 August 1807 wrote: 'Everything must be prepared for the restoration of slavery. This is not only the opinion of the metropolis, but is also the view of England and other European Powers.[45]

Toussaint, who by 1800, had become the undisputed leader of the Revolution, felt that a militarily strong Haiti was the best guarantor for its people's freedom. To build up its armed forces, the country had to have the financial resources. Toussaint decided that agriculture, which had made Haiti the envy of France's rivals in pre-revolutionary times, would have to be revived. Unpopular though it was, he insisted that the large plantations had to be held together and small holdings discouraged. To get the newly liberated Africans to return to the plantation was most problematic because of their abhorrence of the gruelling nature of plantation life. Drastic measures had to be taken to compel the ex-slaves to return to the plantations.

> The agricultural workers were given eight days to return to their plantations. Every person who did not enlist in the army or who could not prove that he possessed a legitimate trade was by definition an agricultural worker. Severe penalties were meted out for those who helped agricultural workers to hide from the authorities. The workers were forbidden to leave the plantations to which

they had been assigned unless equipped with a legal permit. A rural police was created which was to run *vagabonds* down and return illegally escaped workers to the plantations[46].

Thus did Toussaint build his war economy. The country was at war and the freedom of the newly liberated slaves had to be protected. Work was organized in a military fashion and a stern discipline was maintained. 'It was rumored that when faced with an inspection by Dessalines, who was military commander of the West and in charge of the South as well, ten agricultural workers would do more work and cultivate more land than thirty slaves during the colonial period.'[47] These measures did not meet the approval of many. Toussaint's nephew, General Moyse, led an uprising in the North against his uncle. It was put down and Moyse executed in 1801.

Haiti was able to survive because of the measures taken by Toussaint, despite the people's resentment to them. Without them the leaders of the Revolution would have been unable to purchase badly needed arms, ammunition, and other materiel from the sympathetic John Adams, President of the United States. The victory, however, was a very costly affair for the Haitian people. Tens of thousands of men, women and children were butchered by the merciless French generals, Jean Baptiste Rochambeau and Victor Le Clerc. The Haitians retaliated by killing and expelling every European from Haitian soil. This response, albeit mild in comparison to the actions of the French, was extensively portrayed as an expression of African barbarism and savagery.

Although successive Haitian leaders invited European Catholic priests to return to the country, the Papacy, which found African rule in Haiti unacceptable, refused to recognize the Haitian state or permit European priests to work in the country. Roman Catholicism, therefore, was developed and maintained in the country by local creole priests. During this period, Vodun, which had played a significant role in the organization and battle-readiness of the Africans in the struggle for freedom, emerged as the popular alternative to Roman Catholicism.

The adherence to Vodun by the country's majority did not help the international image of Haiti. It must be recalled that all African religions, including Vodun, are even today characterized by Europeans as "witchcraft," "sorcery" and "superstition." Haiti was perceived as a country of wanton lawlessness, its people immersed in idolatry and sorcery. Edwin Fagg wrote:

> The only Negro republic in the world, it mocked those who advocated freedom for colonies; "Haitianization" became an opprobrious term in other countries. The population probably enjoyed lives of peace, freedom, and idleness, not caring if the world disdained them. Voodoo flourished, almost replacing the traces of Catholicism left from colonial times, and Rome had no influence on the remaining Catholics.[48]

Strangely enough, no Haitian ruler, except the Emperor Soulouque, ever publicly embraced Vodun. Dessalines and Christophe outlawed it, and Petión and Boyer allowed it to co-exist with Roman Catholicism. These leaders, partly because they subscribed to the perception that Vodun is superstition appealing only to the ignorant; and partly because of their concern about Haiti's international image, kept their distance from the religion. And yet Vodun is as authentic a religion as Judaism, Christianity or Islam, and is no more superstitious than any of them. Leyburn underscores this point:

> The word "superstition" is relative. It is a subjective

term, being generally applied to beliefs which we consider ourselves too wise, too advanced, to cling to. The sophisticated skeptic calls the belief in miracles superstition; the Christian regards the reverence for certain animals in India superstition: it is all a matter of view. Using the greatest number of criteria available for the definition of religion as distinct from vague superstition, religion may be said to be a set of beliefs about spirits or gods and their nature, about the origin of the world, about good and evil, about man's relation to the universe he knows; it includes a set of practices of worship; it is an attempt to ward off misfortune and to get good; it treats of what happens after death; it is a system of seeking security, solace and support in the face of a supposed supernatural. Vodun is all of these.[49]

The practitioners of Vodun were not averse to embracing and integrating into their religion the beliefs of others. Therefore, while the rites and ceremonies of Vodun are predominantly Dahomean, the ethnic group with the largest representation in the country, there are many that are derived from other ethnicities, as well as from Roman Catholicism. This practice of ritualistic integration, over the years, led to the development of a very complex, highly syncretistic religion. Leyburn wrote:

The Dahomean spirits or gods were Vodun; the dance in which the worshipper sought the inspiration of the spirits was a Vodun dance. Like all but the highly organized religions, this one recognized the validity of other beliefs. Its practitioners were not bigots. No hierarchy existed to keep out new accretions. Imperceptibly these were added to the original basic form: here an Arada spirit, there a Congolese prayer, and in many instances a Catholic saint, until the composite Vodun religion began to take shape.[50]

Unlike Christianity and other officially recognized religions,

Vodun has no hierarchical structure. Each houmfort (temple) has two organizational structures; one for the religious leaders, and the other for the lay members. The man (houngan) or woman (mambo) who is the chief religious leader of a Vodun temple is considered something akin to royalty. Their symbol of office is the asson – a gourd rattle with beads and snake vertebrae with an attaching small bell.[51] The emperors or empresses, as these leaders are called, should not be compared with the priests or priestesses of any other religion.

Further, their titles (emperors and empresses) were conscious and deliberate assertions of equal status with even the highest positions in European society. Their role in real terms can best be compared with that of the Pope in Roman Catholicism[52] or the Archbishop of Canterbury in Anglicanism. And even then that comparison is not quite accurate. For unlike the Pope or the Archbishop, the houngan and mambo have to serve in an apprenticeship capacity before assuming their duties. They have to cultivate and demonstrate community leadership and accountability because advice on practically all matters affecting the community is expected of them. Thus, Vodun is not just a living religion, but also a well-defined system of social practices and cultural values.

The houngan and mambo must be versed in the knowledge of herbs because they are the pharmacologists, physicians and psychologists of the community. They must be versed in the rituals associated with offerings and all other aspects of the religion. As Rodman observes, houngans must know how to cure colds with infusions, shock with salt, bleeding with spider-web applications, infections with garlic. He made reference to a case of a houngan on La Tortue who is said to have cured yaws with poultices of mould – the basis of penicillin.[53] The houngans and mambos are like the parents of the community. In fact they are called *papa* and *mama*. Their authority and power are also derived from their direct interfacing with the loas or *mystères,* the gods, and with the departed ancestors. According to Rigaud:

> Contrary to general opinion, among the countries where the Voodoo mystères originated must be included Judea and Ethiopia, for both the Jewish and the Ethiopian cults hold their origin to be from the sun. Among the Jews, the sun is represented by a serpent upon a staff – the serpent called Da(vid); among the Ethiopians, the serpent is represented by a lion – David – the Lion of the solar house of Judah (a title preserved by the Emperor of Ethiopia). In Voodoo the same serpent, likewise called Da, and the same lion, called *Legba,* preside at the head of the cult.[54]

There are hundreds of loas who receive deification from Haitians. Each district has loas whose existence is unknown outside the boundaries of that particular community. If Vodun ever reaches the stage of founding a seminary of sacred theology, one of its basic functions would be the collection, classification, and metaphysical and theological explanation of the attributes of the hundreds of loa, specifying whether they are Haitian or African in origin, Petro or Rada, powerful or complaisant, inclined prevailingly to benevolence or to malice.[55]

There is a small number, however, which is widely known and honored not only throughout Haiti but also in Africa where they had their genesis. These include Legba, the interlocutor between humans and god, guardian of thresholds, highways, gates, and crossroads; Erzulie or Aida Wedo, the moon, identified with the Queen of Sheba and the Virgin Mary, invoked by those who desire a change of fortune or who wish to become wealthy; Damballa, the

Vodun ceremony. Photo by: George E. Simpson. Courtesy of the National Anthropological Archives, Smithsonian

bringer of rain and fecundity, whose symbol – the serpent – is benign, not evil; Ogun, the god of war, who offers protection against the hazards of the battlefield; Baron Samédi, guardian of the cemeteries – the resting-place of the ancestors; and Agwe, god of the sea and ocean.

> Apart from the *loa*, there are two other categories of divinity which figure in the *rada* ceremonies: the *zaka* and the *guede*. The order of their invocation during these ceremonies (and consequently of the possessions induced) is clearly defined. First come the *loa*, whether African or creole, then the *zaka*, and last of all the guede. The *zaka* were originally Fon Vodun, responsible for agriculture...... The *guede* are divinities from Dahomey, but have no connection with the Fon; they belong to a people known as the *guede-vi,* whom the Fon conquered, and made into their grave-digging caste.[56]

These loas manifest their powers to humans in many ways. Spirit possession is one of the most common forms of such revelation. Possession in Vodun is similar to that of Santería, Shango, Winti or Kumina. The body of a 10 year-old, 100 year-old or a lame and infirm person is entered by a spirit which results in the total transformation of that individual. The person, or 'horse' as he or she is called, will vigorously engage in activities – dancing, jumping, wheeling, spinning and leaping – which would have been inconceivable prior to the possession. When the spirit departs from the body – the 'horse' – like one coming out of a hypnotic trance, experiences a great deal of fatigue but has no knowledge of what had transpired. Bastide wrote:

> There is the gods' chapel (*caye-mystère)*, with a stone-built altar on which sacrificial food offerings are laid out. There is a special chamber (*djévo)* in which the

*Haitian Vodun Drummers. Photo by: George E. Simpson.
Courtesy of the National Anthropological Archives, Smithsonian*

secret part of the initiation ritual takes place. There is an open peristyle or cloister, where public ceremonies are held; in the middle of this stands a central post, the *poteau-mitan*, round which the *hounsi* dance, and at the foot of which the priests (using fine flour for the purpose) trace out the various symbols of the *loa* on the ground. These symbolic patterns are known as *vévés*, and their function (like that of the music) is to make the gods 'descend' on their 'horses'.[57]

Depending on the loa, sacrificial offerings of chickens, goats or bullocks are made. However, human sacrifice is not and was never a feature of Vodun rituals or those of any other religions in the New World. These sacrifices are intended to appease an angry loa or to show gratitude to a generous one. The loas are conceived in much the same way as humans. Hence, they are not immutable. Some are more to be feared than others, some may be regarded with tender affection, but all are capable of working both weal and woe.[58]

Vodun became the galvanizer of the hopes and aspirations of the masses of Haiti . Its function was both religious and secular. It healed the sick, tended their physical and psychological wounds, protected its members from the cruelty and oppressiveness of successive Haitian rulers, rewarded do-gooders and punished the guilty, provided help to the very poor and destitute, and assisted in the funerals of those whose relatives were unable to do so.

Vodun was treated with contempt and dismissed by Europeans and the ruling class Mulattoes in much the same way as the practitioners themselves. Ignorance about the religion continues to this day, and has provided a fertile field of operation for the imagination of divers movie makers, novelists, journalists and ethnographers. Haiti – because it was an independent country ruled by Africans, and because a majority of its people embraced a religion, Vodun, which Europeans associated with idolatry – was depicted as a backward, lawless and superstitious country. The accession to power of the African general, Faustin Soulouque, who coronated himself Emperor Faustin I, was used by the enemies of Haiti and Vodun as further proof of the authenticity of their negative portrayal of the country. The fact that Soulouque was illiterate and an ardent believer in, and practitioner of Vodun helped to strengthen these prejudices.

In 1847, the President of Haiti, Jean Baptiste Riché, who had been selected for the office by the Council of State the previous year, died and was succeeded by Faustin Soulouque. The Mulatto ruling class was quite happy with the selection of the illiterate Soulouque whom it believed would keep the black masses happy without any disturbance to the status quo. In this they were terribly mistaken. By April 1848 Soulouque began a general massacre of all who opposed his will, including his Mulatto patrons. Planters, officials of previous governments, businessmen, and others were gunned down in cold blood. In turning against his patrons, Soulouque was motivated neither by class nor racial sentiments, but by sheer ambition and the lust for power.

In 1849 he proclaimed himself emperor and for the next ten years squandered the country's sparse resources in majestic extravagance. Several unsuccessful attempts were also made by him to reconquer Santo Domingo which had been conquered by Brigadier-General Toussaint L'Ouverture in 1800 and ruled by Haiti until 1844 when it liberated itself from Haitian rule. The last attempt in 1855 was defeated when France, Britain, and the United States intervened "on behalf" of Santo Domingo.[59] The 12 years of Soulouque's reign (1847-1859) represented the heyday for the practitioners of Vodun. For the first and only time in their history they were accorded official respect. Haiti's first three great leaders – Toussaint, Dessalines and Christophe – had all proscribed Vodun, partly because they understood and feared it and partly because they were seeking European and North American recognition of the republic.

The Emperor, however, and most of his officials openly practiced Vodun. Even members of the elite who were opposed to the religion had to keep their resentment to themselves for fear of offending the Emperor, a devout practitioner. For the first time also Vodun lost its anonymity and became known to the Haitian ruling class and the world at large as an authentic African religious expression, albeit synthesized, that had survived the rigors of the plantation system, French colonial oppression, and Christian missionaries. Leyburn wrote:

> As Soulouque had broken with the tradition of presidents who wished Haiti to be recognized as one of the community of civilized Western nations, so he allowed the traditional respect for Catholicism to die. As an emperor, he was a transplanted African chief; as a believer he was a follower of Vodun. The rites were practiced and the sacrifices made openly now. Men in high places dared to reveal their belief in native tenets. For twelve years Vodun flourished with official approval.[60]

Soulouque's Santo Domingo adventure was very costly to him. He had exhausted the country's resources and his soldiers were chastised on the battlefield. His military defeat in 1855 greatly contributed to his subsequent fall. Thus, in 1859 he was overthrown by the Mulatto general, Fabre Geffrard, who, on his accession to power, immediately entered into negotiations with the Papacy to have Roman Catholicism restored to Haiti as the official religion. The overthrow of Soulouque was simultaneously a dethronement of Vodun. Geffrard introduced a series of far-reaching and hitherto unprecedented political and religious changes in the country which contributed significantly to the pariah status of Haiti to the present day.

During Geffrard's rule, the country was opened up to foreigners, primarily investors and missionaries. It became the object of a host of foreign intrigues – U.S., British, French, Spanish, German, and Italian. From 1867, the year Geffrard was overthrown, to the end of the century, there were consequently several wars of presidential succession in which competing foreign interests were deeply involved. As a result, there was very little economic development. The country was making money, but it was not being used for development. It went into the pockets of foreign individuals, corporations and the local elites.

> The elite...naturally came to regard the government as the patrimony of their own class. They alone possessed the education and the intelligence which were required in official positions. The Negro military chiefs who generally occupied the Presidency were compelled to rely upon them for the greater part of the work of administration. As the native businessmen found themselves unable to compete with German and other foreign merchants who appeared in increasing numbers with the development of commerce, and who derived great advantages from the protection afforded by their own governments, the Haitian upper class were forced more and more to depend upon the public treasury for their livelihood. ... The ruling class had little interest in the construction of roads or the improvement of conditions in the rural districts, and the revenues were expended almost entirely for the benefit of the city population.[61]

In spite of the reforms, it was too late for Roman Catholicism. All the peasants were by this time thoroughly imbued with the ideas of Vodun, as were the lower orders in the towns. Most of the elite either clandestinely practiced Vodun or ignored religion altogether.[62] The changes instituted by Geffrard did little to help the image of the country as the myths and fantastic tales about Haiti persisted. For example, in December 1863 a young girl from the village of Bizoton was kidnapped and offered as a sacrifice by a group of religious fanatics. Eight persons were arrested and, after pleading guilty to the crimes of murder, sorcery and cruelty, were sentenced to death and executed.

This story was publicized not so much for its gruesomeness as for the fact that the people involved were Africans who claimed to be practitioners of Vodun. The sensationalist treatment that was accorded this incident by foreign journalists falsely asserted that the ritual murder was one of the features of Vodun. Some of these journalists came from countries where scores of people are ritualistically butchered each year by Satanists, necromancers or extremist Christian religious sects. Indeed, fanatics, claiming to be impelled by some supernatural power, have even killed and eaten the flesh of their victims. No one would suggest that because of these occurrences Europe and the United States have a culture of religious savagery and cannibalism. Yet the entire Haitian population was at once depicted as blood-thirsty cultists.

To this day Haiti continues to be dogged by these negative images. Adventure seekers, particularly those with a penchant for the exotic and the occult, find the country an irresistible magnet. They visit the country with the expectation of hearing eerie, mysterious drumbeats and blood-curdling screams, observing frenetic dances, zombies stalking their prey, orgies, sorcery and so

Vodun musicians in front of a chapel. Photo by: George E. Simpson. Courtesy of the National Anthropological Archives, Smithsonian

Vodun ceremonial parade. Photo by: George E. Simpson.
Courtesy of the National Anthropological Archives, Smithsonian

forth. No amount of public relations on the part of Haiti's leaders and well-wishers has been able to shake the prevailing deep-rooted misconceptions and myths about the country. In like manner, no amount of proscriptions and denials has been able to shake or destroy the legacy, strength and tenacity of Vodun among the Haitian masses.

Winti

In Surinam and Cayenne the victories of the Maroons enabled the Fanti-Ashanti religions to flourish in a relatively non-hostile environment. This resulted in the creation of Winti, the purest of all the surviving African religions in the New World. The Maroons, or "Bush Negroes" as they are called, consist of four major groups – Saramaca, Djuka, Boni, Paramacca, and a number of smaller groups – who successfully fought against the Dutch and the French and established their independent communities. These communities are located in both Surinam and Cayenne (French Guiana) and the groups or "tribes" are divided into clans or *lo*. Bastide wrote:

> At the head of the tribe is the supreme Chief *(gran man)*, who doubles the roles of civil leader and High Priest. For secular matters, judicial decisions in particular, he has the help of the *gran fiskari*. In charge of each *lo* we find a *gran kapiting*, assisted by a deputy captain and a forest officer. The *lo* is a social rather than a geographic unit; each one includes several villages, these being in the charge of a *basia* ... who acts as combined mayor and police chief. What gives the *lo* unity is its connection with some totemic creature (frog, parrot, etc.) which protects it, and which it is *kina* (i.e., taboo on religious grounds) to kill. Despite this hierarchy of officialdom, the political organization of the tribe is

essentially democratic. In every village there is a council of elders (*g'a sembi*), and also the Assembly, open to all grown men (*lanti krutu*); in the last resort decisions rest with the latter.[63]

Bush Negroes believe in a supreme being whose name varies according to the different groups. The dominant Saramacas, like the Maroons of Jamaica, call this deity *Nyame* or *Nyan Kompon*; the Aucas, *Nana*; and the Boni, *Masu Gadu*. As in Santería, there are lesser deities called *Winti*, a name most in use among the Saramaca, or *Gattu*, the term preferred by the Djukas.[64] "Winti" means wind, and the gods are as invisible as the wind. Gods of the cosmos, the earth, the forest and the water live in a stratified order that parallels the structure of human society. These gods were created by God or Anana (Nana is the name of a Dahomean deity).[65]

The Christian god was seen as the god of the Whites, with the potential of depriving traditional Bush Negroes of their obia and their freedom. Obia is considered a wisdom, a power the god gave the slaves to maintain themselves in life.[66] The *obia-man* (obeah man) in Bush Negro culture has the power to remove spells placed on individuals by the *wisi-man* (conjurer and sorcerer) who performs evil on others through the agency of malevolent spirits. While both the obia-man and the wisi-man have a knowledge of herbs and medicine, it is the *luku-man* who is the healer and doctor. In Jamaica, there is no distinction between wisi-man, obia-man and luku-man. The obeah man is identified with and performs all three functions. Bastide underscores this point:

> Magic is in the hands of the *obiaman*, in contradistinction to the *lukuman*, who are priests. However, it is important to distinguish, equally, between white magic (*obia*), and black magic (*wisi*). The former

takes two forms, one defensive, for protection against sorcerers (*tapu*), the other offensive known as *apo* by the Saramacas and *sabi* among the Djukas, this being employed to win someone's love, succeed in one's activities, and so on. Black magic is that practiced by genuine sorcerers (*wisiman*), who call up the spirits of the dead, render them slaves to their malevolent will, and force them to work for evil purposes. These enslaved spirits are known as *bakru*, and recall the famous *zombies* of Haiti.[67]

The victory of the Maroons was made possible with significant support from the Amerindians. Having been maltreated for longer and with greater severity by the Dutch in Surinam than the French and British in the other Guianas, they were loath to render the White man services or return runaways to him. In the 1670s it became abundantly clear that the Indians, antagonized by the Whites, were luring the Blacks to their side.[68]

[The Africans]... sought refuge and protection in the darkness and solitude of the inaccessible jungles farther inland. There, when left alone, they gathered again according to their original African tribes, founded their "clans" and settlements and with a courage born of despair defended these against the full-scale retrieving expeditions organized by their former masters and army detachments.[69]

Victory for the Maroons of Surinam, like elsewhere in the Caribbean and the New World, did not come easy. Not only did the Africans have to contend with a hostile and merciless enemy, they also had to survive in unfamiliar surroundings whose dangers were hitherto unknown to them. This point was underscored by Goslinga:

It is quite true that black ingenuity turned many of the disadvantages of jungle life into assets: they learned to turn the harshness of their abode to their advantage with respect to defense and concealment. They discovered many edible seeds and fruits in the forest, which were good substitutes for their regular food. They learned how to extract salt out of the various kinds of trees whose trunks contained this mineral. Their women learned how to make clay pots -- big ones to hold water, and smaller ones. But there always remained some basic problems which could only be solved at the risk of their lives. Agricultural implements were needed. To build a community that would have continuity they also needed women. Most runaways were men, and rarely did women voluntarily leave the plantations for the hazards of the unknown and uncertain life in the jungle. They were carried off together with tools and foodstuffs in many pillaging raids; any slave who refused to go off into the bush was killed.[70]

The shortage of women remained a serious problem for the Maroon communities throughout the period of slavery. Although this was somewhat mitigated by the institution of polyandry in the community, the need to conduct raids on the plantations for women was ever present. Matrilineality thus became the principal form of descent and social organization among the Maroons. The mother-child relationship took precedence over the father-child. In fact the father-child relationship itself is uncertain in such social structures. Bastide wrote:

A child belongs to its mother's clan, and is a member of her village. The family is of the 'extended' type, comprising not only mother, father, and children, but also grandparents, uncles, and aunts on the maternal side. Marriage involves free consent on the part of the bride, and obligatory gifts to her parents (substantially higher in value if she is a virgin); but it does not constitute a 'purchase' in the strict sense. All it implies is some sort of compensation to the parents for all the trouble they took in rearing the child - and to the group as a whole for the loss they sustain through being deprived of one of their members' labour.[71]

Today the Bush Negroes live as hunters, fishermen, lumberers and river freight carriers, maintaining in each of their communities, the manners, customs and traditions of their forefathers, shrouded in the fascinating, magical mystery of the African continent.[72] In Cayenne, their chiefs are "recognized" by the French government which also gives the tribes -- Boni and others -- its "protection". Approximately 10,000 to 15,000 of these Africans live in the hinterland of Surinam and Cayenne. Like the Amerindians, they are exempted from taxation and are not governed by the laws of French Guiana or Surinam. Their major contact with the rest of the society is by way of trade and transportation which they provide to travelers along the rivers. The Maroon communities were able to survive in Surinam because of the ingenuity, courage, skillfulness and perseverance of the Africans and, above all, the guidance, purpose, cohesiveness and stability provided by Winti.

Kumina, Convince (Bongoism) Pukkumina and Revival Zion

In Jamaica, Myalism was forced to make a retreat during the late eighteenth and early nineteenth centuries. It suffered a further decline after Emancipation when thousands of ex-slaves became Baptists and Methodists. In the 1850s and 1860s it was revived by the arrival of thousands of Kongos and Kromantin laborers into the colony and by the disenchantment and disaffection of the ex-slaves with the Baptist Church. It continued to operate as a secret society promising death to the white "sorcerers" and to those Africans who had substituted their cultural heritage for that of the enemy. Many black Christians who respected and feared the powers of the myal-men renounced Christianity altogether, while others retained a relationship with Christianity, but strengthened their links with their own culture.

The colonial administration reacted by strictly enforcing the laws against Obeah, and the akomfo, obayifos and myal-men were again on the run. In the meantime, Christianity, now strengthened by newer sects, continued its advance through the media of evangelism and education. By the last quarter of the nineteenth century the syncretization process which had been slowly taking place since the 1840s between Myalism and Non-Conformism ultimately gave birth to a new religious expression – Revivalism. "Angel-men" – African Christian priests – the products of this fusion, became the chief practitioners of the rituals and ceremonies of Myalism, which was severed into two parts – Revivalism and Convince (Bongoism). The angel-men evolved into the Revival Shepherd; and the traditional myal-men into the present day bongomen.

Kumina, a fusion of a number of African religions (especially that of the Akan-speaking peoples), Myalism and Protestantism, developed among the Maroons of Eastern Jamaica. The victories of the Maroons over the British in the seventeenth and early eighteenth centuries had enabled religion among the Maroons to flourish without interference from the colonizers or from Christianity. However, the defeat of the Maroons in 1795 and the subsequent banishment of hundreds of the survivors, first to Nova Scotia, Canada, and thence to Sierra Leone, West Africa, was a serious setback for Kumina.

Malachi "Kapo" Reynolds with staff and followers at Revival Zion ceremony. Photo by: George E. Simpson. Courtesy of the National Anthropological Archives, Smithsonian

There is a strong relationship between Convince and Kumina. This is quite understandable because both religions evolved from the same source and had their most significant presence in Eastern Jamaica. Additionally, both religions have had considerable myal influence. According to Mervyn Alleyne:

> Convince is clearly related to Kumina and Myalism. This link is illustrated by the lyric -- consisting of one line sung repeatedly -- of an important Bongo song. The lyric, "John see the kuruma home on a limbay," was recorded by Moore at a Convince ceremony. According to Moore, kuruma was sometimes replaced by its synonym *kumina* in the lyric, which refers to spirits that inhabit the limbs of trees (especially silk cotton trees). Such spirits are part of the belief system of many West African religions, as well as of Myalism and Kumina. This suggests that the terms *kumina* and *myal* mean "spirit", an interpretation supported by the fact that *myal* is apparently synonymous with "angel".[73]

In reference to the indentured Africans who arrived in Jamaica after Emancipation, Alleyne indicated that there was a sizable number of Kongos among them and that they were responsible for the re-Africanization of Myalism by the introduction of Kongo religious elements and Kikongo language into it. He argues that Myalism was given a Kikongo name by them which has come down to us as Kumina. He also credits them with the prevention of the further movement of Myalism away from its African origins, and the adoption of the term Convince to refer to it.[74] Hence, the link between Convince, Kumina and Myalism and the Kikongo influence, which led Schuler to conclude that the Kongos were most influential in the development of Myalism.

By the end of the nineteenth century some of the younger Maroons had migrated to the cities and non-Maroons and Christians had gained a firm foothold in Maroon country. A further merger between Christianity, Convince and Kumina took place, resulting in the formation of a revivalist-type religion, Pukkumina, or *Pocomania*, as it is derogatively called. Kumina and Convince continue to exist in Jamaica, but as dying religions, disintegrating before the irresistible advance of their former rival – Christianity.

A similar syncretization also took place between Shango and the Baptist Society in Trinidad, giving birth to Shouterism, another revivalist-type religion; and to Shakerism in St. Vincent, as discussed in a previous section. In Puerto Rico, Spiritualism was the product of yet another fusion between Santería and Roman Catholicism. These religious expressions are fundamentally similar in their ceremonies and rituals. They all believe in the existence of supernatural beings and good and evil spirits. Drums, cymbals, tambourines, chac-chacs, singing, possession, hand-clapping, and speaking in tongues are integral parts of their ceremonies and rituals.

Many of the traditional African deities were retained in their pure form. The ancestors, however, no longer had Africa as their abode. Adaptation to the new environment became a necessity because the involvement of the ancestors in the lives of their descendants was a crucial one, and because a return to Africa was not among the priorities of the post-Emancipation creole Africans. The Caribbean and the New World became their new home. Ultimately, all spirits, including the ancestors, immigrated to the new territories and were joined by those of other races, namely, East Indians, Chinese, Indonesians and Europeans.

*Three Pukkumina practitioners in ceremonial robes. Courtesy of
the National Library of Jamaica*

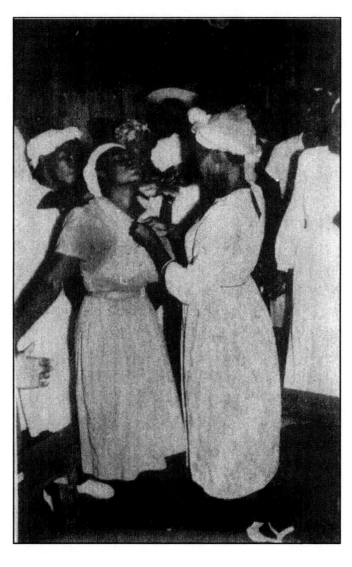

Possessed woman at Revival Zion ceremony. Courtesy of the National Library of Jamaica

Ill-disposed spirits that frequented rivers, streams and cotton trees in Africa were also to be found in the new environment. The spirits were identified as good and evil spirits and became known as *duppies* in Jamaica; *boumbas* in Cuba; *zombies* in Guadeloupe, Martinique, Haiti; *zumbies* in Aruba, Curacao; *bakrus* in Surinam; *ol' higue* in Guyana, Jamaica; and *jumbies* in Trinidad, Guyana Grenada and elsewhere. The priests of the several sects, as well as the sorcerers, adept in the art of healing, divination and conjuring, are often consulted by adherents who believe that spirits are utilized to play a role in the daily affairs of individuals, for better or for worse, and who believe that their failures or misfortunes in life are the work of malevolent spirits.

The Shepherds or leaders of Revival Zion and Pukkumina, like the obeah men, are powerful figures in their communities, feared and respected for their roles as the local doctors, psychiatrists, counsellors and oracles. They are said to have the capacity to conjure up the dead (duppies) and use them as agents. In casting or removing a spell, they have at their disposal vast quantities of herbs and the knowledge of their respective properties. Some herbs are for drinking; others for bathing. Some are for purifying the body; others for poisoning the body. Some are for wrapping the body; others for wrapping the head, and so forth. Some herbs, along with a variety of oils, powders and miscellaneous incense, are used specifically for making or breaking spells.

Revival Zion and Pukkumina have retained in their pure form some of the old African deities such as Oshun, Ogun, Nyame, Obatala and Shango. The two sects are rivals and each has said many disparaging things about the other. However, Pukkumina, the more African-oriented of the two, has been severely maligned not only by Revival Zionists, but also by broad sections of the society. According to Edward Seaga:

> Status-conscious Jamaicans will often disguise their true religious allegiance by claiming to be members of one of the orthodox and accepted churches e.g.,Baptist or Anglican, in order to enhance their status. In addition, the census has used the term Pocomania referring to Pukkumina to which many persons will not admit membership, classifying themselves somewhat euphemistically as "Revivalists". This is especially true of Pukkumina members who rarely use this term in reference to themselves. Zionists, on the other hand, are not as particular and will acknowledge membership as Zionists or Revivalists.[75]

Notwithstanding the rivalry between the two groups, there is a measurable degree of collaboration and cooperation between them. This is inevitable because they are both derived from the same source and there are many similarities in their ceremonies and rituals.

> Despite their many fundamental agreements on doctrine and ritual forms, Zion and Pukkumina exist almost independently of each other. The primary area of association is on matters of healing and obeah; Zionists regard Pukkumina people as better practitioners of obeah, since they deal with 'ground' spirits constantly and these are considered evil by the Zion cult; on the other hand, Pukkumina regard Zionists as more experienced in matters of healing.[76]

In his attempt to distinguish between Revival Zion and Pukkumina, Simpson has repeated some of the false stories about Pukkumina: that its Shepherds use large doses of ganja and rum in their rituals; that fruits and candles are deliberately disarranged and thrown out of place; that fruit are hurled at onlookers; that the

Alexander Bedward.   Courtesty of the National Library of Jamaica.

groups are joined for the purpose of working towards an evil end; and that there are indications of homosexuality among Pukkumina followers.[77] It is enough to say that anyone familiar with the rituals of Pukkumina, and has attended its ceremonial feasts or "tables" as they are called, knows that these charges are false and that the dissimilarities between the two sects are minor. For purposes of historical truth, Simpson's statement regarding the "indications of homosexuality" among Pukkumina followers is highly implausible. While such a statement would seem more credible in regards to some of the leaders of the *de facto* Established Churches, given the relative level of tolerance existing among the middle and upper classes to which these religious leaders belong, it is unlikely among Pukkumina followers, all of whom are from the working class, which remains not only intolerant, but violently hostile to homosexuality.

In spite of their rivalry, both sects take their place with the several others which have collectively contributed in a significant way to the preservation of many of the African cultural forms that exist in the Caribbean today. The contemporary songs and music in the Caribbean contain elements of Kumina, Shango, Convince, Vodun, Santería, Revival Zion, Pukkumina, Rastafarianism and other religious expressions. They also reflect features of the tradition of militancy inherited from Myalism, Shango, and Vodun.

In 1894, Alexander Bedward, a Revival Shepherd, founded the Jamaica Native Baptist Free Church and began preaching in his home community of August Town, in the parish of St. Andrew. He demanded land for the landless, food for the hungry, and jobs for the unemployed. He also asserted the right of all Africans to return to the continent [of Africa], if they so desired, at the expense of the British government which had violently uprooted them from there.

Thousands of people were said to have been healed by Bedward through immersion in the waters of the nearby Hope River. This is most revealing because the belief in a priest's capacity to heal by immersion in the river is intrinsic to Myalism and the religion of the Fanti-Ashanti people.

Bedward was able to attract tens of thousands of followers, religious as well as secular, within a few years. The multitudes and the excitement that his message and healing generated are reflected in the song *Dip Dem, Bedward,* a song that is still sung by many of the older people in Kingston and St. Andrew.

An' me always go up a de Augus' Town,
But me nevva go up a Mona;
One day I was invited
By a ole man dem call Jonah;
When me go up a Mona,
Me see Bredda Bedward standin',
Him tek Sista Mary, pull 'im han',
An' dip her in de healin' stream.

Chorus:
Dip dem, Bedward, dim dem!
Dip dem eena healin' stream!
Dip dem sweet, but not too deep!
Dip dem fe cure bad feelin'!

Some ride jackass, but dem caan get a pass
Fe go dip eena de healin' stream;
Some carry jimmy john,[5] wid dem face favah pan,
Fe go dip eena de healin' stream.

Some come from de Wes' like a perfec' pes',
Fe go dip eena de healin' stream;

---

[5] jimmy john -- A demi-john container for storing liquids and preserves.

Some come from de Eas' like a big leggo beas',[6]
Fe go dip eena de healin' stream.

Some come from de Nort' wid dem face full a wart,
Fe go dip eena de healin' stream;
Some come from de Sout' wid dem big yabba mout',[7]
Fe go dip eena de healin' stream.

Sometime in 1897, Reverend Captain Charles C. ("Warrior") Higgins came to Jamaica and began to preach in the city of Kingston. He too was a member of the Baptist Free Church and he referred to himself as a British and American Evangelist (B.A.E.). Before coming to Jamaica, he resided in England and was a member of the Evangelical Mission Ethiopia. According to him, his mission was to aid and rescue, through the gospel of Baptism, "all people who may be sick and needing financial assistance, and generally to be of some good to the poor who are unable to help themselves."[78]

Higgins would revile the King of England, the Pope, the Anglican Bishop of Jamaica and all other symbols of colonial and racial oppression. It should be noted that during that period and more than half a century later it was a criminal offense to speak disparagingly about the British monarch, the Pope or the Anglican Bishop. As a street preacher, Higgins, like Bedward, had thousands of followers. They were indeed the forerunners of Marcus Garvey. Sometimes Bedward and Higgins would hold joint baptismal services at Hope River in August Town. During one of his sermons

---

[6] leggo beas' -- An aimless, unsupervised or good-for-nothing person.

[7] yabba mout' -- A person whose mouth is likened to the calabash, a drinking or eating vessel made from the gourd.

in 1902, Higgins stated that "the people should obey Christ instead of man. White men murdered the son of God, and God damned them for their wickedness."[79] Higgins was severely castigated by the press after this sermon. Shortly thereafter, he was physically attacked without provocation by a group of thugs and severely mauled. As a result of the injuries sustained from the violent attack, he died in July 1902.

Within the first two decades of the 20th century, Bedward's popularity increased greatly among the masses. It was alleged that he predicted that he would lead the African people out of bondage to their own vine and fig tree by the year 1920. Like Higgins, Bedward was a target of reproach by the colonial administrators and the Christian Churches. He was accused of inciting the people to breaking the peace and deceiving them with false promises[8]. Ultimately, a different and even more cruel violence was inflicted on Bedward. As they would later do in the case of Leonard P. Howell, a co-founder of Rastafarianism, and many other critics of the secular and spiritual order, the colonial administration declared Bedward insane and placed him in the mental institution where he ultimately was driven insane. The movement subsequently disintegrated and some of its followers later joined Garvey's Universal Negro Improvement Association and the Rastafari Movement. The movement, whose political and religious content had enabled it to survive for twenty-six years, collapsed. But the legacy of Alexander Bedward lives on among the masses of Jamaica in general and Kingston and St. Andrew in particular.

---

[8] Among the accusations made against Bedward is that he allegedly promised to take Africans back to the continent on wings that he himself had designed.

The African religions in the Caribbean have played three very important roles. They protected and preserved the culture of the people. They provided some semblance of social order, dignity and self-respect in the face of some of the harshest types of treatment ever inflicted on human beings. Finally, they planned, organized and led revolts and other forms of resistance against the enslavers and colonizers. After Emancipation, their successors continued the struggles against colonialism and Christian hypocrisy. They fought against the social system of education because it taught the children to despise their languages, religions, heroes and history, and because it taught them to despise themselves and their ancestry. Some of these religions have perished; others have survived in new forms, but as objects of derision, scorn and vilification by Africans who are non-conversant with their own history, the role of these religious institutions, and the contribution they have made to our people's struggle for freedom and human dignity.

Since the 1959 Revolution in Cuba, Santería has been accorded the respect that it deserves. It has received technical and material assistance from the government to record its beliefs and practices so that Cubans and non-Cubans can benefit from and develop a greater appreciation of an important part of Cuba's cultural heritage, and, so that its participation and reflection in the society's contemporary cultural history – art, drama, music, dancing, and so forth – can be assured. The idea is to encourage and promote Santería in a positive way and help it to attain a new and contemporary relevance. The promotion of African religion and culture by the Cuban Government is itself an expression of the Revolution's program of social emancipation for the African population. Dr. Moya Pons stated:

And what is curious, too, is that the Cuban Revolution, with its social emancipation of its colored population, has also contributed a greater political relevance to the race question. Sometimes I think that much of the popularity enjoyed by the Cuban Revolution in the English-speaking Caribbean is due more to the revolutionary Cuban politics favoring equality promotion of colored workers than to the ideological acceptance of Cuban communism.[80]

In Grenada the efforts of Christine David, Principal of Harvey Vale Government School, to promote the Big Drum dance in the schools in the island of Carriacou had received the support and encouragement of the People's Revolutionary Government of Maurice Bishop. Until the destruction of the Revolution, the children and adults of the community were taught the historical significance of their music, dances, art and religion. This, in turn, helped them to develop a new understanding of, and respect for, the Big Drum and Shango which still survive in the islands. In Jamaica, Rex Nettleford and the National Dance Theatre have honored Kumina by adding to their repertoire some of the religion's ritualistic dances.

The efforts by Cuba and the former Revolutionary Grenada to give new relevance to the surviving African religions, embrace historical truth, respect and honor the people – their culture, traditions, heroes, institutions, and past and present contributions to the society's development – have not been followed to any great degree by other Caribbean countries.

Judaism

Most of the Jews in the Caribbean today are descendants of the Sephardim of Spain and Portugal who came to the Western Hemisphere from as early as 1509. Under Moorish (African) rule, commencing with the Caliphate of Al-Walid who established an Islamic state in Spain (705-717 A.D.), large numbers of North African Jews and Muslims, many of whom arrived as soldiers, administrators, merchants, artisans, scholars and professionals, settled in Spain and Portugal. Some became important government officials and officers. The high level of literacy, culture, industry and scholarship brought to the Iberian peninsula by the Moorish Muslims of Mauritania and Morocco and by the Arab Muslims and Jews who migrated there served to rescue Spain and Portugal from the Dark Ages that had engulfed the rest of Europe and transform the region into cultural and intellectual centers of both European and Islamic civilization for more than 700 years. Indeed the Islamic states in the Iberian peninsula were the most advanced on the European continent representing an alternative to the Christian feudal system.

The defeat of the Moors in 1492 ushered in a period of military, political and religious repression and ethnic cleansing by the Catholic victors. Roman Catholicism, under whose banner a crusade had been waged against the Moors, became the accuser, censor, persecutor and expropriator of non-Christians – Muslims and Jews alike. The terror of the Roman Catholic Inquisition forced many Jews and Muslims whose families had lived in Spain and Portugal for centuries to pull up roots, return to Africa, or seek asylum elsewhere in the Ottoman Empire or Europe. Many Jewish refugees settled in the "Free Cities" and States of the Netherlands, a possession of the ruling Hapsburg dynasty in Spain, as well as in Hamburg and other "Free Cities" of the German Empire.

The expulsion of the Muslims and Jews from Portugal took place five years after that of Spain. Their possessions were plundered by the Spanish and Portuguese; some Jews and Muslims were forced to convert to Christianity; and children were stolen from their parents to be brought up as Christians. A number of Sephardim, in order to survive, became converts of Roman Catholicism and adopted Portuguese and Spanish names. Some of these Jews – *New Christians, Conversos* and *Marranos* – as they were called, escaped or were exiled to the Portuguese colonies, especially Brazil, where they established new communities. Some became plantation owners, and some became involved in import and export, including the Slave Trade. In Brazil the enforcement of ecclesiastical laws against non-Christians were lax and many *New Christians* reverted to Judaism and assumed their former identities, although discretely maintaining a low profile.

> For a considerable time in the 16th century Portugal sent annually two shiploads of Jews and criminals to Brazil, and also deported persons who had been condemned by the Inquisition. The banishment of large numbers to Brazil in 1548 is especially mentioned. Jews or Marranos were soon settled in all the Portuguese colonies, and they carried on an extensive trade with various countries. "As early as 1548 (according to some, 1531) Portuguese Jews, it is asserted, transplanted the sugar-cane from Madeira to Brazil." Some of them began to feel so secure that they dared to profess Judaism openly.[81]

The Portuguese policy was cruel and vacillating, only a little less so than that of its larger and more consistent neighbor, Spain. The Sephardim who settled in the United Provinces of the

Netherlands provided financial and intelligence assistance to the War of Independence against Spain. Prince William of Orange (1533-1584) rewarded them for this assistance by declaring that "he should not suffer any man to be called to account, molested or injured for his faith or conscience."[82] In spite of the alliance between the Dutch and the Sephardim, however, the latter did not have the full rights of citizenship. They could not serve in the military, engage in the mechanical or retail trades, or intermarry with Dutch citizens. This latter restriction corresponded with their own self-imposed rule and, as such, was of minor concern to them.

In 1580, Portugal was inherited by the Spanish Hapsburg dynasty, through King Phillip II of Spain, and all its colonies, including Brazil, came under Spanish jurisdiction. The laws against infidels were rigorously enforced in Portugal, as well as its vast colonial empire. The Spanish Inquisition made no distinction between Jews and *Marranos*. As a result of this persecution, there was another exodus of Jews to the Netherlands and other areas. Within a few decades the Sephardim represented an important and powerful minority within the banking and merchant sectors, and among the artisans, craftsmen, scientists and scholars of such cities as Amsterdam, the Hague, Zealand and Rotterdam. Their arrival coincided with the rapid economic and political emergence of the United Provinces of the Netherlands, which transformed the new Dutch republic into one of the Great Powers of Europe.

In 1624 the Dutch seizure of the city of Bahia from the Portuguese was facilitated by the logistical intelligence provided by the Sephardim. In 1629 the Dutch conquered a large portion of Brazil and Sephardim were among the colonists that went there. In fact "the Dutch West India Company, which was formed in 1622 in furtherance of the project of conquering Brazil, had Jews of

Amsterdam among its large stockholders, and several of them in its Board of Directors."[83] Two years later, Recife (Pernambuco) was taken by the Dutch and a special appeal was made by the Sephardim to their co-religionists in Europe to settle there. Indeed the fortunes of the Sephardim became inseparably linked to those of the Dutch.

Within a few years, Recife became the first genuine Jewish settlement in the New World. While there were sizable Jewish communities in cities such as Rio de Janeiro, Parahiba, Itamarica and Mauritsstad, Recife was the center, and its fame soon spread even into the Old World.[84] The Sephardim of Brazil were soon among the leading sugar and cotton planters. They were significant contributors to the economic and cultural development of the colony and, while it lasted, their lives were virtually free from persecution. However, all of this came to an end in 1654 when the Portuguese army drove the Dutch out of Brazil. The Sephardim were ordered to leave the colony at once and were obliged to leave their valuable possessions behind. The engine of the Roman Catholic Inquisition was revved up once more and the Sephardim had to flee again -- some to the "old country" (the Netherlands); some to Curacao, Surinam, St. Eustatius, New Amsterdam (New York); and others to Bermuda, Barbados, St. Kitts, Nevis, and Jamaica.

As the years went by, Sephardic planters and merchants in Curacao and the Netherlands were to be found among the important Dutch financiers of maritime commerce, including the Slave Trade. In the British colonies, particularly Jamaica, Nevis and Barbados, the Sephardic communities have been longstanding. In fact the Sephardim in those colonies are direct descendants of Spanish and Portuguese Jews. In Jamaica they were among the earliest Spanish colonists. According to Bisnauth:

Although at that time (1509) their co-religionists were being persecuted in Spain, Jews who settled in Jamaica enjoyed the protection of the Spanish discoverers and conquistadores. As a special favor to Christopher Columbus, the Spanish Crown had forbidden the Inquisition to operate in the island in the way it did in Hispaniola and Cuba. Thus, from its early history as a European colony, Jamaica was to be a refuge for Jews. Later, immigration from the Netherlands and England increased the number of Jews who settled in Jamaica.[85]

They were permitted to reside as merchants and planters, participate in the Slave Trade with their British counterparts, establish their synagogues and practice their religion. Neither the British ruling class nor the Churches of England and Scotland regarded the Jews and Judaism as a threat to their interests. Moreover, the Sephardim did not challenge the leading English and Scottish banking and slave trading companies in Edinburgh, Liverpool, London, Plymouth, and elsewhere; and proselytizing was not a characteristic feature of their religion.

The Sephardim's knowledge of Dutch, Spanish and Portuguese, their commercial links with the South American and West Indian colonies, and their artistic and professional skills contributed to the wealth and prosperity of the British colonies. As the principal brokers and money-lenders in the colonies, they were sought out by many planters whose lavish lifestyles and ambitions obliged them to sometimes take advantage of their readily available loans. In his commentaries on the role of the Sephardim in Jamaica, Edward Long wrote:

The Jews were very early settled in this island, attracted no less by the quantity of gold and silver brought into circulation here, than the mild disposition of the government towards them. In some of the other sugar islands they were proscribed, by admitting the evidence of pagan slaves against them in the court of justice. Yet, although this government was comparatively lenient, they were oppressed, in some instances, conformably to that persecuting spirit which zealous Christians used anciently to manifest towards all those who differed from them in matters of faith, particularly Jews, Turks, and Infidels. But it must be owned, that the rascally tricks, for which both ancient and modern Jews have always been distinguished, may have served not a little to embitter the popular hatred against them.[86]

Long's highlighting of roguishness and dishonesty by the Sephardic merchants as a whole, past and present, is somewhat undeserving. They in fact represented a small percentage of those engaging in corrupt practices that pervaded the colonies. The number of Sephardim who were involved in dishonest commercial transactions appeared large only because of the social make-up of most of the Jews residing in the colonies. A most significant distinction between the Sephardim and all other ethnic groups and races that came to the Caribbean is the fact that the overwhelming majority of Jews were merchants, professionals, artisans, and planters. Accordingly, while a majority of the European nationals came to the Caribbean as small farmers, soldiers, sailors, clerks, and laborers; the East Indian, Chinese, and Javanese as indentured servants; and the African nationals as slaves; there were very few Sephardic small farmers and laborers. Additionally, some Jews were bankers or intermediaries for bankers in Europe, a condition that attracted the attention of Christian plantocrats who were experiencing financial difficulties.

Jews resided in the French and Spanish colonies, but they could not openly practice their religion. Indeed the policy of excluding non-Catholics from these territories remained virtually intact into the nineteenth century. The Lutheran Danish monarchy adopted an open-door policy which attracted merchants of all nationalities and religious persuasions, including some non-Sephardic European Jews, to the Virgin Islands. The Sephardim were also prominent among the merchants in the island of St. Eustatius, the leading "emporium" in the Caribbean during the eighteenth century. Thus, like their Protestant counterparts, the Sephardic merchants and planters felt no remorse in attending their places of worship, reiterating their thanks to god for leading them out of bondage in Egypt and for rescuing them from the terror of their enemies, and later inspecting their warehouses to ensure that their merchandise – African slaves – was secure.

Slave trading with the Spanish colonies in South America was the principal business of the emporia of Curacao, St. Croix, Aruba, St. Eustatius and St. Bartelemé. And Sephardic merchants represented a small, but significant percentage of the traders. Thus, it was a crushing blow to them when Admiral George Rodney, acting on behalf of British imperial interests, levelled the city of Oranjestad, St. Eustatius, during the American War of Independence, looted the warehouses and then burned the shells to the ground. Hundreds of Sephardic Jews fled to other parts of the Caribbean – St. Croix, St. Kitts, Curacao, Antigua, Nevis, Jamaica and other colonies.

In the British colonies, despite a number of restrictions, the Sephardim operated under economic, political and social conditions that were among the most favorable to them in the New World. Commenting on the Sephardim in the colony of Jamaica, Long stated:

> They traffic among the Negroes chiefly in saltfish, butter, and a sort of cheap pedlary wares, manufactured by their brethren in England. But among the chief men are several very opulent planters, and capital merchants,

who are connected with great houses in the city of London. It has been a very striking remark, that the multitude of them settled in this island, the purchases they are continually making both of houses and lands, and the vast wealth they collectively have staked here, are sure indications that they are delighted with the mildness and equity of the government, and rest satisfied, that their property is entirely safe, and securely held; from a conviction, "that a place of such great importance to the mother-country will never be neglected, nor fail of receiving all due care and protection".[87]

Few restrictions, if any, were placed on the Sephardim in the area of commerce. It was largely in the political and judicial arenas that they encountered their greatest difficulties. In 1701 the French Guinea Company was awarded the coveted *Asiento de Negros,* a slave-trading monopoly to Spain's vast dominions. Britain, resentful of the superior advantage that its major competitor had obtained, went to war. In 1712 the English Sea Company was granted a similar award and the war came to an end.[88] Sephardic merchants were among the beneficiaries of the lucrative *Asiento de Negros* concession. Bisnauth wrote:

> When Spain granted the *Asiento* to the English in 1713, a lively trade sprang up between Jamaica and the Spanish islands and mainland in slaves and manufactured goods. Much of this trade was in Jewish hands. Jews were allowed to own landed property, but they were excluded from the political franchise – a factor which caused them much dissatisfaction.[89]

Although they had representation among the wealthiest people in the colonies, they were not allowed to vote nor hold political office until the first half of the nineteenth century. They could, however, serve as police constables and thus were among the tenacious defenders of the colonies from enemy invasions, protecting their vast holdings and complying with the mandatory law which required all able-bodied free men to defend the colonies against enemy incursions and slave uprisings. Significantly, they were not allowed to serve in the judiciary and, unlike their European counterparts who were immune from such testimony, African slaves could testify against them in the courts. It was not until 1831 that, as a result of the first Jewish Emancipation Bill in Britain, all legal disabilities were removed from the Jews of Jamaica.[90]

The Jewish community in Surinam was established during the period when Recife flourished as a Jewish settlement. It grew in size and prominence after the fall of Recife. In 1664 when the French captured Cayenne which later became French Guiana, the Sephardim who were the early colonists there fled to neighboring Surinam. The Jews of Surinam were then chiefly engaged in agriculture, the wealthy among them being large planters and slave holders.[91] The British Government of Surinam guaranteed the Sephardim unrestricted religious freedom, voided summons that were served on them on their Sabbaths and holidays, exempted them from public duties on those days, except in emergencies, permitted their Elders and magistrates to decide simple civil suits, and permitted them to bequeath their property according to their own laws of inheritance. They were also granted ten acres of land for the erection of a Synagogue and such buildings as the congregation might need.[92]

In spite of the above mentioned rights and privileges accorded to the Sephardim, it still fell short of full citizenship. The Sephardim were treated as a separate entity within the colony and Jews were not allowed to intermarry with the European Christians.

They did not find these restrictions offensive because they had an isolated social existence as a matter of course. At the Treaty of Breda in 1667, the Dutch ceded New Amsterdam (New York) to the British in exchange for Surinam. When Surinam became Dutch, the Sephardim were granted all the rights of full citizenship. In spite of this, a number of them departed with the British to Jamaica. The Jewish historian, Peter Wiernik, explains this phenomenon by arguing that "the English were less sentimental and more business-like in their dealings with the Jews than the Dutch, and were probably on that account more trusted."[93]

In 1682 Samuel Nassi, a Sephardic Jew and the richest planter in Surinam, gave to the Jews an island on the Surinam River, which they developed and named *de Jooden Savane* (Savannah of the Jews) and which became the principal seat of the Jewish community in Surinam. It was there that the Congregation Berakah-we-Shalom built its splendid Synagogue in 1685.[94] The Sephardic planters of Surinam, however, were not always on good terms with their Christian counterparts or with the Dutch administration. In 1690, for example, Immanuel Machado, a Sephardic Jewish planter renowned for his cruelty to his African slaves, was killed by his slaves who escaped into the woods. The Sephardic leaders demanded an immediate response from Governor van Scharphuysen, who failed to act because of his unhappiness with the Jewish community and Machado himself. He, however, granted the Jewish community the right to avenge the death of any co-religionist killed by rebellious slaves. Goslinga wrote:

> Such was Surinam's society in those days that the Jews took the Governor at his word and took revenge into their own hands. They organized a force which sought out the nearest Maroon settlement, killed many of its members and brought some women and children back as

trophies, whom they tortured and executed. This Jewish initiative was followed by several others.[95]

The atrocities carried out by the Sephardic Jews against the Maroons, who had nothing to do with Machado's death, in this and other excursions set the stage for a bloody conflict between Sephardim and Africans that would last for approximately eighty-five years. Jewish military commanders such as Jacob d'Avilar and David Nassi distinguished themselves during these campaigns. Nassi inflicted considerable punishment on the Maroons, destroying their provision plots and killing many of their people. In 1718 he participated in a very successful raid and gained so much fame that the Spanish-French poet Ben Venida del Monte glorified him in several of his poems.[96]

In 1743, after more than thirty excursions against the Africans, David Nassi was killed in battle by the Maroons and was succeeded by Capitein Isaac Carvalho.[97] The Sephardic dislike of the Maroons was reciprocated. According to Goslinga:

> The latter, with a kind of sadistic delight, selected Jewish plantations as objects of their raids. The Jewish planters used spies, and so did the Maroons. The latter's forces, constantly reinforced by newly arriving runaways, became more and more adept at this kind of warfare. In the years 1728 to 1776 they conducted some brilliantly led attacks on several estates in which they decisively defeated formidable opponents.[98]

The war between the Sephardim and the Maroons was very destructive and painful to both sides. The Maroons were fighting for their very existence, for the right to live as free humans, and to be left alone to establish their communities. The Sephardim and European Christians were opposed to these goals and both sides were prepared to achieve their ends in a sea of blood.

The Sephardim considered themselves at war with the Maroons and attacked them with a vengeance. And while the Maroons regarded the Dutch Christians as their enemies and routinely raided and plundered their plantations, they singled out Jews and Jewish plantations for death and destruction. In 1750 young Isaac Nassi and three hundred of his men were wiped out in a battle with the Maroons. The punishment inflicted on the Sephardim by the Africans was so devastating that the former was obliged to put vengeance aside, abandon the conflict and sue for peace. In 1774 they erected forts and drew a military line from the Savannah of the Jews along the river Commoimber to the sea.[99] They terminated their excursions against the Africans and the war came to an end.

By the first half of the eighteenth century, German Jewish settlers – the Ashkenazim – arrived in the colony of Surinam. It was not long before disputes between Sephardim and Ashkenazim arose. The latter requested and were granted permission to form their own separate community. They were, however, prohibited from owning any possession on the Jewish Savannah, and were not allowed to have their own jurisdiction.[100] Both groups were profoundly orthodox, differing from each other primarily in the area of liturgy.

> The Sephardim and Ashkenazim differed, for example, in the recital of the *piyyutim*. They differed also in the number of benedictions recited while they were putting on the *tephillin*; the Ashkenazim preferred two recitations while the Sephardim thought that one was enough. The Sephardim turned their eyes downwards when saying, "Kadosh, Kadosh, Kadosh." (Holy, Holy, Holy."). The Ashkenazim, on the other hand, looked upwards. In their study of the Bible (i.e. the Old

Testament) the Ashkenazim preferred a homiletical and literal approach; the Sephardim tended to be allegorical in their interpretations of the Bible and the Talmud. But as far as the central beliefs of Judaism were concerned, there were little, if any, differences between the Sephardim and the Ashkenazim.[101]

The religious differences between the two sects, albeit relatively minor, were exacerbated by ethnic and cultural differences, which resulted in the creation of separate communities in the colonies in which the two groups resided. And this separation would continue until the latter part of the nineteenth century.

The Sephardim came with the first Dutch colonists to Curacao after the island was seized from Spain in 1634. Their numbers were greatly increased after 1654 when Brazil was reconquered from the Dutch by the Portuguese. Some of the Brazilian Jews who came to the colony in that period brought with them considerable wealth, and they laid the foundation of that prominence in the commerce of the island which they have since retained.[102] The Sephardic entrepreneurs in the colony first tried their hands at agriculture. When this failed, they became traders. So well did they do as traders that some of their members replaced most of the Protestant merchants there in wealth and prominence within a very short time. Jews were even sent on trade missions to the Spanish Main by the Dutch West India Company.[103] They built their synagogue; a theatre; and schools for their children. According to the Jewish historian Wiernik:

By 1750 their numbers had increased to about two thousand. They were prosperous merchants and traders, and held positions of prominence in the commercial and political affairs of the island. By the end of the century they owned a considerable part of the property in the district of Willemstad; and as many as fifty-three vessels are said to have left in one day for Holland, laden with goods which for the most part belonged to Jewish merchants.[104]

The Jewish community in Barbados was one of the oldest in the British Caribbean. The Sephardim settled in the island as early as 1627 when it was seized and settled by the British. The Jewish community in Barbados was never as large as that of Surinam, but at the height of its greatest prosperity, it had its own synagogue and boasted a congregation of 147 members. The Sephardic merchants suffered great losses during the devastating hurricane of 1831 and the community experienced a continuous decline since that time. A number of Sephardim left for the island of Jamaica and an even larger number migrated to the United States. In 1848 there were only 71 Jews left. In 1873, those remaining petitioned for relief from taxation of property held by the congregation. The census of 1882 showed 21 Jews, and the number was still smaller at the end of the nineteenth century.[105]

During the seventeenth, eighteenth and nineteenth centuries Judaism played an important role in the lives of the Sephardim. The Sephardim's Talmudic interpretation of the Torah – the first ten books of the Bible – was their frame of reference. The head of the extended family was patriarch, spiritual leader and guardian of the group's customs and traditions. Marriage between Jews and "Gentiles" was strictly forbidden and whenever it did occur, ostracism was the punishment meted out to the transgressors. This factor was also noted by Long:

> They are consequently contented and happy under this government; and would be more so, if it was not for their own little schisms in religious matters; for they are divided into two factions, or sects; one of which, called the Smouse Jews, are not acknowledged orthodox by the

rest, on account of their having, through the rigours of the Inquisition in the Portuguese and Spanish dominions, relaxed in some indispensable rituals, or intermarried with Christians; by which abomination, they have polluted the pure Israelitish blood with the corrupt stream of the Gentiles. The Smouses have therefore a distinct conventicle, or meeting of their own, at a private house, where they vociferate, to the great disturbance of the neighborhood.[106]

The Smouse Jews, condemned as *Marranos* or *New Christians* by their Jewish co-religionists, included offsprings of mixed marriages, as well as offsprings of Sephardim who, for survival during the persecutions, or for survival against persecution, changed their names outwardly, adopted Christianity, or reconverted to Judaism. Those who intermarried with non-Hebrews, or were reconverted *Marranos*, were discriminated against by the orthodox Sephardic elders who placed a special emphasis on the preservation of Hebrew exclusiveness as a guarantee for the group's distinct existence. Indeed, so strict were the rules regarding marriage that the offsprings of the appreciable number of "wayward" Jews who married outside of the group were also ostracized, notwithstanding their retention of the family name and Jewish religious practices and beliefs. The Sephardim even regarded as outsiders the Ashkenazim who migrated to the Caribbean from East and Central Europe during the eighteenth century and they frowned upon intermarriages between the two sects.

There were at least three factors underlying the sectarian and ethnocentric existence of the Sephardim. In the first place, they feared that their culture and identity as a people would be absorbed by the dominant culture. Additionally, because of their North

African origins, they would not have been accepted by the colonial rulers as equals even if they had tried to assimilate. Finally, they subjectively believed that as "God's chosen people" they had a duty to retain their ethnic and religious "purity". To help ensure this purity and protect their social status, the Sephardim placed a high priority on education. Even before public elementary schools were established in the nineteenth century, Sephardic children attended the *Midrasj*, an elementary school, and the *Jesivah*, an academy. Hence, the Sephardim lived according to their customs and values and, in general, kept to themselves.

According to Frances P. Karner, the relationship between Sephardim and Africans was positive and most beneficial to the latter. She wrote:

> The individual famiya,[9] in addition to the Yaya,[10] also counted other peripheral members. Some families took Afro-Caribbean children under their protection and provided for their education. These youngsters were appointed as helpers in the house, and the children of these domestics often continued to fill the same positions in successive generations of the same family.[107]

Besides being shamelessly paternalistic, the above quote stands in antithesis to the common sense proposition that no relationship between two peoples can be deemed "positive" when successive generations of the one occupy the role of masters, and those of the other, the role of slaves or servants. Such a relationship is intrinsically oppressive. However, while it is historically true

---

[9] *The extended family*

[10] *Nanny, mammy, nurse*

that there were Sephardic families who manumitted their slaves in accordance with the mandates of the Mosaic Codes and might have felt some compassion for Africans, the Sephardic planters and slave traders, in general, were just as cruel as their Christian counterparts in the colonies. Like their non-Hebrew plantocratic colleagues, they resisted every measure that was proposed by the colonial regimes to ameliorate the condition of the slaves.

In 1751, for example, the Sephardic planters in Surinam went so far as to petition the Staats-Generaal in the Netherlands to have Governor Johan Mauricius removed from office on the grounds that he was interfering in the affairs of the Raad (local council), as well as in the master-slave relationship. The indictment of Mauricius was a direct response to his introduction of a number of modest legislative measures calculated to reduce abuses in the master-slave relationship. The commission appointed by the Staats-Generaal to investigate the charges reported that they were all based on falsehood.

At no time during their entire history in the Caribbean did the slavemasters, including the chiefs and elders of the Sephardim, treat the African as anything other than a slave or a servant. Karner herself acknowledged this fact when she wrote:

> Although some Afro-Caribbeans were gaining economic ground as compared to former years, and thereby high status within their own segment, they failed to achieve social prestige in the entire heterogeneous structure of the Island. "Equal level" contact with either the Sephardics or the Protestants was still an "impossible dream".[108]

This appraisal of the relationship between the Dutch and Jewish ruling class on the one hand, and the Africans on the other is true not only of Curacao but also of the entire Caribbean. Even in those instances where Africans and Sephardim have, by necessity, fought as allies, the master and servant contradiction between the two groups was never absent. After all, if the Sephardim did not consider the Ashkenazim and other Jews their equals, why would they treat as peers their servants and former slaves?

In the second half of the nineteenth century the leaders of the Sephardim joined the colonial rulers to enact legislation calculated to exclude the ex-slaves and Asians from the political process. In Surinam and the Netherlands Antilles they were signatories to the Tripartite Kingdom "Agreement" with the Netherlands, which sanctioned the perpetual colonial status of those territories. In the British and Dutch colonies they fought against universal suffrage to deny political representation to the African majority. In 1969 the Africans had to put the torch to the city of Willemstad, Curacao, before the Dutch Christian and Sephardic Jewish ruling class would acknowledge their right to be represented in the government.

In 1865 Governor Edward John Eyre of Jamaica was commended by the Sephardic leadership and the European business community for his butchery of hundreds of innocent African farmers, the public whipping of hundreds of men and women and the burning down of their houses. They applauded the hanging of Paul Bogle and George William Gordon, whose only "crime" was their support of the severely abused farmers and their families. In the 1920s they were bitter enemies of Marcus Garvey whom they maligned and disparaged in their newspapers in most of the colonies,[11] notwithstanding Garvey's well-known high regard for Judaism.

Towards the end of the nineteenth century Judaism lost the importance it once exercised over the lives of the Sephardim. The old patriarchal order succumbed to the dictates of corporate big business. The rivalry between the Sephardim and Ashkenazim broke down and a closer relationship developed between the two groups. The building and opening up of the Panama Canal, the establishment of oil refineries in Curacao and Aruba, the discovery of bauxite in Jamaica, British Guiana, Surinam, and Haiti, and the discovery of oil and asphalt in Trinidad created an unprecedented prosperity for the business communities in the region. The European Christians, Jews, Syrian and Lebanese Christians were among the principal local beneficiaries of this economic boom. Orthodox Judaism suffered a further decline as the demands of competition unceremoniously forced it into the background. Karner wrote:

> Services in the synagogue, less frequently held and yet less regularly attended by the members of the congregation than in former centuries, started taking on more definite characteristics as a social gathering. Direct evidence of this decline may be witnessed by the fact that the Sephardic merchants started placing business obligations before religious mandate. Where before firms had remained closed on the Sabbath, a few merchants now decided to open shop on this "day of rest" as well. During World War I ships and mailboats would happen to arrive on Saturdays and they felt it advantageous to be open for them. A strong and old tradition was thereby quietly being sacrificed to the

---

[11] Paul Bogle, George William Gordon, and Marcus Garvey are now national heroes of Jamaica.

Golden Calf. Gradually other Jewish enterprise followed this pattern, and in 1932 the last Sephardic business capitulated to the demand of competition and ceased to observe the Sabbath closure.[109]

Religion had never played a central role in the lives of the Syrian and Lebanese, mostly Maronite Catholic, Christians who came to the Caribbean during the nineteenth century as merchants specializing in haberdashery, footwear, jewellery, and other merchandise. Thus, it was relatively simple for them to take full advantage of the benefits to be derived from the business boom. Unrestrained by the Judaeo-Christian commandments, the Jewish, Syrian and Lebanese Christian capitalists became powerful, formidable, ruthless and reactionary political factions in the colonies and neo-colonies in which they resided. Indeed they exercised a power far in excess of their actual population size. In Curacao and Aruba, for instance, these minorities constitute about one percent of the population, but are by far the most powerful, organized local economic and political force in those colonies. In Jamaica they account for a majority of the most economically powerful families, although they represent a mere 0.05 percent of the population. To this day Africans, approximately 85 percent of the population, have no representation among the most powerful families.

The Jewish, Syrian and Lebanese business communities in the Caribbean remain not only racist but are also the chief subscribers to the prevailing system of corporate privileges and monopoly. They continue to show hostility to any movement – secular or religious – that seeks to change the system. Thus, they were bitterly opposed to Garvey's Universal Negro Improvement Association (UNIA), the trade union movement, the Rastafari

Movement and the Grenadian Revolution. They were hostile to the Surinamese Revolution and they manifest a strong aversion for the Cuban Revolution. Indeed it was the Jewish, Syrian and Lebanese business elite and their local allies who, in collusion with US corporate and political circles, brought the government of Michael Manley to its knees during the years 1974-1980, ending that government's modest attempts to improve the social condition of Jamaica's poor.

Judaism in the Caribbean, as elsewhere, sought no converts and operated in a sectarian manner. The explanations for the political and social behavior of its leaders range from the insecurity of the colonial powers to the subjective notion that as "God's chosen people," they [the Jews] had a special interest in the preservation of their material and spiritual purity. The Jewish community in the Caribbean manifested itself as a highly disciplined society of people who thrived as a result of the ostracism of non-conforming Jews and the exploitation and oppression of others. This resulted in the absence of collaboration with the working class in the Caribbean region, or the majority African population, in contrast to the prominent roles of Jews in trade unionism and social reform movements elsewhere in the world.

In general, the role of the Jews, and Syrian and Lebanese Christians in Caribbean history has been one of crude self-interest, and exploitationism. In spite of historical changes, they continue to represent a major stumbling block to the attainment of a just, peaceful, and economically advanced Caribbean. Whatever the aversion of the Sephardic capitalists to social justice, the significant influence of the Judaic religious liberation legacy on the Caribbean people is reflected in many ways and, perhaps most prominently, in the Garvey and Rastafari Movements. The Caribbean people have somehow been able to distinguish between Judaism as a religion with liberating qualities, and the exploitative capitalism of those who also happen to be Jews.

The Religions of the East Indians

As previously stated, at the end of the apprenticeship system in 1838, the plantocracy and its religious allies in the British Caribbean were developing strategies to enable them to sustain a declining sugar industry and retain or increase their profit margin at the expense of the ex-slaves. The recommendations of Lord Howick, the British abolitionist, to destroy provision grounds and institute measures to make it very difficult or impossible for the ex-slaves to abandon their regular industry were adopted and put in place. In Barbados, British Guiana, Jamaica and Trinidad, the garden plots that the Africans had cultivated to augment their miserable income were destroyed by the planters. Wages were severely reduced and laws were passed against loitering and vagabondage. All of these measures were intended to coerce the Africans to remain on the plantations in virtual servitude under a new system of peonage. And the Africans rebelled. Rev. Harricharan noted:

> The sugar industry continued to decline and the tiny planter class could have averted the crisis by rationalization of the sugar-industry with the introduction of new technology. The other alternative was to diversify the monocrop economy by the introduction of other cash crops. Instead this oligarchy was bent on maintaining its position in the society. This meant then the perpetuation of the plantation system. To continue its dominance over the labouring classes, the planters decided that immigration of labourers would be the best method to ensure an adequate supply of labour and reduce the high level of wages.[110]

Consequently, between 1837 and 1917 when the practice was terminated, hundreds of thousands of Asians were brought into the Caribbean to work on the sugar plantations. These included 239,000 East Indians to British Guiana, 134,000 to Trinidad, 78,000 to Martinique and Guadeloupe, 35,500 to Surinam, 33,000 to Jamaica, and 19,000 to Cayenne (French Guiana). Between 1852 -1874, 125,000 Chinese were brought to Cuba and 14,000 to British Guiana between 1853-1912 as indentured laborers.[111]

The East Indians who came to the Caribbean were themselves actually going through a second phase of colonization. Their own country, India, had been colonized in the eighteenth century by the European powers -- Portugal, France and Britain. The British ultimately emerged as the sole exploiter of that vast country. They ravaged the society, trampled upon its customs, pitted Indians against Indians, and relegated the Indian masses to a state of abject poverty. Like their Chinese counterparts at the turn of the twentieth century and the continental Africans, the Indians became strangers in their own land.

> The economic exploitation of India by the British led to disastrous consequences for that society. Britain turned India with a self-sufficing economy into a supplier of raw materials especially cotton to feed the machines of Lancashire and other industrial towns. The influx of British manufactured goods rendered millions of Indian workers employed in the various arts and crafts, jobless. The introduction of the notion of private-property by the British and the Permanent Settlement of Bengal in 1893 adversely affected the majority of agricultural workers. A new class of landowners (zamindars) arose at the cost of the tenants (ryots). Besides, recurrent famines in North India and floods made agriculture an extremely depressed sector in the Indian economy.[112]

It was from this background of deprivation, famine and destitution, largely created by the very people who were now recruiting the victims for a new type of exploitation in the Caribbean, that the East Indians came. A majority of the recruits came after having been given a rosy picture of life in the Caribbean and the benefits to be derived from indentureship. It was not difficult for the recruiters to have persuaded them because, given their desperate situation, any job which at least guaranteed food for themselves and their families would have been an improvement.

They had no idea of the life that awaited them. Besides, a sizable number of East Indians were simply kidnapped and taken to the Caribbean. Just as poor Europeans were snatched from the streets of Le Havre, Lyons, London, Edinburgh and other towns, and Africans from their towns and villages throughout West Africa and brought to the Caribbean as indentured laborers and slaves respectively, so were East Indians kidnapped from their villages and from the streets of Lahore, Madras, Calcutta and Bengal and forcefully relegated to a life of indentureship.

Islam

Muslims represented approximately one-quarter of the East Indians brought into the Caribbean by the European powers as indentured laborers. And it is to them that credit is due for securing for Islam a lasting and significant communal presence in the Caribbean. However, they were merely reintroducing Islam to the region. Islam was first introduced into the Caribbean region by the Fulanis, Mandingos, Hausas, Wolofs, Nagos, and other Africans from the earliest days of the African Slave Trade. The African Muslims found the institution of slavery particularly offensive to their spirit and they did not hesitate to show their resentment at every opportunity.

Accordingly, they were among the most militant of the slaves in the New World and were the collaborators, co-conspirators, organizers, and leaders of numerous revolts, particularly in Cuba, Surinam and Brazil. Mandingos in Jamaica reportedly practiced circumcision, recited morning and evening prayers and fasted on Friday, the Islamic holy day. They were also literate in Arabic.[113] In Cuba, where Islam had established a foothold, many of the Imams were either executed or deported elsewhere as punishment for their belligerency. Commenting on the role of Islam in the revolts in northeastern Brazil, Bastide wrote:

> Those [revolts] of 1807, 1809, and 1813 were all carried out by Hausas, while the latter ones, in 1826, 1827, 1828, 1830, and 1835 were all the work of Nagos. But in every case the organization and cadre leadership was provided by Muslim or 'fetichist' holy men.[114]

The losses sustained by the Muslim freedom fighters in these battles were staggeringly high, and they suffered further losses by executions and deportations to Africa. Muslims in Surinam were completely absorbed into the dominant Fanti-Ashanti culture; while those in Brazil continued to exist until the first half of the nineteenth century. By the end of the century, however, those who had survived were ultimately absorbed into the Yoruba culture.

Unlike the indigenous African religions, however, Islam required a less rigorous, less hostile, and less restricted environment in which to thrive. The conditions of slavery did not allow for prayers five times per day; nor for the practical application of any of the other Five Pillars (al-Arkan) of Islam[12]. In any event, the

---

[12] The Five Pillars (al-Arkan) of Islam include the following:
(1) All Muslims must pray five times daily – at dawn, mid-day, mid-afternoon, sunset, and before retiring to sleep, with their face turned in the

assembling of persons from the same ethnic group for whatever purpose was strictly prohibited. Bisnauth underscored this point:

> The development of Islam in the Caribbean would have demanded Mosques around which the religious life could center, *imams* who could expound the Qu'ran and give guidance to holy living according to Qu'ranic prescriptions and, above all, freedom in which the Islamic community could shape its life according to the teachings of the mosque, the *imam* and the Qu'ran. The plantation which was geared exclusively to sugar production gave no scope for the development of Islam as the African village did.[115]

For the foregoing reasons, Islam did not survive as a coherent religious expression, at least in the first two centuries.

Islam means submission and peace. But it is submission to Allah (God), the Omnipotent, and the Creator of all things, including humans. African Muslims did not interpret Islam to mean submission to the institution of slavery or racial inequality. Their adherence to Islam became the source of their belligerency and *liberty or death* the motto of their struggles. Those who did not die in battle or, as prisoners, banished from the colonies, were absorbed into the dominant animistic Yorubas and Fons. As a consequence, the emergence of Islam as a communal religion of the Caribbean people had to await the abolition of slavery and the advent of the East Indians.

---

direction of Mecca (towards the East)

(2) All adult male Muslims are expected to attend prayers at the mosque.

(3) All Muslims are required to perform zakat, i.e., the giving of alms to the poor and needy.

(4) During the holy month of Ramadan, all Muslims, except pregnant women and the sick, are obliged to fast.

(5) Every Muslim is expected, unless it is impossible, to make a pilgrimage (hajj) to Mecca at least once in his or her life-time.

In the Caribbean the indentured Asians -- East Indians and Chinese -- were described as "White". This classification included the black-skinned Dravidians from Calcutta and elsewhere. In Cuba they were classified as "White" and "free". But according to Franklin Knight, the system of indentureship differed from the institution of slavery only in name. He wrote:

> To the speculating capitalists involved in the importation schemes, anyone not coming from Africa was regarded as "white." In this way, a vast array of non-Europeans and non-Africans, including brown Mexican Indians, black East Indians, and "yellow" Chinese, became classified for statistical purposes as "white." Nor were those contracted to work "free." They were tied to the sugar estates, and forced to work for periods ranging from four to ten years. In the Cuban context, they became subject to almost the same forms of police measures as the African slaves they were supposed to replace. Asians who thought that the terms of their indentures allowed them to change masters found on their arrival in Cuba that they were virtually sold to the planters.[116]

A majority of the East Indians went to the British, French, and Dutch colonies and the Chinese to Cuba, but their contract of indenture was the same. They were brought in to ensure that the plantocracy maintained or maximized its profit margin and simultaneously to undermine and frustrate the efforts of Africans to obtain higher wages for the improvement of their economic and social conditions.

Islam was reintroduced into the Caribbean by the East Indian Muslims. The Asian Imams, however, unlike their earlier African counterparts, did not follow the militant tradition of using Islam as a tool of struggle against slavery and colonialism. This may be explained within the context of Islamic development in India. The Turkish, Persian and Moghul conquerors of Northern India did not introduce Islam to the Indian people by way of an ultimatum, as was the case of the peoples of the Arabian Peninsula and Central Asia who were given the choice of complete submission to Islam or death. In India, Islam was interpreted in Hindu terms which enabled the converts to retain their social and cultural identity within the prevailing Hindu framework. This included a continued acceptance of the socio-political and religious caste system which humiliates and strips the poor of their dignity. Bisnauth wrote:

> The conversion of Hindus to Islam did not seriously affect the lifestyle of many of the converts. In the villages of Northern India, there was little to distinguish the Muslims from the Hindus. Not only were the former of Hindu descent, but their conversion to Islam did not prevent them from observing Hindu festivals and customs and even from worshipping at local Hindu shrines. In addition, most Muslim villagers observed the rules of caste to which their Hindu forebears belonged.[117]

The tendency of the East Indian Hindus and Muslims to accept and submit to oppression represented a sharp contrast to the militancy of Shamanism and the several African religions that came to the New World. This, however, does not mean that the East Indians offered no resistance to the system of indentureship. Imams (Muslim priests) and Brahmins (Hindu priests) organized work stoppages and led labor strikes in the colonies of British Guiana, Surinam, Martinique and Trinidad. There were many instances in which resistance expressed itself in the form of riots, strikes, desertion, and the 'killing of particularly oppressive' managers and overseers.[118] But for the most part, the Indian laborers, at least for the first few decades, were very much resigned to their condition of indentureship. They kept to themselves and did not interface with the other racial and ethnic groups – Chinese, Africans, Javanese, Europeans – in the colonies, partly because they were unaccustomed to the new environment, and partly because they had not yet forged the cultural tools and language skills with which to function in the broader society.

The European rulers saw no distinction between Muslims and Hindus. In accordance with their arrogance, they considered the Hindus and Muslims "heathens" and "barbarians" because they were not Europeans and did not embrace Christianity – the "vanguard of civilization." And whereas the Europeans did painstakingly try to eradicate the religions, languages and culture of the Africans, they did not as a policy interfere with the religious practices or ceremonies of the East Indians, except on those occasions when labor strikes or work stoppages influenced them to do so as acts of vengeance. The East Indians did, however, experience certain restrictions that greatly impeded their religious practices. For example, like the Baptists, Methodists, Moravians, and Roman Catholics in the British colonies but a few decades earlier, they could not conduct legal marriages.

> Asian religious practices were generally tolerated (with the exception of Hindu cremation and Javanese coffin-less burials), but none of the Hindu or Moslem sects received governmental subsidies as did the Christian or Jewish religions, nor were marriages, conducted solely according to Hindu or Moslem ceremonies, given legal recognition.[119]

Therefore, Muslims in Guyana, Surinam, Martinique, Cayenne, and Trinidad were able to build mosques, establish social and cultural organizations and schools for the teaching of Arabic and to proscribe non-orthodox Islamic practices. But it was not until the 1940's that government aid was granted to the Islamic and Hindu schools. The Muslims, like their co-religionists elsewhere, were not free of sectarian cleavages. The two major rival sects that had their genesis during the seventh century War of Caliphate Succession -- the Sunnis and the Shi'ites -- were also present among them. One Muslim event -- known in Trinidad as *Hosein* or, more popularly, as *Hoosay* -- has been co-opted by non-Muslims and even non-Indians into a version of Carnival, much to the resentment of pious Muslims.[120] This festival, also known as *Tadjah*, was celebrated by the Shi'ites during the Muslim month of Muharram in all of the colonies in which they resided. It was in memory of Hassan and Hosein, the sons of Ali and grandsons of the Prophet Muhammad, who were slain during the War of Caliphate Succession. The Sunnis held the festival in disdain and in the 1880s lobbied the colonial government of Trinidad to ban its celebration.

The Tadjah festival was celebrated in Jamaica for many years. East Indians in Cockburn Pen, southwest St. Andrew, as well as other East Indian communities, could be seen dressed up in bright costumes and carrying what appeared to be a large tomb-like contraption. As the procession headed towards the sea, men and women wailed loudly, while a few of the male participants literally dueled with each other (stick-fighting). When they arrived at their destination, they walked into the water until they were about waist high, dumped the cask-like contraption into the water, wailed for a little while longer and then departed. The local Africans called this festival *Coolie Hoosay*. This, of course, was their understanding of the Shi'ite festival to mourn the death of Hassan and Hosein.

The orthodox Sunaat-ul-Jamaat, the principal organization in Trinidad, advocates a strict religious observance of Islamic beliefs. Many of the schools and mosques in the island were built by this group. It also has a strong presence in Guyana, Surinam, Martinique, and Cayenne. The largest Islamic organization in Guyana is the United Sadr Islamic Anjuman, but the Ahmadiyah, a reform movement founded in India in the late nineteenth century, has had considerable successes. It even has some Afro-Guyanese among its converts. The rites of orthodox and reform Islam are similar, but the reform movement allows the Q'uran to be read in English and women to enter a designated section of the mosque.[121]

A majority of the East Indians (Muslims and Hindus), unlike the Africans, remained tied to the sugar estates for a source of income even after indentureship had ended. Approximately 17 percent have taken up residence in the towns. Hence, the East Indian Muslims and Hindus constitute the bulk of the rural laboring classes. In the final decades of the nineteenth century, however, East Indians settled on Crown Land, frequently in swampy areas not especially suitable for the growing of sugarcane but capable of supporting other crops -- most particularly rice and other subsistence foods.[122] Today most Muslims earn their livelihood from either working the agricultural lands or operating small businesses. Like the Hindus, most are involved in rice or sugar cultivation, truck farming, or in the operation of small stores and other small community businesses.[123]

Despite the apparent differences between the Hindu, Christian, and Muslim East Indians and their respective denominations, they were all perceived by the Europeans and the Creole African population as one homogeneous entity. While it is true that haughtiness and indifference might have contributed to this misconception, there were objective and subjective bases for the belief. The Hindus and Muslims had the same cultural background, lived in the same communities and, for the most part, shared the same lifestyle.

Hinduism

The Hindu beliefs that first appeared in the Caribbean were those of the Sri Narayana Panth or Sieunarainis or Ramanandis as they were called in Guyana. This group, unlike other Hindu polytheistic sects, believes that there is one Omnipotent and Loving God.

> God is not impressed with the external forms of religion -- the performance of rituals, the reading of scriptures, asceticism, pilgrimages, ablutions in the Ganges -- unless the worshipper is truly devout and unless his devotion is matched by moral living. It is God alone who frees men from the Law of Karma and brings to an end the cycle of reincarnation in which a man might be caught. Freed from the karmic wheel, the soul is absorbed into the Absolute. This absorption or salvation comes to the man who has a simple, complete love for God.[124]

The Law of Karma was used to rationalize the status of each believer. It was very beneficial to the Brahmins who occupied the highest status in the Hindu caste system because they could "have their cake and eat it at the same time." Central to the Hindu belief system is the principle of reincarnation. On the basis of this belief, the Brahmin (priestly caste), Kshatriya (warrior-noble-merchant caste), Vaisya (peasant-artisan caste), and Shudra (lowly, untouchable caste) occupied their respective status either as a reward or punishment for his or her deeds in a previous life. Respect and status among Hindus are accorded to the caste to which one belongs, not to the person; and caste is derived from birth.

Since caste is ascribed and not achieved, one is unable to change one's caste through any effort of one's own.[125]

Accordingly, a Brahmin could arguably have been a member of a lower caste in his previous life and was rewarded with a higher status in his present life because of his good deeds. Conversely, a Shudra or Untouchable could have been a Kshatriya or even a Brahmin in his previous life and, because of his evil deeds, is condemned to live the life of an Untouchable. What seems more than a coincidence, though, is the fact that the Brahmins, Kshatriyas and Vaisyas tend to originate from Aryan stock and are fair-complexioned, while the Shudras or Untouchables are from the indigenous Dravidian stock and are very dark-complexioned.

A Hindu's status within the caste system is directly related to the Law of Karma and consistent with the Divine Will. Therefore, a devout Hindu, even the wretched Untouchable, is expected to endure his or her oppressive condition of existence without protest. If Untouchables were to struggle to change or ameliorate their social and political condition, they would be deemed apostates and heretics and condemned for attempting to usurp the power of Brahman who alone can change one's karma. In this way the Law of Karma serves as a formidable shield to protect the status quo and enable the Brahmins and Kshatriyas to enjoy their wealth and power with impunity.

The orthodox Hindu sect of Sanatan Dharm Maha Sabha, the group to which most Hindus belong, brought with them to the Caribbean this adherence to the Law of Karma. Among the Vaishnavite Hindus the higher castes worship the classic pantheon of Vishnu and Shiva. During the indentureship period, the East Indian caste system, with its reinforced variations of rites and beliefs within the Vishnu cult, broke down. Hinduism was redefined, and caste-distinguishing practices were eliminated.[126] This became inevitable because the new environment and the social dictates destroyed the old caste system.

> As the East Indian became more immersed in Creole society, he ignored many of the caste laws, restrictions and cultural norms.... Marriage by East Indians was usually through child wives and child husbands. These unions were family and religious arrangements, decided for the benefit of the minors, by adults. This long established system was slowly eroded as the participants in many cases openly flouted these marriages and sought fresh matrimonial arrangements at a maturer age.[127]

For the first few decades they kept to themselves and made no attempts to change the oppressive condition of indentureship or to participate in the democratic struggle being waged by the Africans. The reason for this is the fact that the East Indians saw themselves as transients whose ambition was to make some money and return to India. However, of those who were able to make the return passage to India at the end of their indenture, a significant number came back to the Caribbean after experiencing difficulties in readjusting to the old society.

The immigrant mentality of the East Indians suffered a further erosion when, under the auspices of the Secretary of State for the Colonies, African and East Indian squatters were given title to the lands they occupied. Unoccupied Crown lands were also divided into ten-acre lots and many East Indians who had completed their contracts of indenture opted to purchase these lots in lieu of the return passage to India. East Indian settlements such as Oropouche, Calcutta and Coolie Town in Trinidad were the products of this process of land allocation. Thus the end of the nineteenth century and the beginning of the twentieth saw the establishment of a class of Indian peasant farmers who, in league with the estate-oriented communities of Indians, would wield tremendous political power with the introduction of universal adult suffrage in the post World War II period.[128]

In the early years, therefore, as a form of protection, East Indians had very limited contact with the broader society. They displayed no interest in integrating with the other ethnic groups. As a consequence, they were able to retain not only their racial identity, but also their religious integrity. To protect Hinduism from further Christian encroachment, the Brahmins had to do away with certain age-old practices in order to make their religion more attractive. The Brahmins, for instance, began administering spiritual rites to all Hindus regardless of caste, a taboo in India, once the Christian missionaries started proselytizing in the villages, hastening the breakdown of the caste system. After the 1930's, Hindu conversions to Christianity slowed because the status of Hinduism had improved and discrimination against Hindus had diminished.[129]

By the turn of the twentieth century, public criticism in Europe and India of the indenture system, particularly by the educated classes and legislators, had reached a high pitch. 'The built-in contractual impedimenta denied the worker freedom of choice in selecting his employer, his length of service and his place of residence. One of its severest critics was Mahatma Gandhi.'[130] The government of India was obliged to abolish the indenture system in 1917 and no more Indian laborers were allowed to enter the colonies. The Dutch government, however, continued the importation of Javanese into Surinam until 1937.

Hinduism was strengthened with the formation of the Arya Samaj, a reformist group which was formed in India about 1875 and in 1910 brought to British Guiana by one Dayanand. This sect rejected the caste system entirely, the authority of the Brahmins, and the polytheistic nature of Hinduism. The Arya Samaj instead advocated strict monotheism, the worship of one god. However, this sect indirectly helped to further strengthen Hinduism in the colonies because it influenced the formation of the orthodox sect, Sanatan Dharm Maha Sabha. Visits by Hindu and Muslim scholars and holy men to the colonies and visits to India by local religious students also had a positive effect on the effort to strengthen the religions. According to Brimsley Samaroo:

> In the religious sphere the Indian connection has been strong and continuous. Between the Caribbean visits of Bhai Parmanand, an Indian mystic, in 1910 and that of Sant Keshav Dass in 1977, there has been a constant flow of Indian religious leaders to the Caribbean. But the movement has not been one-way; over the years a number of Hindus and Muslims have gone back to the sub-continent for training and inspiration. As early as 1888 Yacoob Ali of Princes Town went to India where he spent nearly a decade studying Islamic theology.[131]

East Indian Hindus and Muslims in the Caribbean and elsewhere also gained a new sense of importance from the successful independence struggle that was unfolding in India during the 1930s and 1940s and which culminated in the victory of the Indian people over British imperialism in 1947. During this period, several Hindu shrines, mosques, and schools teaching Hindi, Sanskrit, and Arabic, among other secular subjects, were built. East Indians were euphoric from the liberation of their homeland. Indian movies began to arrive and became very popular in the colonies. Extended visits in the early 1950s by Indian missionaries (known as "Swamis") resulted in an increased interest in Hinduism on the part of many young people.[132]

By the 1940s the East Indian population in Guyana had become larger than that of the African. In Trinidad, the Indian was approximately 5 percent (5%) less than the African population. In Surinam, East Indians represented roughly thirty-five percent (35%) of the population; but when combined with the Javanese population, constituted close to an equal percentage to that of the Africans. On the basis of the foregoing, East Indians gradually began to lose their traditional aloofness. They were beginning to feel their economic strength and were now prepared to protect their political interests. Additionally, literacy among East Indians, which was at one time lower than among Africans, had begun to increase as the former began to realize the importance of education.[133]

In the 1940s the United States was permitted by the British government to build a military base in the island of Trinidad. The base provided a source of income to many who previously had none or had to rely on the meagre earnings from the plantations. Better roads were built, transportation improved, and isolation decreased as people in rural areas, mostly East Indians, went in search of and, for the first time, found employment other than in the cane fields.[134] Among the individuals to share in the "Yankee Dollar" through his dealings with Americans, acquiring considerable wealth in the process, was Bhadase Sagan Maraj, a Brahmin and an early sugar-union leader, who later became a leader in East Indian political and religious affairs. As head of the Sanatan Dharm Maha Sabha, the most influential Hindu religious organization, he fostered the construction of schools and temples throughout the island.[135]

Thus, by the 1940s East Indians in the colonies had adopted a new posture. The image of the immigrant pinching pennies in order to save and return to India had become a thing of the past. They now saw themselves as Caribbean citizens who had every right to share in the resources of the colonies. India, however, remained their source of inspiration. And when Muslim Pakistan broke away from India and declared its own independence, the allegiance among East Indians of different faiths in the Caribbean also became divided: the Hindus gave their allegiance to India and the Muslims to Pakistan. Strangely enough the contradictions between India and Pakistan which gave birth to two wars and a continuously hostile relationship between them were never present among Hindus and Muslims in the Caribbean. Muslim, Hindu and Christian East Indians, despite their differences and orientation, were now poised to challenge the status quo and compete with the other ethnic groups in the creole society.

East Indian Social and Political Relationships

It should be emphasized that the East Indian communities in the Caribbean actually consist of Hindus (the majority), Muslims and Christians (significant minorities). The overwhelming majority of the Christians were converted from Hinduism. As such they possess a mish-mash of Hindu and Western culture and are largely centered in the urban areas. Of the relationship between the Hindus and Indian Christians in Trinidad, Gosine stated:

> The Hindus, mostly a rural enclave who cling steadfastly to their religious and cultural beliefs, look towards India for their general orientation towards life. From their Western orientation, East Indian Christians look down on Hindus as inferior for not conforming to Western tastes and life-styles. Hindus, on the other hand, see East Indian Christians as "deviants" of Hinduism who have denied the true faith in the interest of Christianity. Hindus believe that most Christian converts were low caste Hindus who simply converted to Christianity to hide their caste identity. They see East Indian Christians

as having "sold out" to Christianity to seek more equitable economic opportunities. Hindus, therefore, pride themselves in the fact that they have not converted to Christianity simply for the sake of economic opportunities or material gain.[136]

The contradiction between East Indian Christians and Hindus was absent among the Muslims because practically all of the Christians were converted from Hinduism. According to Gosine, Muslims in Trinidad see themselves as being closely related to the African community because "a majority of Africans throughout the world belong to the Islamic faith."[137] In the political arena the differences among East Indians tend to disappear as a majority of them vote for Indian candidates, independent of their platform in most cases. The middle class Hindus, Muslims and Christians, however, will generally vote and make alliances in accordance with their economic and social interests.

Thus, an appreciable number of East Indians, mostly Christians and Muslims, voted for and associated themselves with the then ruling People's National Movement (PNM) of Trinidad, an African-dominated party, rather than the opposition Hindu-dominated Democratic Labor Party (DLP). Yet, for cultural reasons, many of them, especially the Christians, feel a need to deny that affiliation. Even in Guyana where the racial cleavage between Africans and East Indians is sharper, the People's National Congress (PNC), an African-dominated party, enjoyed moderate support among the East Indian middle class. However, unlike their Trinidadian counterparts, they were less inclined to make excuses for or deny their affiliation. Rather, they would more readily rationalize their non-support of the Indian-dominated People's Progressive Party (PPP) on the grounds that the party was "communist".

The situation in Surinam was somewhat different. In 1945 Surinam had a population of approximately 100,000 and only 2,000 exercised the voting franchise. In December 1942, Queen Wilhelmina of the Netherlands, exiled in London since the German occupation of her country in 1939, made a radio announcement promising autonomy to the colonies after the war. This created a lot of political activity in Surinam, and by 1946 several political parties had been formed. These included the Moeslim Partij (Moslem Party--MP), the colony's first political party, which appealed to Javanese and East Indian Muslims and had universal adult suffrage and a decentralized economy among its demands; the Oranje Hindoe Groep (Orange Hindu Group -- OHG), a Hindu party which demanded universal adult suffrage and close ties with the Netherlands; the Progressieve Surinaamsche Volkspartij (PSV -- the Progressive Surinamese People's Party), a party formed by the Catholic Priest, Father Weidman, which, *inter alia*, demanded universal suffrage for men and women, educational scholarships for students, government action against usury, and limitation of imports in favor of local production; the Nationale Partij Suriname (National Party of Surinam -- NPS), a party consisting of Dutch, Jewish, Mulatto and dark-skinned African professionals, with a sprinkling of Asians and Javanese, which rejected universal adult suffrage on the grounds that the high level of illiteracy existing among the masses rendered them incapable of intelligently exercising the franchise; the Surinaamse Hindoe Partij (Surinamese Hindu Party -- SHP), a Hindu party which shared the views of the NPS; and the Hindostans-Javaanse Politieke Partij (Hindustani-Javanese Political Party -- HJPP), a party consisting of East Indian and Javanese Muslims under the leadership of Jagernath Lachmon, which advocated universal adult suffrage, proportional representation on a district basis, and local self-rule in the districts.[138]

All of the above mentioned parties, without exception, were created by and for the middle class. With the exception of the Brahmin SHP and the Jewish and Mulatto-dominated NPS, all of them advocated universal adult suffrage, not because they were more democratic than the NPS and the SHP, but because they could not compete with those two parties without mass participation in the political process. None of these parties demanded jobs, land, housing, education (Father Weidman's PSV excepted), vocational training, medical and dental care -- issues that directly affected the material and spiritual well-being of the working poor. This omission resulted in the formation of the Neger Politieke Partij (the Black Political Party -- NPP) and the Kaum Tani Persatuan Indonesian (the Indonesian Peasants' Party -- KPTI) in 1948 and 1949 respectively.

In 1949 the Dutch colony of Indonesia (the East Indies) rebuffed the Dutch ruling class, rejected its so-called "Kingdom Charter" and, when it resorted to violence, chastised its soldiers on the battlefield, and proclaimed its independence. Frightened by these developments, the Dutch monarchy feverishly tried to secure the remainder of its colonial empire. In February 1950, two months after its humiliation in Indonesia, a draft for the proposed Charter was hastily presented to the Staten of the Netherlands Antilles and Surinam for ratification.

In April 1950 Surinam's representatives -- J. Buiskool (European), David Findlay (Mulatto), Johan Adolf Pengel (African), all of whom were opposed to universal adult suffrage, and Jagernath Lachmon (East Indian), who was passionately opposed to Surinamese independence; and the Dutch Antilles' Moises Frumencio Da Costa Gomez (Jewish) and Efrain Jonckheer (Jewish), both of whom were opposed to universal adult suffrage, met with the Dutch government in the Hague and finalized the "Tripartite Kingdom Agreement", the intent of which was to bind Surinam and the Antilles to the Netherlands in perpetuity. There were no referenda in the Antilles nor in Surinam on this most important issue.

Between 1963 and 1967 the number of political parties and groups had grown considerably. Every disagreement or dispute between party members was the occasion for the formation of a new organization. The most important among the new parties were the Partij Nationalitische Republiek (the Republican Nationalist Party -- PNR), which was formed by E.J. Bruma and advocated independent republican status for Surinam; and the Progressieve Nationale Partij (the Progressive National Party -- PNP), which was formed by former NPS members.

This inordinate number of political parties is not unusual in colonial countries where politics serves as the central vehicle for social mobility for the colonized. This is also true of those colonies and independent countries in which two or three parties have been able to exclude all others. Intrigues, bribery, intimidation, dishonesty, treachery and even murder become the *modus operandi* of political parties and politicians as they vie with each other for control of the government, the country's treasury, and for the opportunity to serve metropolitan and local big businesses and make a fortune from graft, franchise payments, and so forth.

The African politicians had been well schooled by the European Christians and Jews in these political vulgarities. And it did not take a long time for the Asians to become adept in them also. And yet there was a time in Trinidad and even more so in Guyana when Africans and Asians struggled together for a just society. East Indians, for example, were highly represented in the labor movement of Captain Arthur Cipriani of Trinidad between the years 1919-1934. Many became members of Cipriani's Trinidad Workingmen's Association (TWA) which advocated constitutional decolonization; but they were divided in their political sentiments. The East Indian business community expressed satisfaction with the Crown Colony system. The East Indian National Congress wanted communal representation on the grounds that the economic, political and cultural interests of East Indians could not be protected in any other way. The Young Indian Party (YIP) desired the electoral system of representation on the grounds that East Indians had no unique interest to protect. It expressed the view that Indian culture and identity were worth preserving, but not by political means, and that the East Indian poor should identify with other poor ethnic groups in the society and protect their collective interests in this way.

Adrian Cola Rienzi, an East Indian, worked side by side with Cipriani and the African labor leader, Tubal Uriah "Buzz" Butler. He was one of the chief architects in the formation of the All Trinidad Sugar Estates and Factory Workers Trade Union (ATSEFWTU) and the Federated Workers Trade Union (FWTU). A majority of the East Indians, however, especially Hindus, were under the influence of the most backward section of the middle class. The most prominent member of that class and reputedly one of the wealthiest persons in Trinidad and Tobago was the Brahmin Bhadase Sagan Maraj, President of the All Trinidad Sugar Workers Union (ATSWU), and President-General of the Sanatan Dharm Maha Sabha.

In 1957, Maraj, Radranath Capildeo, and other Hindus formed the Democratic Labor Party (DLP) as a federal opposition to Dr. Eric Williams' People's National Movement (PNM). The DLP, which campaigned on a platform of race, defeated the over-confident PNM in the elections of 1958 and became a part of the short-lived West Indian Federal Government. Williams reacted by appealing to Africans and defeated the DLP in 1961 to become the first Prime Minister of an independent Trinidad-Tobago.

The leaders of the DLP consider it a betrayal for any East Indian – Christian, Hindu or Muslim – to support the PNM. In spite of this, some do, but express denials when confronted; others do so overtly and unapologetically. What all East Indians, including those who support the PNM, seem to agree on is the need to protect their cultural identity against absorption in the creole society. For all three religious groups, being East Indian is more important than religious or cultural differences. This may account for the fact that inter-caste marriages among East Indians, an uncommon feature of the past, is today quite common and acceptable in Trinidad.[139]

Approximately sixty five percent (65%) of the 239,000 East Indians that were taken to British Guiana were Hindus, with the remainder divided between Muslims and Christians. Like their kinfolk in the other Caribbean territories, they remained aloof and kept to themselves for the first few decades after their arrival. Africans resented East Indians for having broken their hold on the labor market, but since most East Indians lived on the estates and most Africans in the Negro villages, there were few clashes between the two groups.[140]

When the East Indians did break out of their isolation, their relationship with Africans was a positive one. During the years 1906-1916 an appreciable number of East Indians, in spite of the prohibition in their contract against striking, participated in the strikes staged by other sugar estate workers. The British Guiana Labour Union (BGLU), founded in 1919 by Hubert Critchlow, the father of trade unionism in the Southern Caribbean, included in its membership African workers of all categories and East Indian sugar estate workers. In 1946 Dr. J. Lacthmansingh and Amos Rangela formed the Guiana Industrial Workers' Union (GIWU) and demanded that the colonial government recognize its right to represent East Indian estate workers.

In that same year, 1946, Dr. Cheddi Jagan, his wife Janet Jagan, Ashton Chase and Jocelyn Hubbard established the Political Affairs Committee (PAC). It adopted an anti-colonial platform and condemned the social and political conditions of the African and East Indian masses. In 1949 Linden Forbes Samson Burnham, a budding African leader, joined the British Guiana Labour Party (BGLP), which was being organized by Dr. Jai Narine Singh. In January 1950 the PAC and the BGLP dissolved and formed the Peoples Progressive Party (PPP), with Dr. Cheddi Jagan as President. Within the next two years several leaders and members of the labor movement had joined the PPP. A powerful democratic political movement of Africans and East Indians was born.

In the elections of 1953, the party won 18 of the 24 seats, but its attempts to implement economic and social reforms were blocked by the British Government which labeled it "communist". On October 9, 1953, 133 days after it had taken the oath of office, the PPP Government was thrown out of office by British troops and the constitution suspended. The reforms that the PPP attempted to institute and for which it was labeled "communist" were, for all intents and purposes very modest.

[The PPP attempted] to bring all schools under the

supervision of the government and local education committees; to reform local government so as to provide for universal adult suffrage without property limitations; to appoint working people to government boards and committees; to revise the fees of government medical officers in order to make medical care possible for the poor; to curtail unnecessary expenditure of public funds; to provide more scholarships; to bring about social security and workmen's compensation; to improve drainage and irrigation; to make available and usable large tracts of land then uncultivated; and to review and act on the recommendations of the Central Housing and Planning Authority.[141]

Modest though they were, these reforms came into collision with powerful and diverse economic, political and social interests in the colony. Thus, the attempt by the PPP to implement the above "communist" measures, among others, served as an excuse for the British colonialists to overthrow the government. Yet these same "communist" measures, as one observer noted, existed as a matter of law in the United Kingdom and the United States.[142] Subsequent to the PPP's ouster, a state of emergency was declared; an interim government of nominated legislators and ministers established; and several PPP leaders arrested and imprisoned for violation of the emergency regulations. The Robertson Commission which was appointed "to investigate the British Guiana situation" reported that no constitutional progress could be made in the colony as long as the PPP retains its "extremist leaders." The extremism of the leaders consisted of their demands for an end to British colonial rule, and the right of the people of the Caribbean in general and British Guiana in particular to determine their own destiny.

What is most remarkable is that there was hardly any opposition by the middle class, Christian and non-Christian, to

British colonialism throughout the years of its oppressive rule. Yet, no sooner than an organization emerged to unite the African and East Indian masses under one umbrella and challenge the colonial hegemony of the British ruling class, the middle class politicians, local business leaders, the major Christian denominations, the British Guiana League of Coloured People, the Imams and Hindu Brahmins vehemently condemned the new organization. The leaders of the Christian denominations, especially the Anglican, Presbyterian and Roman Catholic churches, opposed universal adult suffrage. Their opposition to the PPP became even more bitter when the new government put into operation its stated principle of bringing all schools, hitherto within the exclusive domain of the churches, under the supervision of the government. Cheddi Jagan wrote:

> The Churches' hostility to us was mainly due to our policy with respect to the control of schools. We had stated categorically that we were in favour of the abolition of the system of dual (church-state) control of schools. The organized Hindu and Muslim groups -- the Hindu Maha Sabha, the Pandits' Council, the United Sad'r Islamic Anjuman and the Muslim League -- also attacked us.[143]

The PPP was faced with a political dilemma. The League of Coloured People condemned the African leaders as stooges who were being used by the Indian-dominated PPP. On the other hand, the Hindu Pandits and the Hindu United Farmers' and Workers' Party led by Daniel Debidin told the East Indian masses that the East Indian leaders of the PPP were selling out their interests to the Africans. To further excite East Indian passions and destroy PPP popular support, Debidin adopted the slogan *Apan Jhaat* (literally, own race).[144] It was because of these maneuvrings and the seeds of division that were planted in the political soil of British Guiana why the country did not participate in the Federation of the British West Indies, although the PPP government itself supported it.

Since the PPP still had the African and East Indian masses behind it, the strategy was to destroy that unity. Linden Forbes Burnham, Dr. Lachtmansingh and Dr. Jai Narine Singh proved to be the weak links in the chain. In 1957 they were induced by the British and Americans to form the People's National Congress (PNC). In the elections of that year, the PNC won 3 of the 14 seats to the Legislative Council, as opposed to the PPP's 9. In 1961 the PPP won 20 of the 35 seats. The British and their American allies concluded that new tactics had to be employed to oust the PPP from power. Thus, by February 1962, Debidin's slogan of *Apan Jhaat* became a battle cry; the unity between Africans and East Indians was shattered; and the country plunged into racial war. Workers and unemployed persons, bribed and instigated by the CIA-connected American Institute for Free Labor Development (AIFLD), demonstrated against government legislation, looted and rioted.

The wildcat strikes, arson, looting and wanton murders continued through 1964. When the carnage between African and East Indian sufferers was over, approximately 200 people were murdered, 1,000 injured, 1,400 homes destroyed, several million pounds in property damage sustained, and more than 15,000 people forced to vacate their homes and re-establish themselves in communities in which members of their race and ethnicity predominated. The people of Guyana have yet to recover from this cleavage and the social devastation it created. But the party favored by the British and Americans -- the People's National Congress -- was still unable to win fairly at the polls, because East Indians represented approximately fifty-three percent (53%) of the population. Under the guidance of its metropolitan patrons, the PNC was able to overcome that hurdle and "win" successive elections for the next two decades. Among the ballots cast in its favor were those of "voters" who had died in the previous centuries and "voters" who had never been born.

The racial violence in British Guiana was vulgarly used by the politicians in neighboring Surinam during their election campaign. It was reported that East Indian women from British Guiana were displayed at public meetings by the East Indian parties in an attempt to persuade East Indian voters about "what could happen in Surinam if they were to allow the black-dominated National Party of Surinam (NPS) to win."[145] The NPS did win the elections and formed a government. There were no murders, beatings, or violence because the NPS did not threaten the status quo. The new government simply continued the corrupt, dishonest and nepotistic practices of its predecessors.

In fact misappropriation of public funds, bribery, nepotism, and intimidation became the *modus operandi* of the European, Jewish, African and Asian politicians. Thus, by 1980 strikes and demonstrations had disrupted the economic life of the society and the government, too corrupt and insensitive to the just demands of the people for jobs, wage increases, and improved health, housing and social welfare, resorted to violence against them. It was this seemingly endless abuse of the people's trust; the political and moral fraudulence; the unfettered avarice, corruption, class and racial divisiveness; and the politicians' indifference to the welfare of the people and the national interests as a whole that led to the overthrow of the Henck Arron regime in 1980 by a group of patriotic, reform-oriented military officers under the leadership of Desi Bouterse and the establishment of a civilian-military government

From the foregoing, it is clear that the anti-colonial movement was weakened by the non-involvement of the Asians during the nineteenth century. It is true that at the time of their arrival in the Caribbean, there was mutual resentment between Africans and Asians. The Western-oriented Africans were hostile to the East Indians whom they identified as strike-breakers. They resented their presence on the grounds that they were a threat to their newly won "freedom"; they depressed wages; they were regarded as "heathens"; and their customs and behavior were strange. The Hindus, on the other hand, resented the Africans because they feared defilement as sanctioned by their caste system; and they felt superior to the Africans whose manners they found awkward, vulgar and savage.[146]

However, this feeling of resentment was short-lived as Africans and East Indians in all of the colonies in which they resided began, at the turn of the twentieth century, to struggle together for an amelioration of their conditions. Believing that isolation was a necessity to protect and preserve their religions and culture, some of the Brahmins and Imams unwittingly aided and abetted the Europeans in the exploitation of their own people. And in later years when this type of protectionist measure was no longer necessary or even desirable, some of the Asian religious leaders were still intimately bound up with sectarianism. This in turn objectively complimented the colonial policy of dividing and ruling the subject peoples and maximizing profits for the colonial rulers.

In the first half of the twentieth century, every attempt by Africans and East Indians to create a united front against colonialism was effectively blocked by the colonialists and the religious leaders themselves, especially the Brahmins of the Sanatan

Dharm Maha Sabha, whose philosophy was that the economic, political and cultural interests of the East Indians would be best protected under colonialism. The cleavage created and nurtured by the colonizers, aided and abetted by the middle class Brahmins, Imams, Christians, and Jews, and exploited and encouraged by their African counterparts has not only retarded and stultified the hopes and aspirations of the Asian people but also served to fan the flames of division and discord between the African and East Indian poor.

In spite of this, East Indians and Africans have collaborated and struggled together for their collective interests. East Indian leaders like Raffique Shah, a former lieutenant in the army of Trinidad-Tobago and a principal in the mutiny of 1970, contributed greatly to the unity of Africans and East Indians. As leader of the Islandwide Cane Farmers Trade Union (ICFTU), he and other East Indian leaders such as Basdeo Panday, the then President of ATSEFWTU (former Prime Minister of Trinidad and Tobago), worked together with African leaders like George Weekes, President-General of the Oilfield Workers Trade Union (OWTU) to organize East Indians and Africans at the workplace and in the United Labour Front (ULF), which became a political force in the 1970s.

Over the last three decades there has been an influx of reform Hindu and Islamic movements, especially in Trinidad-Tobago and Guyana. Their aim is to strenghten Hinduism and Islam and to counter the influence of Western values and interests. The reform movements, particularly the Islamic, have had considerable success, gaining converts not only from among East Indians but also Africans. In Trinidad-Tobago, many of the Africans associated with the National Joint Action Committee (NJAC), founded by Geddes Granger – the organization that spearheaded the movement in 1970 that almost toppled Eric Williams' regime – became converts of Islam. And over the last two decades, many Africans who have become disenchanted with the social and political system and with Christianity have increasingly looked to Islam and Rastafarianism as alternatives.

In 1988 the Jamaat Muslimeen, an organization of African and East Indian Muslims under the leadership of Abu Bakr, was formed in Trinidad. During this period, Trinidad's per capita income fell from $12,000.00 in the 1970s (one of the highest in the world) to $5,095.00 in 1988. In 1980 Trinidad, producing about 150,000 barrels per day, was receiving $35.00 per barrel for its crude oil, which accounted for $10 billion in export sales. By 1988, oil prices fell to $9.00 per barrel and export earnings to $5 billion. As a consequence, Trinidad, a former lender, became a borrower; and by 1988 the national debt stood at $18 billion.

The Coalition government of Arthur N. R. Robinson, which came to power in 1986, opted for a self-imposed austerity program. The brunt of this program, however, fell on the shoulders of the poor. And this situation was greatly aggravated when Robinson agreed to the structural adjustment program of the International Monetary Fund (IMF). Government spending for social programs such as education, housing, transportation and assistance to the elderly, and so forth, were severely reduced. The Trinidad and Tobago dollar was devalued from T&T$1.00 to US$.42 in 1980 to T&T$1.00 to US$.23 in 1988.[147] Unemployment rose to 30 percent, crime and violence increased, the country's unemployed and underemployed professionals migrated to North America in droves, and the tens of thousands of poor Africans and East Indians who could not flee lived as squatters and vagabonds, some of them obtaining their food from the garbage.

Accordingly, when the Jamaat Muslimeen was formed, its first acts included building a mosque, food kitchens, day care centers and a school. It wanted to do more. Consequently, on Friday, July 27, 1990, a number of its members, mostly Africans, tried to seize political power. The police and the security forces retaliated and approximately 30 persons were killed, including a minister of government. The Muslimeen took and held 40 hostages, including the Prime Minister, Arthur N.R. Robinson, and several members of his cabinet for five days. During the intense negotiations that followed, the Prime Minister conceded to the demand of the Muslimeen, in a signed document, to resign and set up an interim administration leading to new elections.

On the fifth day 141 Muslimeen gave themselves up and were taken into police custody. During the five-day stand off, scores of desperate people in the capital, Port-of-Spain, took advantage of the event to loot and burn numerous businesses, mostly owned by Jews, Syrians and Lebanese, with damages estimated at approximately US$100 million. The other demands of Abu Bakr, namely, amnesty for the Muslimeen, new elections in Trinidad-Tobago in ninety (90) days, and permission for the Muslimeen to keep their weapons, were rejected. On his release, the Prime Minister also repudiated the signed agreement for his resignation on the grounds that it was done under duress.

Abu Bakr and the other members of the Muslimeen were tried and convicted as criminals. They successfully appealed their convictions, which were overturned. They then sued the government for unlawfully seizing their property and imprisoning them and recovered a portion of their real estate and approximately T&T$5 million in compensation. The action taken by Abu Bakr and the Muslimeen received tacit support from East Indians and

Africans throughout the country. They did not approve of the strategy employed by them to redress the glaring social discrepancies within the society, but they felt the same anger and frustration that underlay their action.

There has also been a measure of cultural exchange between African traditionalists and East Indian Hindus and Muslims. The Africans have added East Indian spirits to their roster of *jumbies* (spirits) in Trinidad-Tobago and Guyana, *zombies* in Martinique and Cayenne, and *duppies* in Jamaica. In fact an East Indian ("Coolie") *duppy* or *jumbi* is one of the most feared and dangerous spirits in the service of a sorcerer. In turn, East Indians have also attributed some of the powers of the babalawos, santeros, shepherds, mayomberos, and obeahmen -- healing, making and breaking spells, and divination -- to the Brahmins and Imams.

> A feared *bhut* was the *chureil,* the ghost of a woman who had died during pregnancy. Chureils and 'tree' bhuts were known in North India. Not known there, however, was the peculiarly Negro spirit called 'ol' higue' in Guyana, and 'sukuyan' in Trinidad. This spirit was credited with the ability of being able to shed its skin, fly through the air and suck the blood of its victim. Many Indian immigrants quickly came to fear this Creole spirit. East Indians in the Caribbean came to believe too in the powers of the obeahman -- a figure from the world of Negro folk beliefs. It was not long before they began to credit Brahmin priests, mahants and Muslim Imams with the powers of the Negro obeahman, and to solicit from them charms, amulets and potions against the mischief of real and imaginary enemies.[148]

Thus, on the basis of their individual, collective and interracial struggles, East Indians have been successful in impressing upon the colonial and post-colonial governments the need to give equal respect to their culture so that the diversity of the society can be truly reflected. As a consequence, today in Guyana Hindu holidays include *Holi*, the spring festival, and *Divali*, the festival of lights. Muslim holidays include *Id al Fitr*, the end of Ramadan, the sacred month of fasting; *Id al Adha*, the feast of sacrifice; and *Yaum an Nabi*, the birthday of Muhammad. The dates for these holidays vary. An East Indian heritage day is celebrated on May 5, and an Amerindian festival is held on Republic Day, in February.[149]

Buddhism, Taoism and Confucianism

From all accounts the Chinese in the British, French, and Dutch colonies were considered poor agricultural laborers. A variety of reasons have been given to explain why this was so. The views of the planters, as articulated by Roy A. Glasgow, are that "the growing disenchantment with instances of petty theivery, rum smuggling and gambling houses, plus the movement from the farms into small country businesses, was responsible for the termination of this source of labor supply in 1878."[150] There is merit to the arguments that the Chinese engaged in gambling and that they left the plantations and went into small businesses, but there is no evidence to substantiate the views that thievery and rum smuggling were any more widespread among Chinese than any other ethnic group. Thomas A. Shaw, on the other hand, pointed out:

> There are many accounts of mistreatment and abuse of the Chinese as contract laborers on the sugar estates in Trinidad, Jamaica, and British Guiana. Many disputes were about wages although, unlike in Jamaica or Trinidad, the Chinese in British Guiana did not join other laborers in strikes against plantation owners. In all three regions the Chinese left the estates as quickly as possible -- either as deserters before their contracts were up, or as soon as they had fulfilled their original agreements -- and found their way to the villages and towns.[151]

Eric Williams concurred with Shaw that the planters were unimpressed with the performance of the Chinese in the fields and that the Chinese were severely maltreated by them. He stated that the Chinese Imperial Government, angered by the maltreatment of its nationals, especially in the Spanish colony of Cuba, demanded better treatment for them and return passage for those who had completed their period of indentureship.[152] Hence, the demands of the Chinese Government, the poor performance of the Chinese laborers, and the availability of East Indian substitutes resulted in the ultimate discontinuation of the importation of Chinese laborers.

In the colony of Cuba, the planters' overall impression of the Chinese was markedly different. The Cuban merchants, who primarily controlled the "trade" in Chinese indentured labor, and the planters who ultimately profited from that labor were mostly satisfied with the system. Julián Zulueta of Zulueta & Co., a Spanish-born slave trader, merchant and multiple plantation owner, 'was in many respects representative of the great planters, the prospective millionaires, ... which included the Aldamas, the Poeys, the Diagos and the Torriente families.'[153] These were the Cuban tycoons who reaped an enormous sum from the Cuban trade in Chinese indentured labor. Comparing the African Slave Trade with Cuba (especially after the 1807 Abolition), and Chinese indentured labor in Cuba, Mary Turner wrote:

> The subsequent development of the trade seems to have remained largely in Cuban hands and the profits accrued to Cuban capitalists. In this the Chinese contract trade contrasted with the slave trade which, although it involved important Cuban interests, was dominated by the Americans. The Havana trade, 'could not be called a Cuban trade at all: it was financed by American capital carried in American ships, manned by American seamen and protected by the American flag.[154]

The contract of indenture for both Chinese and East Indians in the British, French, and Dutch colonies included the payment of $6.00 per month, medical care, and a quantity of rations for the first three months. In addition to these provisions, the East Indians also were given the option of return passages to India or parcels of land at the end of their indenture. The Chinese 'were contracted to work at 4 pesos a month for 8 years. They were to work at the order of their 'patrono', the contract holder, at any kind of work, for 12 hours a day in the country, or more in domestic service, for four pesos a month, 2 changes of clothing a year and food; 12 pesos were paid in advance (an incitement to indebted peasants) to be deducted from wages in Cuba.'[155] In the British, French and Dutch colonies, the Chinese had the option, after one year of service, to shorten their indenture by paying $12.00 for each unexpired year. Many Chinese took advantage of this option and established themselves as gamblers, launderers, and petty traders. Indeed very few Chinese completed the five-year period of indenture.[156]

The mortality rate among Chinese was very high. Twenty percent of those who landed from the ship *"Australia"* in 1853 were dead within the year. The twin scourges of ulcer and fever took their usual heavy toll. Additionally, for the Chinese, there was the added hazard of opium which could easily be bought in the colonies. At the time of the 1861 Census in the colony of Trinidad, only 461 Chinese were enumerated, although it is likely that some were not counted.[157]

Like the East Indians, many Chinese were tricked into coming to the West. Some had never worked on plantations and were not told that they were being recruited to perform agricultural labor. Many artisans and tradesmen to whom agricultural labor was a social disgrace committed suicide. Some were simply kidnapped from their villages and cities, placed on a ship, or *Shanghaied,* as it became known, because of the prevalence of kidnapping in that city, and transported to the West. Turner noted:

> Although the Chinese government issued warnings against pig-stealers', it is clear that kidnapping and

intimidation were common and torture not unknown. The Cuban investors and prospective buyers were only concerned that their agents should have enough expertise to avoid shipping the old and the sick.[158]

Hustlers and tricksters, who were themselves tricked, "vanished" from the estates. The Exchange Estate at Couva, Trinidad, for example, had been allotted 112 Chinese. At the end of the year only 19 had worked regularly, 49 had been in prison, and 44 had disappeared.[159]

The reluctance of the indentured Chinese in the British and Dutch colonies to engage in agricultural labor made them economically risky to the planters who began to look to the East Indians as their chief source of indentured labor. In Cuba the economic risk was greatly lessened by the fact that indentured Chinese labor operated side by side with African slavery and, for that reason, it was more risky for the Chinese to break their contract. If and when they did, they were hunted down in much the same way as runaway slaves were. The punishment meted out to Chinese runaways was as severe as that inflicted on the African slave. Turner underscored this point:

Discipline was to be enforced in the terms of official regulations which subjected the Chinese to the same discipline as the slaves. The regulations of 1849 permitted 12 lashes for disobedience, 18 lashes for persistent disobedience, the stocks and shackles for recalcitrance. Runaways were given bouts of this punishment for two, four or six months according to the frequency of the offence.[160]

Aside from the consequences meted out to runaways, the existence of slavery side by side with Chinese indentureship in Cuba had other features discouraging to Chinese abscondence from the plantations. As small entrepreneurs, the Chinese did not have the huge market of ex-slaves that their counterparts in the British colonies had.

By 1871, however, when the practice terminated, approximately 50,000 Chinese had been brought to the British and Dutch colonies and 125,000 to Cuba. The Chinese population in British Guiana, at its highest level, was about 12,000. However, one-half of that number had departed from the colony at the termination of Chinese indenture. In 1872, about 2,500 Chinese and 480 Portuguese Madeirans were recruited by the Dutch Government for indentured labor in Surinam. But within a short time, they abandoned the sugar estates and established themselves as small independent merchants and farmers even before the expiration of their contracts. In Surinam and British Guiana the Chinese shared the retail trade with the Portuguese. In Jamaica and Trinidad they dominated it.

The Chinese in the Caribbean were less attached to Buddhism, Taoism or Confucianism than were the East Indians to Islam and Hinduism. This, of course, was largely the result of three very important factors. In the first place, the Chinese religions do not have deities or god-heads to command the kind of loyalty and adherence from devotees as do the other religions. Additionally, very few, if any, Buddhist priests accompanied the indentured laborers to the New World. And finally, the indentured population was relatively small and, without the priests to organize and propagate the religions, particularly among the *t'usheng* – those who were born in the colonies – they [the religions] ceased to play a central role in the lives of the Chinese. Indeed, even in Cuba where the indentured Chinese population was at its highest, a figure that was more than twice the combined Chinese population in the rest of the Caribbean, there was an absence of a strong Buddhist, Taoist or Confucianist tradition.

An attempt to establish a Chinese settlement in British Guiana, by O. Tye Kim of the Church Missionary Society, failed and the members gradually filtered into the capital, Georgetown.[161] In any event, Kim and his followers were Christians and, accordingly, Westernized. Shaw noted that the *t'usheng,* who retained recognizable Chinese names rarely could write the characters for their own surnames.[162] Indeed if the Report of the Society for the Propagation of the Gospel in Foreign Parts (SPG) is to be believed, a considerable number of Chinese in the colony of British Guiana had become Christian converts. The SPG, an arm of the Church of England, made the following boast in its report to the head office in London:

> The Chinese Missions have been a great success. Very few heathen Chinese are left in the colony. It may be stated that the new generation of Chinese is all Christian. In the opinion of the writer and nearly all colonists they are the best Christian element in the colony. They are generous to a degree, honest as "day", and altogether to be relied upon.[163]

The level of integration between Chinese and Africans was far greater than that of East Indians and Africans. And this was primarily due to the fact that relatively few Chinese women accompanied their men to the New World. This resulted in frequent confrontations between Africans and Chinese males as the latter tried to win the affections of African women. Daly noted that there were clashes between Africans on the one hand, and Chinese and East Indians, on the other. The Africans blamed the East Indians for breaking their hold over the labor market. The Chinese brought few women with them and in their attempt to get African wives they clashed with African men.[164] This accounts for the large number of persons in the Caribbean with Chinese names but predominantly African features.

The rivalry between Chinese and African males was carried over into other areas. In 1865 and 1866, for example, there were a number of serious clashes between Chinese and Africans in the colony of Trinidad. These confrontations ostensibly resulted from the apprehension of alleged Chinese malfeasants by the local police. Whether or not there was a legitimate reason for arresting the Chinese, their countrymen came to their aid and the Africans came to the aid of the local African police.[165]

The Chinese universally commuted their indentureship or simply broke their contract and began to pursue the trades or occupations of their choice. They made a concerted effort to preserve their culture -- values, language, customs, and so forth. By the turn of the twentieth century they had become, to a greater or lesser degree, an economic force in all of the colonies in which they resided. They were most successful in the colony of Jamaica where they established their own community, printed a newspaper, and organized a Benevolent Society, among other things. Indeed they even created a number's game, *peaka-peow,* as it became known, which did a thriving business among Africans. Shaw noted:

> In Jamaica, a Chinese community emerged, and in 1891 the Chinese Benevolent Society was organized to perform charitable work among the aged and the poor. Not until 1922, however, did it become much of an integrating force in the community, with the Chinese Poor House, a sanatorium for general respite and recuperation, a Chinese cemetery, a Chinese public school, and a Chinese newspaper under its control.[166]

In this way the Chinese were able to maintain their cultural distinctiveness, at least until the first half of the twentieth century. Chinese from all walks of life appeared to be united under the banner of Chinese ethnicity. Shaw stated that Jamaican nationalism forced them to abandon much of their ethnic identity and to accept West Indian "creole" cultural symbols by the second half of the twentieth century.[167] This, however, is only partially true, because by 1949 the People's Republic of China was proclaimed by the Communist Party of China and its leader, Mao Tse Tung, and many Chinese either lost touch with the families they had left behind or had no desire to re-establish their roots in the new socialist republic. As a consequence, the efforts at cultural retention suffered. Few, if any, indigenous Chinese were migrating to Jamaica and, with the passing of the older Chinese, the process of creole assimilation began to take firmer roots. By the 1960s when Jamaican nationalism became most strident, the Chinese were well on the road to assimilation.

At the same time, they had endeavored to learn the language of the colonizers in order to take advantage of the more favorable economic opportunities made available to people of their race and pigmentation. Thus, for several decades, the children of Chinese, many of whom attended some of the prestigious Christian and secular high schools, were able to speak English and Chinese. By the 1950s a growing number of Chinese children were unable to write or speak the Chinese language in much the same way as their counterparts in British Guiana in the nineteenth century. Therefore, the Chinese were less resistant to Christianity and the Christian-dominated school system than the East Indians. This was because of the absence of their priests and a god-head that could command loyalty from adherents wherever they happen to be. As a consequence, Buddhism, Taoism, and Confucianism, having failed to establish a foothold in the Caribbean -- even in Cuba, Jamaica, and Guyana where they had their strongest representation -- have had a relatively minor impact on the social, cultural and political life of the region.

Rastafarianism

When Marcus Garvey returned to Jamaica from the United States in 1927 and launched his political movement, he had the overwhelming support of the masses whom he had earlier influenced with his teachings. His political party failed because the masses did not have the voting franchise. For them, however, he was much more than a political leader. He was their teacher, hero, philosopher, and prophet. He is alleged to have made several "prophesies" concerning various historical events, personalities and politicians. And it is one of these "prophesies" that gave birth to a movement – the Rastafari Movement – that was destined to reshape the social fabric of Jamaica, the rest of the Caribbean and other parts of the world.

Garvey is alleged to have prophesied that an African prince would be crowned and would become the redeemer of the African people. On November 2, 1930, Ras Tafari, son of Ras Makonnen, was crowned Haile Selassie I, Emperor of Ethiopia, King of Kings, Lord of Lords, the Conquering Lion of the Tribe Judah, the Elect of God and the Light of the World. This event did not escape the vigilance of Garvey's disciples who hurriedly consulted their bibles to determine whether this was the prince of whom Garvey had spoken. Revelations 5:2, 5 convinced them that Ras Tafari was indeed that man:

> And I saw a strong angel proclaiming with a loud voice: who is worthy to open the book and to loose the seals thereof? And no man in heaven, nor in earth, was able to open the book, neither to look thereon. And one of the angels saith unto me: weep not! Behold the Lion of the Tribe of Judah, the Root of David, hath prevailed to open the book, and to loose the seven seals thereof!

The undisputed report that Selassie's family line extended to Makeda, Queen of Sheba, and King Solomon, son of David, served to dismiss any lingering doubts these Garveyites might have had about the "prophesy." They argued that since Jesus Christ, who is also a descendant of the House of David, is deemed to be the son of God, then Haile Selassie, the Lion of Judah and the Root of David, is the reincarnation of Jesus Christ – Almighty God.

It was of little relevance to them that Menelik II, Emperor of Ethiopia (1889-1913), and other emperors before him, also had the title "King of Kings, Lord of Lords, Conquering Lion of Judah," and were descendants of Solomon and Makeda. What was of importance to them is that Garvey had spoken about the coming of Selassie, like John the Baptist did of Jesus, and the Bible had confirmed it. Thus arose the Rastafari Movement which, in its development, incorporated the aims and aspirations of Marcus Garvey, the militancy and perseverance of Myalism, and the revolutionary-democratic principles of Jesus Christ.

The Rastafari Movement arose during the height of the Great Depression (1929-1933) when famine and misery stalked the land. It arose when the pro-colonialist and anti-African orientation of the Christian Churches had produced widespread disenchantment with Christianity among the predominantly African population. Finally, it arose when the colonial government and its religious and secular allies were deeply engaged in the process of victimizing the symbol of African pride, respect and dignity -- Marcus Mosiah Garvey.

Rastafarianism was a response to economic, political and spiritual oppression and it developed among the most disadvantaged section of the working class. What is noteworthy is that a number of persons had conducted independent investigations and had individually concluded that Haile Selassie was indeed Almighty God. These individuals included Leonard Percival Howell, Joseph Nathaniel Hibbert, and Henry Archibald Dunkley; and their earliest disciples included Robert Hinds, Altamont Reid, Paul Earlington and Ferdinand Ricketts. These men were largely poor, unemployed persons who had been greatly inspired by Garvey's teachings.

Dr. Robert Hill, a well-known authority on the life and philosophy of Marcus Garvey, in his work *Leonard P. Howell and Millenarian Visions in Early Rastafari,* disputes the alleged link between Garvey and early Rastafari philosophy. He expresses the view that the prophesy pertaining to Haile Selassie's coronation is a myth and that there is no evidence to substantiate the alleged prophetic pronouncements of Garvey. He also denies that the belief in Selassie's divinity originated with Leonard Howell, Nathaniel Hibbert and Archibald Dunkley, but rather that it was the product of an Ethiopianist consciousness that flowered in the United States between 1925-1935. He argues that divers persons, mostly African-Americans, associated with that consciousness, were in fact the actual advocates of this belief.

Dr. Hill, however, has overlooked the fact that every religion has its myths which, through the passage of time, are transformed into truths. Rastafarianism, like other religions, including the relatively new Christian and non-Christian sects, such as Bahai'ism, Mormonism, Sun Yung Moonism, and Zen Buddhism, which have made significant inroads among the white middle class, is no exception. Whatever the relationship that existed between Garvey and the propagators of Rastafari in Jamaica, he holds a central place in the religious and secular lore of the Movement and enjoys canonical status in the theology itself.

It has been alleged that when the Buddha was born the nocturnal owls moved about in broad daylight and flowers bloomed in winter; and that when Jesus was born a star led three wise men, the Magi, to the manger where he was hidden, although King Herod's most diligent spies were unable to find him. It has also been said that shortly before the birth of the Prophet Muhammad, his hometown of Mecca was invaded by Ethiopians whose elephants, brought along on the raid, refused to take their riders near Muhammad's future birthplace and, that when force was employed against them, they turned on their riders and trampled them to death. In like manner much symbolism has accompanied the allegation that when Ras Tafari was a baby he was missing from the palace for several hours and, after a long and fruitless search by his distraught parents, he was seen returning to the palace with a pride of lions walking behind him like lambs.

Not surprisingly, the secular and clerical rulers of the colony dismissed the new movement as a manifestation of insanity, in much the same way that Jesus and his followers were dismissed by the Romans and denounced by the secular Hebrew leaders, and the officially recognized priests of Judaea – the Sadducees. Yet, the essence of the Rastafarians' alleged insanity lies in their belief that all the prophets of the Old Testament were black; that Moses, Samuel, David, Solomon, Jesus and the biblical Hebrews were black; and that Haile Selassie – Ras Tafari – is a reincarnation of Jesus Christ – Almighty God. Remarkably, this belief has been characterized as insane by European Christians who for centuries, in writing and by proclamations, have themselves made the even more preposterous averment that the biblical Hebrews, including Jesus and his disciples, were white. In furtherance of this view, they even designed artistic portraits of these biblical figures reflecting European phenotypical characteristics.

The Rastafarians' views regarding the African ethnicity of the Hebrews was strengthened by the writings and proclamations of the Ethiopian World Federation (EWF) which was founded in New York in 1937 by a cousin of Haile Selassie and which had chapters in a number of cities in the United States and in the Caribbean. Horace Campbell wrote:

> These adherents [Rastafarians] of black nationalism accepted literally the claim of the Ethiopian World Federation that Haile Selassie was the Elect of God and Light of the World. When the *Voice of Ethiopia* added that the true Israelites were black and that Africans formed the *Twelve Tribes of Israel,* giving a historical account of the Falashas who, it claimed, had carried the Ark of the Covenant back to Ethiopia, many Rastas believed that blacks were indeed the children of Israel.[168]

The Rastafarians, therefore, believe that Africans are the true Israelites who have suffered another period of captivity by the modern Babylonians, i.e., Europeans; that man is God and not a spirit in the sky as the false prophets teach; and that Jah Rastafari is omnipresent and omnipotent and dwells in the hearts of all men, including *bald heads* (non-Rastafarians). It is their belief that there will be a day of Armageddon when the forces of Babylon will be finally vanquished by the mighty power of Jah Rastafari; and that on that day of Judgment the evil shall pay the price of their iniquities and every man and woman will return to his and her own vine and fig tree.

Therefore, to Rastafarians who consider themselves "prisoners" in Jamaica, repatriation to Ethiopia (Zion) is not a privilege to be granted by some benign ruler, but a natural and divine right. These ideas are reflected in the song *By the Rivers of Babylon:*

By the rivers of Babylon,
There we sat down,
And there we wept
When we remembered Zion;
For the wicked carried us
Away in captivity,
Required from us a song;
But how can we sing King Rasta's song
In a strange land?
So let the words of our mouth
And the meditation of our hearts
Be acceptable in Thy sight, O Fari!

In the song *Back to Ethiopia* the demand for repatriation and the basis for that demand is made:

Take me back to Ethiopia lan'!
Take me back to Ethiopia lan'!
Take me back to Ethiopia lan'!
Oh, yes, Rastafari, oh, yes!

Africa is our father's home!
Africa is our father's home!
Africa is our father's home!
Oh, yes, Rastafari, oh, yes!

Haile Selassie is our God an' King!
Haile Selassie is our God an' King!
Haile Selassie is our God an' King!
Oh, yes, Rastafari, oh, yes!

This was the philosophy that Howell, Dunkley, Hibbert, et al. took to the poor people of St. Thomas, Portland and Western Kingston. Howell, leader of the largest sect -- the "Dreadlocks" -- founded the Ethiopian Salvation Society; Dunkley, the King of Kings Missionary Movement; and Hibbert, the Mystic Order of Ethiopia. Dunkley, who had begun his mission in Kingston in

1934, lacked the charisma and organizational skills of Hibbert and Howell and, as a consequence, his Missionary Movement foundered very early. Most of his followers ultimately joined Howell's movement.

Hibbert, the Master Mason, believed in proper organization and in the immaculate appearance of his followers. He was organizer of a number of chapters of the Ethiopian World Federation in Jamaica and founder of the United Ethiopian Body. He and his followers believed that the hair should be allowed to grow but that it should be combed and neatly kept. For this reason they became known as *Combsomes* in contradistinction to Howell's *Dreadlocksomes.*

Hibbert's sect was also distinguished by its attire. On formal occasions, its members wore long, white robes with red, gold and green (the colors of Ethiopia) sashes around the neck and waist. Hibbert's group, however, failed to attract as large a following as Howell's and continued along a descending line until the 1960s when the Ethiopian World Federation churches, run by Brothers Claudius Stewart and Raphael Downer respectively, were among the only survivors. The death of Brother Stewart and the subsequent displacement of Brother Downer from his base in Davis Lane, Trench Town, in the 1970s, sounded the death knell for the *Combsomes.* The term *Combsomes* came out of use after the disintegration of Hibbert's sect and the *Dreadlocksomes* began to refer to themselves as *Dreadlocks* or simply *Dreads.*

Hibbert's sect lacked an important element needed for survival. It did not have the militant political feature that was prominent in Howell's sect, the Free Baptist Church of Alexander Bedward, and the secret religious society of Myalism. Howell's followers neither combed nor shaved their beards and hair, partly

Leonard Percival Howell, co-founder of the Rastafari Movement (the "Dreadlocksomes"). Courtesy of the National Library of Jamaica

Joseph Nathaniel Hibbert, co-founder of the Rastafari Movement (the "Combsomes"), and family. Photo by: George E. Simpson. Courtesy of the National Anthropological Archives, Smithsonian

because of their belief that all things, from a seed of corn to a lock of hair, should be allowed to grow freely and naturally; partly because it is written in the Book of Numbers that the hair should be grown until it "toucheth the very tip of the garment."

Howell also believed that even though they [the Israelites] were "prisoners" in Jamaica, they had a duty to fight against Babylon and all its iniquities until such time when they returned to Zion. In other words, they were not prepared to let the oppressors "off the hook" while they await repatriation. Thus, they became the standard-bearers in the struggle against colonialism and racism which they repeatedly sentenced to destruction by "lightning and thunder" and "brimstone and fire". Their outspoken criticisms of the political, social and religious improprieties prevailing in the society incurred the wrath of the Christian Churches and the State, which reacted with severe violence against them. The terror unleashed against Rastafarians by the Jamaican ruling class with the tacit approval of the *de facto* Established Christian denominations will be discussed later.

The Rastafarians had hardly formulated their doctrine when a crisis of great magnitude and many ramifications to the young movement developed. In 1935 the armies of Benito Mussolini of Italy invaded and overran Ethiopia, and Emperor Haile Selassie fled with his family to London. In that same year Japan invaded and conquered Manchuria, China. The Soviet Union (USSR), the only country in the League of Nations to condemn Italy and Japan, provided arms and training to the Chinese and Ethiopians and helped them to build their respective resistance movements.

The Ethiopian patriots adopted the name of the anti-colonial resistance movement of Kigezi, Uganda – *Nyahbingi* – and its slogan: "Death to all white oppressors." A considerable number of

African-Americans and other members of Garvey's Universal Negro Improvement Association (UNIA), and Africans from the continent and the Caribbean, answered the call to arms on behalf of their siblings in Ethiopia. Frustrated by the refusal of the governments of the United States and the United Kingdom to allow them to leave for Ethiopia, they staged demonstrations in several cities. African American workers rioted and engaged in pitched battles with Italians in New York City.[169]

Most Africans regarded the invasion as a racist war of aggression. This was quite true; but it involved much more than that. Until the 1860s, Italy, like Germany, was a geographic expression consisting of city states and principalities. Otto Von Bismarck of Germany and Count Cavour and Guiseppe Garibaldi of Italy were instrumental not only in uniting their respective countries but transforming them into major world powers. But by this time, the 1870s, the world had already been divided among the European powers. Accordingly, at the Conference of Berlin in 1885, Germany and Italy demanded what was left of the African continent. Germany got Togo, Rwanda, Burundi, the Cameroons and South West Africa (Namibia). Italy received Libya and portions of Somalia and northern Ethiopia which it called Italian Somaliland and which it decided to use as a springboard to take the bigger prize -- the ancient, majestic kingdom of Ethiopia.

Emperor Menelik II of Ethiopia, realizing that the European predators were closing in on his domains, modernized his army and got his troops into battle-readiness to meet the impending invasion. On March 2, 1896, the event most dreaded by the Ethiopian people came to pass as tens of thousands of Italians invaded their country. The Italians were not only defeated, they were humiliated. More than 1,000 officers of different ranks and thousands of rank and file soldiers were taken prisoners. Adwa, the name of the battlefield where the Italians suffered their humiliation, became a word of opprobrium to Italians.

This indeed was no minor accomplishment. It was a victory by a non-European country over a prominent European nation and a major world power. Italy became the butt of jokes in the courts of Europe and in the diplomatic community. The Italians, smarting under this humiliating defeat, developed what became known as the *Adwa complex* for more than three decades, and were obsessed with a desire for vengeance. Mussolini promised to free them from the *Adwa complex* and restore the pride and glory of Italy. Hence, the invasion of Ethiopia in 1935 was dictated by vengeance as well as a desire for colonial possessions.

Although Ethiopia had been overrun by superior arms and untold atrocities were inflicted on the people, they refused to surrender. The Nyahbingi fighters harassed the Italian army for five years and regained control over large sections of the country. The Italians, in alliance with Nazi Germany, declared war on Britain in 1939 and the latter threw its support behind the Ethiopians' successful war effort in 1940. Britain's entry into the war was decisive in helping to bring about the defeat of the Italians the following year, and Selassie returned from England in triumph to resume leadership of the country.

Many people, including Marcus Mosiah Garvey, associated Selassie's flight to London with that of a general who deserts his army on the battlefield in the face of a punishing enemy bombardment; and with that of the captain of a sinking ship who sails away in a life boat leaving his passengers and crew behind. In a word, they regarded it as an act of cowardice. Garvey went even further. Writing in *The Blackman*, he admonished Selassie for his years of neglect of the masses of Ethiopia; his failure to establish any relations with Africans from the continent and from the diaspora; his pre-occupation in trying to forge links with Europeans at the expense of his own people; and his total unpreparedness to confront the Italian invasion.[170]

To Rastafarians, however, Selassie is Almighty God, Fearsome, Dreadful, and Terrible, and lacks the capacity for cowardice. Consequently, the Rastafarians perused the Holy Bible for an explanation. Revelations 19:19 was used to show that the Italian invasion and Selassie's flight were the result of prophesy.

> And I saw the Beast, and the Kings of the Earth, and their armies gathered together to make war against him that sat on the horse, and against his army.

The subsequent overthrow of the fascist regime in Italy, the arrest and murder of its leader, Benito Mussolini, and the restoration of Haile Selassie's power in Ethiopia were all declared integral elements of that prophesy by Rastafarians. Revelations 19:20 was also used to further substantiate this claim:

> And the Beast was taken, and with him the false prophet that wrought miracles before him, with which he deceived them that had the mark of the Beast, and them that worshipped his image. These both were cast alive into a lake of fire burning with brimstone.

Thus did Rastafarians rationalize what could then have become an ideological problem of devastating proportions. They succeeded in converting the patently questionable conduct of Selassie during the war into a "fulfillment of divine prophesy." Indeed, even today there are in the homes of many a Rastafarian pictures of Selassie with one foot on top of a bomb. The Rastafarians' interpretation of the picture is that Selassie rendered the bomb harmless by stepping on it during the Italian occupation. It was not explained how Selassie could have been residing in the suburbs of London and at the same time "trapping" a bomb in war-torn Ethiopia. However, in the words of the old Afro-Christian spiritual: "All things are possible, if you only believe."

The resistance movement in Ethiopia, which had been closely followed by Rastafarians, had a great influence on their own struggle against British colonialism. They adopted the slogan of the Nyahbingi Movement and changed it from "Death to all White oppressors" to "Death to all White and Black oppressors." They also began to call themselves *Nyah* and *Bongo*. These were not empty, meaningless names; they were fighting names. As you may recall, "Nyah" was the name used by the fighters of the Ethiopian resistance movement. "Bongo" is the name used by the followers of Bongoism or Convince, which is a syncretization of a number of African religions -- especially that of the Fanti-Ashanti people of Ghana -- and Protestantism.

Bongoism, an offshoot of Myalism, had old roots among the fighting Maroons of Eastern Jamaica. It derived from the religion of the great Maroon chieftainess, Nanny, and it still exists, albeit in small pockets, in that section of the country. It was in the eastern parishes of Portland and St. Thomas that Leonard Howell first launched his Mission. The drums used by Rastafarians at their informal gatherings and "groundations", the *bass*, *funde* and *repeater*, are quite similar to those of Bongoism and are, in fact, called Bongo drums. These in turn are identical to the atumpan, apentemma, and petia drums of Ashanti, the three ceremonial drums of Winti, and the *mamam, seconde,* and *bebe* drums of Vodun. Hence, the Rastafari Movement is neither completely new, nor irrational, as some observers and writers would have it. It represents spiritual, political and cultural continuity of the African legacy. This was well understood by the colonial administration.

Howell and his followers, who had commenced their activities in the parish of St. Thomas in 1933, were on several occasions brutalized and jailed by the police. On January 1, 1934, Howell and his lieutenant, Robert Hinds, a former supporter of Alexander Bedward, were arrested and convicted on a charge of sedition. Howell was sentenced to two years imprisonment and Hinds to one year.[171] The Mission in St. Thomas was violently terminated by the police and Howell's followers had to shift their activities to the neighboring parish of Portland. The violence, however, continued unabated and they were forced to leave Portland for Kingston. In April 1937, Howell and 14 of his followers were arrested and sent to the mental institution.

In accordance with scriptural and other religious tenets, Howell believed in the communal ownership of land and rejected the concept of either private or state ownership of the land. In furtherance of these views, he and his followers discouraged small farmers from paying taxes or rent to the government for the lands they cultivated. In short, his position was that the land belongs to the people and should be possessed only by the people.

Shortly after his release from the mental institution in the latter part of 1938, Howell and approximately 1,600 of his followers acquired an abandoned sugar estate called *Pinnacle* in the parish of St. Catherine and commenced the cultivation of yams, bananas, peas and other cash crops. In 1941, less than three years after the acquisition, the police invaded *Pinnacle* and arrested Howell and scores of his followers – this time on charges of cultivating, selling and smoking ganja[13]. They were all convicted and given mandatory sentences of eighteen months at hard labor in prison.

After their release in 1943, Howell and his followers returned to *Pinnacle* and reestablished the community. In 1954 the police carried out a full-scale offensive against *Pinnacle* on the grounds that it was a nuisance to the neighboring residents who allegedly complained of "being victims of Howell's *Ethiopian Warriors[14]*, who coerced them into paying taxes to him;" and that Pinnacle "had become a major drug center." It is ironic that Howell who encouraged the small farmers and sharecroppers to withhold the payment of taxes to the government would in turn be accused by the same government of coercing the people into paying taxes to him.

In any event, the foregoing charges were used as an excuse by the government to launch its invasion of *Pinnacle*. The police destroyed the community and again arrested Howell and an indeterminate number of his followers. They were once more

---

[13] A tall plant from the hemp family brought to the Caribbean in the nineteenth century by the indentured East Indians. Its tough fiber is good for making rope, sailcloth, etc. Its leaves serve as medicine for asthma, rheumatism, fever, colds and other illnesses. Many people from all classes in the society smoke it and find its halucinogenic qualities soothing and desirable. Rastafarians, in general, smoke it, but some also consider it an important source of wisdom, knowledge, and understanding, and sanctify it. Other terms frequently used are "marijuana", "'ily", "colly", "tampi", "herb", or simply "weed".

[14] Name given by Howell to the Rastafarian sentries who guarded the gates of Pinnacle. The name derived from the fighters of the revolutionary Mau-Mau Resistance Movement whose leader, Jomo Kenyatta, was greatly admired by Rastafarians.

declared "insane" and sent to the mental institution[15]. This determination of "insanity" was, of course, not made by psychiatrists and psychoanalysts, but by politicians and Christian Church leaders who decided that the philosophy of the Rastafarians, like that of Alexander Bedward, was a dangerous manifestation of madness. The clear intent, however, was to destroy the Movement by incarcerating and humiliating its leadership.

The period 1940 to 1970 was extremely painful for Rastafarians who had by then incurred the wrath and venom of both the State and the *de facto* Established Christian Churches. The ruling class associated the Rastafari Movement with Pocomania and Myalism and referred to it as "a new-fangled religion reeking with blasphemy and sedition."[172] During this period it took great courage to be a Rastafarian. The added price one paid for embracing the faith was ostracism. Indeed Rastafarians were shunned by families and friends as well as persecuted by the State. Under the flimsiest of pretexts, their homes were burnt to the ground or wrecked by the police with wanton disregard for the legal rights of the occupants or the safety of women and children. Rastafarians had no recourse against those who perpetrated unlawful acts against them. Police officers would physically humiliate and psychologically abuse them just to curry favor the higher political authorities, show off to their

---

[15] In February 1981 Leonard Howell, who had been living in relative obscurity in the parish of Saint Catherine after his release from the mental institution in 1960, was savagely beaten by an irate police officer who accused him of "mashing up" Jamaica with his crazy ideas. Howell, about 90 years old at the time, died shortly thereafter. The police officer was never brought to justice for the commission of this crime.

friends, or satisfy their quota of arrests[16].

There were divers police officers who gained notoriety for their sadistic beating and humiliation of Rastafarians. Such humiliation included the cutting off of their locks and the shaving of their heads with broken bottles. For instance, there was one police officer, Detective Joe Williams, (who later became Chief of Police), who was a scourge to Rastafarians. The officer would "invite" a Rastaman to lunch and specifically request a menu of pork spare ribs, jerk pork, or roast pork, knowing that pork is as offensive to Rastafarians, as it is to Jews and Muslims. When the Rastaman, understandably, declined the offer, he was given the painful choice of either going to jail on some trumped-up charge or eating the pork. Rastafarians would be arrested and charged with the first offense that came to the police officer's mind. The most frequently cited offenses included "disorderly conduct", "resisting arrest", "vagrancy", "possession of ganja", "smoking ganja", "usage of indecent language", "sedition", "blasphemy" and "being a suspicious person".

The nightmare visited on the people of the United States by Senator Joseph McCarthy in the 1950s, when the finest citizens in labor, politics, law, the arts, academia, and other disciplines were persecuted for espousing and advocating the very democratic principles on which the American Revolution was based, was by no means confined to the shores of that country. In Jamaica the repression against Rastafarians intensified as a result of McCarthyism, which pressured the colonial government of Norman Manley not only to expel the progressive members of his own

---

[16] As late as the 1960s a police constable was promoted on the basis of his arrest record.

People's National Party (PNP)[17], but also to terrorize Rastafarians whom it considered "dangerous and subversive." The two main Rastafarian communities at the time – Wareika Hills and Back-O-Wall – were repeatedly razed by bulldozers and the furniture of the occupants destroyed or confiscated by the police. These abuses, however, were by no means the only tribulations Rastafarians had to bear. Their non-adherence to Christianity's interpretation of Judaeo-Christian ethics and their rejection of the prevailing social values served to seal their fate as outcasts in the society.

Before the advent of the Rastaman, African children had been taught to fear black men with beards and long hair. This was intended to coerce the African population into conformity with the colonial norms of social conduct, which required all African adult males to have their hair closely cut and their faces and chins clean shaven. The failure to conform could cost one his job or his social relationships. Those who dared to grow beards and long hair without "acceptable" reasons ran the risk of being associated with the mythical "Blackheart Man" – a black, dangerous, vile and evil man – who seized unsuspecting children, took them to his lair in the gullies or in the bushes, killed them and extracted their hearts for his own consumption.

---

[17] In 1951, under the pressure of McCarthyism – the rabid anti-Communism that terrorized the people of the United States during that period – Norman Manley and the right wing members of his party (Noel Nethersole, Florizel Glasspole, Allan Isaacs, et al.) set up a Commission of Enquiry to investigate the degree to which the PNP was "infiltrated by communists." On the basis of this "investigation", many of the party's most devoted, dedicated, and committed members, including Richard Hart, Arthur Henry, Frank Hill, Ken Hill – leaders of the hitherto popular Trade Union Congress (TUC) – were expelled.

Consequently, little children became terrified when left alone. And they trembled with fear at the sight of a bearded black man. Therefore, when the Rastaman came on the scene with his dreadlocks and long beard he became the Blackheart Man incarnate and all the attributes and characteristics of the latter were transferred to him. Bunny Wailer eloquently describes this phenomenon in his song *Blackheart Man:*

Tikya[18] the Blackheart Man, children!
I say don't go near him!
Tikya the Blackheart Man, children!
For even lions fear him!

Growing in a neighborhood for such a long time,
That is filled with fear;
I can't go here, can't go there,
And I ain't supposed to go anywhere;
When I ask my mom if she could let me go out and play
Like little children do;
She said be careful of the stranger
Giving candies to children
And then take them away.
He lives in the gullies of the city!
He's the Blackheart Man! The Blackheart Man!
Even in the lonely parts of the country!
The Blackheart Man! The Blackheart Man!
He's got no friend, no home, no family!
He's the Blackheart Man! The Blackheart Man!
He is famed to live just like the Gypsy!
He's the Blackheart Man! The Blackheart Man!

Growing and learning and gathering
For myself a little more experience
Jumping over the fence;
Curiosity has brought me, yes it's brought me

---

[18] Be careful of, beware of

A little common sense.
Trodding the road of life,
I've come to this one conclusion
That everything is equal under the sun,
All that is created by Jah mighty hand.
And he said: "Knock, and it shall be opened!
Seek, and ye shall find!
Wisdom is found in the simplest of places
In the nick of time!"

And now I trod the same road of afflictions,
Just like the Blackheart Man!
Just like the Blackheart Man!
Getting my share of humiliation,
Just like the Blackheart Man!
Just like the Blackheart Man!
You'll find me even in the prison or the dungeon,
Just like the Blackheart Man!
Just like the Blackheart Man!
I even get blamed without a reason,
Just like the Blackheart Man!

No cross, no crown, no sorrow, no laughter,
Trial and crosses in a I way;
But the hotter the battle
Is the sweeter Jah Jah victory!
Ancient children used to say if you want good
Yuh nose got to run, run, run;
How could the world go free
And let Jah bear the cross alone?
And them that drink of the old wine
Hath no place for the new;
And the stones that are head of the corner
Are the same ones that the builders refused.
Now it's the Blackheart Man, Children,
Who've become the wonder of the city!

In the foregoing song Bunny Wailer vividly recalls the pain, anguish and victimization of the Blackheart Man and the trials and tribulations experienced by the Rastaman. He clearly makes a connection between the two victims of class, racial and spiritual oppression. Finally, he identifies them as the "stones that the builders refused" – the corner stones. Hence, the Blackheart Man and Rastaman have today been ultimately vindicated in their becoming "the wonder of the city."

Repression and ostracism dictated a close unity among Rastafarians and obliged them to find solace, comfort and support in each other. Thus, a genuine feeling of love and a strong communal spirit developed among them. No one would employ a Rastafarian, however menial the task. Consequently, Rastafarians had to create their own independent source of employment. They became fishermen, craftsmen, artisans, small farmers, pedlars and handymen. The repression against them did not daunt their spirits nor silence their criticisms of the colonial system. The price for this perseverance and doggedness, however, was extremely high. By 1960 it was virtually impossible to find a Rastafarian who had not served time in prison on at least one occasion.

In 1960 there was an angry altercation between a police constable and Bongo Amos, a Rastafarian, at the Coronation Market in Western Kingston. A fight ensued and the constable got the worse of it. An hour or two later scores of police officers, vowing revenge on Rastafarians, went to Back-O-Wall, about a quarter of a mile to the west, completely demolished the community and carried off most of the male Rastafarians to jail. A similar act was carried out against Rastafarians at Wareika Hills, some four miles to the east. Bongo Wally who lived in Rose Town, more than three miles northwest of Coronation Market, was arrested at his home, severely mauled and carried off to jail. Bongo Color Red who lived in Spanish Town in the parish of St. Catherine, thirteen miles to the west, had to go into hiding to escape arrest for the same incident. Indeed even Rastafarians in Montego Bay, at the other end of the island, were not spared the police's fanatical desire for vengeance.

In that same year a number of academicians from the Institute of Social and Economic Research at the University of the West Indies led by M.G. Smith, Roy Augier, Rex Nettleford and Carl Stone, alarmed by the excessive brutality of the police against Rastafarians, organized a meeting with the Movement's leading spokespersons -- Sam Brown, Mortimer Planner, Samuel Clayton, Douglass Mack, and Philmore Alvaranga, among others. Subsequent to this meeting, the Institute published a report entitled *The Rastafari Movement in Kingston, Jamaica*. It outlined some of the basic tenets of the Movement, including the demand for repatriation to Africa and the recommendation that the government study the matter with a view to assisting those who desired to emigrate to the continent.

Pursuant to the Institute's recommendations, Norman Manley, Premier of Jamaica, organized a delegation of Rastafarians to visit Ethiopia. This served to establish communications between Rastafarians and Emperor Haile Selassie for the first time. It also marked the very first time that anyone with "dreadlocks" was ever officially permitted to leave Jamaica's shores. This seemingly progressive gesture of Manley, however, reeked with political opportunism, because the Henry episode had revealed that internal and external eyes were steadily being focused on the growing Rastafari Movement and its political potentiality.

In 1959 Reverend Claudius Henry, a religious eclectic, whose doctrine reflected strains of Evangelism, Garveyism and Rastafarianism, returned to Jamaica from the United States whence he had earlier migrated. While residing in New York, he had close contact with Garvey's U.N.I.A. and the Ethiopian World Federation. Very soon after his arrival, he revived Garvey's African-oriented platform and mobilized a large number of Rastafarians. He proclaimed October 24, 1960 as the date that all Africans, if they so desired, would return to Africa, and, in furtherance thereof, he collected a very small donation from each person to assist in defraying the costs.

A number of persons sold their belongings in anticipation of the trip. And when it failed to materialize, they were left disappointed and ruined. Shortly thereafter, Henry was accused by the Norman Manley government of converting his home at Rosalie Avenue in the parish of Saint Andrew into an armed training camp and that Rastafarians were being instructed there in the usage of firearms. Henry was also accused of involvement in a conspiracy to overthrow the colonial government, and that a part of that conspiracy involved the poisoning of Kingston's reservoirs. Henry and scores of his followers were arrested and charged with treason and a number of lesser felonies. He was sentenced to 10 years' imprisonment and his followers received sentences ranging from 3 to 5 years.

A few months later, Henry's son, Ronald, and three of his companions and ex-army buddies, Rollins, Morgan, and Jeter, arrived in Jamaica from the United States reportedly with a large shipment of sophisticated arms. They allegedly established contacts with a number of Rastafarians, including one Albert Gabbidon, and commenced military training in Sligoville, in the parish of Saint Catherine. British soldiers stationed at New Castle in Saint Andrew accosted and engaged Henry and his men in military combat and two of the soldiers were killed. Henry and his small band of men

Marcus Mosiah Garvey, leader of the greatest African mass movement the would has ever known.

Rastarfarian elders. From left to right (kneeling) George Bent (Bongo Tony) and Bongo Bigga (deceased). From left to right (standing Maurice Clark (Ras Irice) and Bongo Shefron.

were forced to go on the run, engaging the army and police in sporadic dog-fights. They were eventually captured and charged with the "murder" of the two British soldiers and a dubious Rastafarian called "Thunder". They were found guilty, sentenced to death and hanged shortly thereafter.

Manley was also concerned about the newly formed political party – the People's Political Party (PPP) – the name of Garvey's former party – led by Millard Johnson, whose political philosophy incorporated some of the teachings of Marcus Garvey and anticipated the Black Power Movement of the late 1960's. With this profound African-oriented platform, Johnson expected strong support from Rastafarians and sympathizers. Manley, on the other hand, hoped that by his gesture of "goodwill" to the Rastafarians, they would in turn express their gratitude by voting for his party – the People's National Party (PNP) – in the general elections scheduled for 1962.

Both Manley and Johnson, however, received a rude awakening. Three Rastafarian leaders, including the eloquent Brother Sam Brown of the Nyahbingi Order of Rastafari, were PPP candidates in the general elections. But neither Johnson, Brown, nor Manley received any strong show of support from Rastafarians. In spite of its failure to win a seat in Parliament, the PPP received encouraging support from the general electorate – a support that suggested a promising political future. However, Millard Johnson did not appear to see it that way. He packed up his political kit and disappeared from the scene.

The repression and violence against Rastafarians were heightened following the campaign against Claudius Henry and his son Ronald. In fact they reached a very high point in 1963 in what became known as the *Coral Gardens Incident*. Rastafarians residing in Rose Hall, Montego Bay, had for years exercised an easement on lands belonging to the Rose Hall Estate across which they walked to get to the small plots of land which they farmed for subsistence. In 1963 there was a confrontation between the Rastafarians and a number of real estate developers, who attempted to terminate the easement on the Rose Hall Estate without any consideration of the property rights of the Rastafarians. They also laid claim to the lands being cultivated by the Rastafarians and indicated that they were in fact a part of the development scheme, which they called Coral Gardens.

The Rastafarians, asserting the most fundamental of human rights – the right to work and make a living – resisted this callous attempt to destroy their livelihood. As always, the police, acting in the interest of the developers, resorted to violence. During the altercation, which took place on Holy Thursday during the Easter period, the Kenneth Douglass Service Station, whose proprietor was involved, was burned to the ground and a police officer speared to death. The army was brought in and together with the police wreaked havoc on the Rastafarian community. The assault left eight people dead, including Superintendent Scott and Detective Melbourne, and hundreds of men, women and children were arrested and detained. The make-shift jails were full, and when the heat of the sun caused uncomfortable conditions in the detention centers where the Rastafarians were held, the police turned water hoses on them.[173] Horace Campbell wrote:

> On top of the arrests the *Gleaner* carried stories that the defendants were under the influence of ganja. There was no question of their rights as citizens of independent Jamaica, for the response of the politicians was "de bwoy dem no wan wuk, dem only wan fe smoke ganja." Such a simplistic analysis called for simplistic answers

– the brutal force of the State – and so the war on Rastas and the war on ganja became one.[174]

The delegation that went to Ethiopia reported that the meeting had been successful and that Emperor Haile Selassie had allocated a parcel of land called Shashamani for all Rastafarians who wanted to migrate there. The grant of Shashamani had apparently been made several years earlier and reported in New York by the Ethiopian World Federation. In fact Shashamani was the intended destination for the people associated with Claudius Henry's recruitment. In any event, excitement reigned in the camps of the Rastafarians because their spiritual communication with Zion had now been broadened to include a physical relationship with the King of Kings. And this excitement was transformed into sheer ecstacy and an indescribable euphoria on April 21, 1966, when His Imperial Majesty Emperor Haile Selassie I paid a visit to Jamaica.

Twenty-four hours before his scheduled arrival, hundreds of Rastafarians from all parts of the country converged on the Palisadoes (now Norman Manley) Airport where they kept a vigil until the following day. By the time Selassie arrived the next morning, this number grew into the thousands. Later that afternoon, hundreds of thousands of Rastafarians and non-believers gathered at the National Stadium to see Selassie in the flesh and listen to his message.

It was a "national holiday" for Rastafarians. They lit up their *chalices* (pipes) and puffed their *spliffs* (marijuana cigarettes) into the faces of police officers who were obliged to suffer these affronts in silence. Actually, they had been instructed by their superiors to turn the other cheek to the Rastafarians on that day. However, even in the absence of such instructions, it would have been insane for the police to have reacted in any other way.

The wife of a Caucasian official was chosen to make a welcoming presentation to the Emperor and, in the course of doing so, she bowed before him. At that stage bedlam broke loose. The triumphant shouts of the people, the most distinguishable of which were "Bow, Jezebel![19] Bow before Almighty God!" reverberated throughout the stadium. Rastafarians raucously affirmed their faith with shouts of "Almighty God, Jah Rastafari!" "Upful and Dreadful One, Jah Rastafari!" But Rastafarians were not the only persons who felt that sense of pride and satisfaction. To a people who have been degraded, humiliated, dehumanized, and subjected to the most unspeakable indignities by Europeans, the sight of a white woman, a member of the ruling class, publicly making obeisance to a black man, was indeed a proud moment for Africans, whether or not they believed in the divinity of Haile Selassie.

Mention should also be made of the fact that it was raining very heavily on the morning of Selassie's arrival. About half an hour before the plane landed, the lightning flashed and the thunder rolled somewhat portentously. Then the rain stopped abruptly and the sun shone so brightly that it appeared as if it had not been raining earlier. If these events had occurred on any other day they would have passed unnoticed. However, they assumed ominous proportions on that unforgettable Friday in April 1966. It is extremely difficult to describe the Rastafarians' overt expressions of satisfaction in light of these occurrences. Suffice it to say that the day's events served to vindicate their faith and to dispel the doubts of many skeptics about Selassie's divinity.

---

[19] Wife of Ahab, King of Israel, known for her wickedness and shamelessness. (Holy Bible) I Kings 16:31

The Movement benefitted greatly from Selassie's visit, gaining a large number of converts. Members of the middle class as well as foreign visitors began to frequent Rastafarian meeting places to hold talks with them. It was during this period that the distinguished Guyanese historian, Dr. Walter Rodney, paid several visits to their communities, gained an understanding of their philosophy, shared his knowledge of history with them, and subsequently published the pamphlet entitled *Groundings With My Brothers*. In 1969, one of the oldest Christian denominations in the world, the Ethiopian Orthodox Church, of which Selassie was the head, established a chapter in Jamaica. Hundreds of Rastafarians became members, but the majority, while supporting it, opted to remain independent of it.

In spite of all these developments the repression continued, albeit with less intensity. The social ostracism also remained intact. Until the late 1960s, Rastafarians belonged exclusively to the working class and, as the most outspoken section of that class at the time, they automatically bore the brunt of the economic, political and social oppression experienced by the working class in general. They were singled out for punishment for their militancy and outspokenness.

There were a handful of Rastafarians who came from "good families," like Douglass Swaby and Herman "Woody" King, son of Iris King, a PNP member of Parliament. But the Movement was predominantly proletarian. Swaby and King were on many occasions beaten up by the police and arrested on trumped-up charges, but later released with the most profound apologies from the police when their family backgrounds became known. During the late 1960s and 1970s some of the leading working class singers and musicians such as Bunny and Skully, Tommy McCook, Bob

Marley, Peter Tosh, Bunny Livingston, Max Romeo and others joined the Movement. Within a decade the overwhelming majority of the singers and musicians became Rastafarians and expanded the Movement.

In 1968, Walter Rodney, who had irritated the Jamaica Labor Party (JLP) government of Hugh Shearer, the country's first black Prime Minister, with his advocacy of equality for the African majority, left the island to attend a conference of African scholars in Canada. Although he was a son of the Caribbean (Guyanese) and a professor at the University of the West Indies at the Mona campus in Jamaica, he was denied re-entry into the country. The students at the university protested the government's action and Hugh Shearer, who referred to himself as a "No Nonsense Prime Minister", instructed the armed forces to quell the demonstration.

The students were tear-gassed and savagely beaten. The masses, outraged by the government's action against Rodney (with whom they identified) and the violence of the armed forces against the students, gave vent to the years of pent-up fury and frustration and rebelled. When the confrontation was over, several commercial enterprises were looted and destroyed; scores of buses were seized and burnt; many offices in the city of Kingston were smashed and torched; and Whites and Mulattoes were severely mauled. At least three people were killed and hundreds arrested; and property damages were estimated at more than one million pounds.

After the uprising, the repression against the progressive movement became even more intense. Many middle class radicals from the university, some of whom had participated in the demonstrations, took refuge in and became converts of the Rastafari Movement. By the end of the 1970s, their numbers had multiplied hundredfold. At the same time, the Movement, which had hitherto been exclusively African, now had in its ranks Mulattoes, Whites, and a considerable number of foreign social misfits. To some of these people, Rastafarianism was conceived as a means of gaining easy access to an abundance of marijuana. To others, the mystic Rastaman presented a challenge to their sexual fantasies. It is ironic, indeed incredible, to see Whites and middle class Mulattoes, who but yesterday felt and demonstrated nothing but the most profound contempt for the African working class in general and the Rastaman in particular, wearing *dreadlocks* and making such utterances as "Dreadful One, Jah Rastafari!"

The philosophy of the Rastaman was now being disseminated throughout the country and the world by the singers and musicians, particularly Bob Marley, Peter Tosh and Bunny Wailer. Rastafarians were appearing on radio and television worldwide and were to be found among family members of judges, parliamentarians, doctors and other professionals. The Movement itself now had in its ranks lawyers, doctors, engineers, architects, academicians, visual artists, sports and media celebrities, and people from all walks of life.

Michael Manley's victory at the polls in 1972 -- a victory to which an appreciable number of Rastafarians contributed -- was a significant milestone in the struggles of the Rastafarians. For the first time their contributions to the society's development, particularly in the areas of culture, arts and crafts, were officially recognized. Manley discontinued the repression against them and acknowledged, albeit unofficially, their right to ceremonially use marijuana without being criminally prosecuted.

The Movement had by then spread to other areas of the Caribbean, Africa, and the metropolitan countries -- Canada, the

His Imperial Majesty, Emperor Haile Selassi I, King of Kings, Lord of Lords, Conquering Lion of the Tribe of Judah, The Elect of God, and the Light of the World. Jah Rastafari!

United States, the United Kingdom, France and elsewhere. At the same time, however, its social and political character underwent a metamorphosis as the middle class elements that had joined its ranks sought to bring it into conformity with the prejudices and aspirations of their class. As a consequence, the traditional feeling of brotherhood ("one love"), the spirit of community and the militant rejection of social injustice that had historically characterized the philosophy and social practice of Rastafarians were gradually becoming the exception.

Rastafarians were now being employed and exploited by their brethren in much the same way as non-Rastafarians. Middle class Rastafarians were displaying the same snobbery to their working class brethren as did their "bald-headed" (non-dreadlocks) counterparts. A visitor to a Rastafarian social function could not help but notice the huge crowd of working class Rastafarians queuing up at the gate, unable to pay the prohibitive admission fee. Inside the hall, the White, Mulatto and Black middle class Rastafarians occupied one corner and the few working class Rastafarians the other. Indeed anyone with knowledge of the tribulations endured by Rastafarians cannot help but empathize with pioneers like Sam Clayton, Mortimer Planner and Douglass Mack when they bemoan the new course the Movement has taken.

The influx of the Movement with non-working class elements had the positive effect of enhancing the Movement's collective knowledge, especially in the areas of organization and structure. In the 1970s, therefore, the loose, amorphous Movement began to give way to organized groups and sects. However, it also served to initiate the transformation of Rastafarianism from a Movement to a mere religious expression and simultaneously eclipse the prominence and influence of the traditional working class leaders, rendering them insignificant, irrelevant and obscure. By far the largest and most organized group is the Twelve Tribes of Israel. This group was formed by former middle class radicals from the University of the West Indies and remnants of Brother Downer's Ethiopian World Federation branch at Davis Lane, in Trench Town.

In an attempt to legitimize and give credibility to the group, a working class Rastaman from Trench Town, Vernon "Doctor" Carrington, a.k.a. "Gad", was chosen as the group's leader. Thus, the picture presented was one in which a working class Rastaman with a primary school education, at the time living in a shack with no running water and too poor to even own a bicycle, became leader of an organization in which a considerable number of persons were from the middle class, had university degrees, owned flourishing businesses, lived in mansions and drove Mercedes Benzes and BMWs. However, the people knew that the real leaders of the Twelve Tribes were the middle class Rastafarians, or to use the coinage of a witty brother, the *Jah Rastacracy.*

As an organization, the Twelve Tribes does not participate in secular activities. Invitations sent to it by the country's democratic movement to participate in the convening of rallies and progressive forums in solidarity with various liberation struggles throughout the world, including Southern Africa, were not even dignified with a response. Other groups like Ras Historian's Rastafari Movement Association (RMA), the Mystic Revelations of Rastafari (MRR), the Nyahbingi Order of Rastafari (NOR), individual members of the Twelve Tribes, and other groups and individuals with no connection to the groups mentioned, did continue   the democratic tradition of the Movement, but they represented a minority.

In 1974 the King of Kings and Lord of Lords, Emperor

Haile Selassie I, was overthrown in a popular uprising and placed under house arrest by the new government of Mengistu Haile Mariam. This was very painful for Rastafarians who were hard-pressed to explain this phenomenon to their gleeful detractors. As if this was not enough stress for the embattled Movement, the Emperor died on August 28, 1975. This was by far the greatest crisis faced by Rastafarians during their more than four decades of existence. It was no less severe a crisis than that faced by the followers of Jesus Christ in 33 A.D. when he died; and Rastafarians are ultimately solving it in much the same way.

The news hit the Rastafarian community like a thunderbolt. Initially, there was general denial, consternation and confusion as Rastafarians tried to assess the news report and its implications. In general, a feeling of melancholia commingled with rage and utter disbelief prevailed in the Rastafarian communities. Many Rastafarians angrily dismissed the news report as an outright fabrication of Babylon calculated to destroy the beliefs of "I an' I." It was Bob Marley who introduced an element of calm, placed the reeling Rastafarians on their feet, and created the climate for a spiritual assessment of the situation with his song *Jah Lives.*

> Chorus:
> Jah lives, children, yeah!
> Jah Jah lives, children, yeah!
> Jah lives, children, yeah!
> Jah Jah lives, children, yeah!
>
> The truth is an offense,
> But not a shame;
> It is he who laughs last, children,
> It's he who ends;
> It's a foolish dog
> Barks at a flying bird;
> Our people must learn, children,

To respect the shepherd.

Fools say in their hearts:
"Rasta, yuh god is dead!"
But I an' I know, Jah Jah,
Dread, it shall be dreader dread!

Let Jah arise
Now that the enemies are scattered!
Let Jah arise,
The enemies, the enemies are scattered!

The solemnity of this song betrayed the general consternation and profound anguish that gripped the Rastafarian community. At the same time, however, it contained strong elements of confidence and defiance that provided "Jah Jah" children with the reassurance they desperately needed. "It's a foolish dog [which] barks at a flying bird" represents a rebuke to Rastafarianism's detractors, who felt that Selassie's death would severely weaken, if not destroy, the religion. Bob Marley scoffed at the idea of Selassie's mortality and suggested that it is the enemies of Rastafari who are confused. Note the lines: "Let Jah arise, now that the enemies are scattered!" What did he mean by this? Was he suggesting that Selassie had deliberately deceived the enemies of Rastafari so that he could snatch victory from them even as they disperse in rejoicement of his alleged demise?

Whatever Bob Marley meant by the statement, the song was like a port in a turbulent storm. It was instrumental in mollifying the anger of the Rastafarians who were thrown headlong into a philosophical maelstrom. It took the followers of Jesus Christ a long time to overcome the pain, anguish, disbelief, and ambivalence resulting from his death, before being able to comfortably articulate the view that Jesus lives in the spirit. Rastafarians are currently experiencing that metamorphosis. The more reasonable Rastafarians entertain the belief that Jah had departed from the flesh and was now more powerful and dreadful than before.

Therefore, a very small number of Rastafarians believe, like Christians do of Jesus, that Selassie did not die but assumed a new form and continues to live in the hearts of all people. This view allows Selassie's immortality to remain intact. However, only a few Rastafarians have the courage to articulate it publicly. Silence on the subject is the preferred disposition of the majority. Indeed it will take a long time for most Rastafarians to adjust to and feel comfortable with the new reality (at least those who concede that there is in fact a new reality). But there is a large and vocal group which tenaciously clings to the idea that Rastafari still lives in the flesh.

There is still no central document embodying the philosophy, principles, ceremonies and rituals of Rastafarianism and, as a consequence, each group or individual provides its, his or her own interpretation. Some Rastafarians believe that Haile Selassie is God's chosen representative; most regard him as Almighty God without any reservation. Some regard Ethiopia as Zion, the land of their vine and fig tree; others regard the entire continent of Africa as the land of their vine and fig tree. Virtually all Rastafarians smoke ganja and treat it with sacrosanctity; but some also consider ganja an important source of wisdom, knowledge and understanding. Some seek formal education for their children; others regard it as brainwash. Some believe in formal marriages and in the burial of the dead; others believe in "natural" marriages and in the literal interpretation of the biblical saying: "Let the dead bury the dead and those who go down in silence."

Some Rastafarians believe that meat, especially pork, is unwholesome for the body; others, while rejecting pork, eat other kinds of meat. Some Rastafarians drink wine, beer, ale and stout; others condemn all alcoholic beverages as "Devil's soup". Some believe that Rastafarians should not participate in the country's politics; others believe that they should struggle against all iniquities and improve their condition even while living in Babylon. Some believe that Rastafarianism is the religion of the African people; others are of the opinion that it belongs to all people. Indeed some of the prevailing beliefs and practices of many Rastafarians are so radically different from those of the early Movement that they most surely would have been condemned to "fire and blood" and "lightning and thunder" by the founders.

Thus, Rastafarianism has largely been transformed from a Movement to a mere religious expression. It has moved from a position of revolutionary democracy, brotherly love, and a spirit of community to one accommodating individualism, greed, profound subjectivism and mysticism. The Myalist militancy, which was a major characteristic of the early Movement, is no longer reflected in the contemporary social practices of many Rastafarians. The middle class elements who now influence it have undermined its spiritual-secular-cultural unity by disregarding the secular, social justice dimension.

The struggle waged by Rastafarians against British colonialism, however, is worthy of Nanny, Paul Bogle and Marcus Garvey. They have made an indelible imprint on the culture of Jamaica and the Caribbean; provided their own interpretation of Judaeo-Christian ethics; and created their own mode of communication. Rastafarian liberationist songs, accompanied by the *bass*, the *funde* and the *repeater* drums, have contributed to the sophistication of Jamaica's and the Caribbean region's musical heritage. Their message of peace and love, and their demand for social justice and the redemption of the dignity of African humanity have been a singular contribution to the struggles of the Caribbean people in general and the Jamaican people in particular. The United Nations' acceptance on November 22, 1996 of the Rastafari Movement's application (filed August 26, 1996) for Non-Governmental Organization (NGO) status[20] within that world body is indeed a crowning glory to the years of struggle and martyrdom. Rastafarians have triumphantly overcome degradation, dehumanization, humiliation, and isolation to become not merely "the wonder of the city," as Bunny Wailer proclaimed in the song ***Blackheart Man***, but of the world.

Today a material distinction that once existed between Rastafarian and Christian ideology, namely, that "man is God", has disappeared. The concept of the living god objectively suffered a demise in 1975 along with Selassie, and in its place has arisen a subjective idealist philosophy with little resemblance to the revolutionary democratic ideology of the early Movement. Many foreigners, influenced by the songs of Bob Marley, Peter Tosh, Bunny Wailer, Dennis Brown and others, assume that the progressive orientation of those songs is characteristic of Rastafarianism as a whole. However, the songs merely reflect the social consciousness of the singers themselves and, at best, a small number of Rastafarians. Indeed some Rastafarian singers are today representatives of the backward trend in Reggae. (This is a subject of an upcoming work, ***The Politics of Caribbean Music***, by the

---

[20] The Rastafarian NGO representatives to the United Nations are Bongo Spear of Barbados and Bongo Watto of Jamaica.

same author).

The Jah Rastacracy has so transformed the Movement that the former revolutionary democratic norm has become the exception. In spite of this, the finest expression of that militant tradition continues to exist among small groups and individual Rastafarians in Jamaica and the rest of the Caribbean, the United Kingdom, the United States, the African continent, France, Canada, Japan, Latin America, and elsewhere. However, the prevailing philosophical and organizational looseness still enables a number of scoundrels to find a haven within its ranks. They grow the "dreadlocks", now a mere hair style to an extremely large number of persons worldwide, and mouth certain catch phrases like "irie", "I an' I", and, of course, "Jah Rastafari", while their real objective is to enrich themselves through drug trafficking and gun smuggling, or robbing, raping and murdering innocent, hard-working people, and simultaneously smearing the image and historical legacy of the Rastafari Movement.

CONCLUSION

Much of what is known about Caribbean history since the time of Columbus is derived from the documents, letters, diaries, reports and literature of the conquerors and colonizers. Very little has been preserved from the point of view of opposition to the conquest and colonialism. It was not until the eighteenth century that the beginnings of a Caribbean literature became discernible, but most of it was largely Eurocentric. As a consequence, it is very difficult to write an economic, political, social, religious or cultural history which does proper justice to the Caribbean epic of freedom.

The most fruitful documentation of that epic exists in the various forms of cultural and religious expressions of the colonized, in the folklore and aesthetics (especially music). These, however, constitute the most underutilized data and sources for the interpretation of Caribbean history. With few exceptions, "folk culture" has been selectively utilized by social scientists – anthropologists, sociologists, psychologists and others – and by musicologists and the humanities professions to interpret and analyze the Caribbean from the peculiar Eurocentric vantage point of the respective specializations.

Therefore, Caribbean history became an object of study and analysis that fitted into those hypotheses constructed by the social sciences and the humanities to which Western readers could relate. What resulted, in a general sense, was the portrayal of Caribbean non-Christian culture and religion as examples of "backward", "primitive" or, at best, "quaint" practices and customs of interest to those who had a flair for dabbling in the exotic.

When viewed within the context of such hypothetical

construction, Caribbean secular history becomes so many volumes of distortions. The result is an amalgamation of facts, myths, and prejudices with the latter two assuming a position of greater prominence. Indeed it was not until the twentieth century that many insights on the hidden aspects about the region were uncovered by Caribbean scholars like Elsa Goveia, C.L.R. James, George Padmore, Eric Williams, Juan Bosch, Aimé Cesaire, Fernando Ortiz, Arthur Schomburg, Frantz Fanon, and others.

Christian religious history, on the other hand, is the political history of the official Church-State constitutions and alliances in the Caribbean. The Church establishments enjoyed a political, social and legal status that was equalled only to that of big business. In contrast, the family and the community never attained such status, nor did they ever attain the religious sanction and doctrinal protections that were accorded to State authorities and to businesses. In effect, the Caribbean family and community and their rights were made extraneous to the politics of church affairs and transformed into passive objects of private philanthropy and charity, on the one hand, and faithful attendance at formal church functions, on the other.

The exotic politics of the Established Churches became indistinguishable from the exotic politics of the State and big business. Such political differences as did, and still do exist, between these institutions, are manifestations of the factionalism, sectarianism, and related patronage power politics to which the major Christian churches, business institutions and State bureaucracies have historically subscribed. To speak of "religion" in this context is to speak of the politics and political history of the State and of big business. One can speak of the "religion" and religious history of the State, and of big business without diverging from the secular-political-economic substance of either.

In the post-Columbian history of the Caribbean, the State has been the Father, big business the Son, and the Established Churches the Holy Spirit – a comfortable Trinity incorporated under one monotheistic fat golden calf which the people have been obliged to worship since the days of Columbus. This secular-political-economic conception and manifestation of religion and god is not only idolatrous, but has nothing in common with the aesthetics, ethics, and religion of the Caribbean people whose historical struggle reflects the larger conflict between the universal values of humanity and the peculiar state of inhumanity practiced by Western civilization.

Contemporary liberation theology, in that historical context, is itself a continuum of the struggles waged by the boyez, bohitos, myal-men, houngans, angel-men and women, babalawos, imams, bongos, Rastafarians, and others. This reality has been obscured or disregarded by the official recorders of the region's history who deny the theological legitimacy of Shamanism, Myalism, Vodun, Winti, Shango, Santería, Bongoism, Rastafarianism, and so forth, and instead bear false witness by classifying them as "witchcraft", "black magic", "idolatry", "Satanism" and "heathenism".

In effect, community religion and spirituality of the majority were transformed into the irreligious objects of secular study by anthropologists, sociologists, and others and relegated to the realm of folk psychology, folklore, and pathology. Thus redefined as being devoid of spiritual, aesthetic and ethical dimensions, Caribbean people themselves became depicted as objects, rather than human beings. Yet the diverse expressions of liberation theology have indigenous validity precisely because they evolved from the spiritual and moral struggles of the people themselves. It is an outgrowth of community reflections, an articulation of the values and spirit of Caribbean humanity. Both the aesthetics and liberation theology are very different from the values underlying the idealist and empiricist philosophies of Plato and Aristotle and their modern Christian theological and philosophical successors.

Religion and theology, as they developed in the West, became inextricably bound to the Graeco-Roman aristocratic ethos in general, and the value placed on colonialism, slavery and individualistic property ownership in particular. Thus, whereas Western theology continued to apologize for and participate in slavery, colonialism, masterdom, racism and religious war, the "pagan" and "heathen" religions were engaged in a heroic struggle on behalf of freedom, justice and human dignity. The inescapable conclusion, therefore, is that a god of such Western spirituality is the god of the master, of slavery, and of the golden calf – an anthropomorphized saviour deity at the beck and call of that god's "chosen people." In a word, a god alienated from the spirit of universal humanity.

A theology of oppression, symbolized by the whip, the gun, and the chain is intrinsically a vulgarization of the epic of the ancient Hebrews and is irreconcilable with the Mosaic Commandments and the Sermon on the Mount. However, it is compatible with the "true gospel" according to Thomas Hobbes, John Locke, David Hume, and Adam Smith, whose god aids and abets colonialism and the exploitation of human beings. The Western spirit and ethic are historically represented in the characterization of Francisco Pizarro, Ponce de León, John Hawkins, Francis Drake, Piet Heyn, and the "mercantilists" and plantocrats as exemplary of heroism, progress and civilization. The Protestant ethic and the spirit of capitalism in which exploitation is redefined as entrepreneurship and the "free market" operate according to laws of nature invented for and sanctified by a Western god.

The aesthetic values, ethics, morality and sense of justice underlying the struggles of the Caribbean people and their heroes are derived largely from Shamanism, Vodun, Myalism, Shango, Santería, and others, including the Mosaic epic of freedom and the Sermon on the Mount. The role played by religion in the history and struggles of the Caribbean people is pervasive and predates the secular movement. In fact, secular movements like Garvey's Universal Negro Improvement Association have so strong a religious orientation that some writers have erroneously classified them as religions.

The aesthetic values, ethics, and morality embraced by the Caribbean people are incompatible with the theology of the ruling class, which is so intimately linked to political-economic and racial oppression. This theology continues to seek a hiding-place for its immorality, its vulgarization of Judaeo-Christian ethics, and its twisted sense of justice in the slogan of "separation of the spiritual and the secular," when in practice it makes no such separation. The resistance to this type of interpretation of Judaeo-Christianity by leading members of the Caribbean Conference of Churches and their adoption of the theology of liberation has severely strained the historical State-Church-business relationship and has prompted local and international secular and religious forces of racial, economic, and political backwardness to embark on a campaign of misrepresentation and slander against liberation theology itself.

Peace, freedom and social justice are not abstractions, but important human concerns and goals. They are antithetical to colonialism, racism and authoritarianism. The liberation theologians, like the singers and musicians, perceive that these human goals cannot be achieved within the existing social, political and economic framework. Their skepticism and criticism of the domestic and international policies of the region's ruling economic and church leaders reflect a shared belief that the countries of the Caribbean, Latin America, Africa and Asia will never be allowed to achieve the kind of economic development currently enjoyed in Western Europe, the United States, Canada, Australia and Japan. In fact they do not believe that many of the Caribbean territories will ever develop beyond their present stage without adopting a new strategy.

How can Belize, for example, hope to develop economically and satisfy the social needs of its people when approximately eighty percent (80%) of all freehold land has been appropriated by an oligarchy of foreign corporate interests? How can the systems of poverty and socioeconomic backwardness be abolished in Haiti, the Dominican Republic, Antigua-Barbuda, Dominica and St. Lucia, when the commanding heights of their respective economies are owned by foreign corporations which, for the most part, pay little or no taxes, and when the miserable portion of the gross national product received by their governments is misappropriated by unscrupulous, corrupt officials supported by Western states and corporations? How can they hope to advance into the twenty first century when the economic and political policies of their northern neighbor, the United States, reflect aims, methods, and values calculated to keep them in the early nineteenth?

Unlike the British, French and Dutch colonizers who made no pretenses about their imperial designs, the United States denies that it has any but noble intentions towards the developing countries. Yet, it is patently clear that the principles of liberty and social justice that guided the American Revolution and are embedded, albeit partially, in the Declaration of Independence have long ago been objectively repudiated by successive administrations.

> We hold these truths to be self-evident, that all men are created equal, that they are endowed by their Creator with certain unalienable Rights, that among these are Life, and the pursuit of Happiness. That to secure these rights, Governments are instituted among Men, deriving their just powers from the consent of the governed, that whenever any form of Government becomes destructive of these ends, it is the Right of the People to alter or abolish it, and to institute new Government. . . .

The above principles were negated by the Presidency of Thomas Jefferson which supported French colonialist effort to overthrow the Haitian Revolution and reimpose slavery on the people, and by the Monroe Doctrine which declared the Caribbean and Latin America to be the "backyard" of the United States to control and exploit as it saw fit. These principles were further negated by President Theodore Roosevelt who, as a "Corollary" to the Monroe Doctrine, articulated the view that the US ruling class had a "natural right" to act as international police with authority to dictate the code of political and economic conduct of all countries in the hemisphere.

The principles of natural and international law were negated by the Manifest Destiny doctrine which attributed to the ruling class the "god-given and natural right" to impose its "good concept of government," by force if necessary, on the non-white peoples of the world. The chauvinism, racism, and sectarian Christian arrogance embedded in these doctrines have remained virtually intact and continue to be the driving force behind US policies even today. Yet, they are as repugnant to the spirit underlying the foundation of the United States, as they are to the peoples of the world in general and of the Western Hemisphere in particular.

To conceal their renunciation of revolutionary action as a legitimate recourse against tyranny and blatant oppression, religious, academic, journalistic and other leaders of the United States redefine and mythologize history and transform things into their opposites. The fraudulent character of these revisions of history comes out in bold relief in the U.S. ascription of the name "freedom fighters" to the bands of brigands of, for example, *ARENA* of El Salvador, the *National Union for the Total Independence of Angola (UNITA)* and the *Resistancia Nacional Mozambicana (RENAMO)*. UNITA and RENAMO, strongly supported by Christian Fundamentalists in the United States, not only devastated Angola and Mozambique, destroyed their infrastructure and transportation systems and murdered hundreds of thousands of innocent civilians, they also gave these countries the horrendous distinction of having more amputees and maimed persons per capita than any other country in the world.

The end result of this strategy of turning world history on its head is to allow exploitation to become a sacrosanct feature of human existence and to demonize and treat as outlaws any people who oppose it. The consistent portrayal of the Caribbean as an idyllic region with happy, contented indigenous people waiting impatiently to share their paradise with tourists, and the attempt to bury their struggles in obscurity are expressions of this strategy. Any social or political action at variance with this portrait continues to be targeted for repression. However, the truth is that no people, even in the face of coercion, will submit indefinitely to exploitation as a way of life.

Unable to contain and obscure the struggles of the people

for social justice and to keep intact the idyllic picture of the Caribbean region, secular and religious enemies of human progress propagated the myth that the democratic struggles were the creation of external influences, of "communism," and were, accordingly, manifestations of the "East-West" Conflict. Thus, communism became the scapegoat and anti-communism the mask for perpetuating the bondage of oppressed humanity. Yet the abuses and atrocities committed against the Caribbean people by Britain, Spain, France, the Netherlands, the United States, and Denmark had commenced centuries before the existence of communism.

It would be ridiculous to argue that the heroes of the Caribbean -- Hatuey, Anacaona, Nanny, Cuffee, Boukman, Toussaint, Dessalines, Fedon, Chatoyer, Queen Mary, Betances, Paul Bogle, Antonio Maceo, José Martí, Marcos Canul, Nathaniel Critchlow, Buzz Butler, Marcus Garvey and others – were communists. In fact, what they struggled against were territorial plunder, robbery, rape, genocide, human enslavement, colonialism and racism perpetrated by Western capitalism and imperialism. They fought to secure peace, freedom, human dignity, and democratic self-governance – the essence of the contemporary struggle.

The anti-communist strategy in the wake of World War II was very devastating to the Caribbean and Latin America. Every popular labor, religious or political movement was characterized as "communist" in order to rationalize Western intervention in and control over the internal affairs of the affected countries. Workers and farmers who had never heard of Marx, Engels or Lenin, but who knew that they were hungry, naked, down-trodden and oppressed were branded "communists" and "terrorists" by the dictators who oppressed them with the overt and covert financial and military support of the United States. Parish priests who took their sacred mission seriously and supported their parishioners' struggle for human dignity were condemned as "communists" and "terrorists", some of them murdered with impunity. Liberation theologians, leaders of the World Council of Churches and the World Peace Council were branded "communists" by successive US administrations and their theological allies. United States citizens who refused to be associated with this wanton disregard for natural and international law and the principles of self-determination and national sovereignty were denounced as communist sympathizers and persecuted for "anti-American" activities. At the same time, economic, religious and political hooligans were hailed as standard-bearers of democracy, and those in the developing countries provided with foreign aid and subsidies.

The result was that many democratically-oriented Caribbean leaders, fearful of economic destabilization or a military invasion, rejected developmental strategies which did not meet the approval of the US business, political, and church interests, even though such strategies were undoubtedly in their countries' best national interests. These contradictions placed a great deal of pressure on the religious institutions and further exacerbated the schism between those who associated imperial arrogance with Western democracy and those who saw it as being inconsistent with the Churches' subscription to the form and substance of the international fraternity of humanity.

In contrast to the ruling classes, the ordinary citizens in the Western countries have historically expressed opposition to national chauvinism and imperial arrogance and sympathized with the aspirations of the colonial peoples. The enchantment of the ruling classes, especially those of Britain and the United States, with the "good old days" of Victorian impudence and Theodore Rooseveltian swashbuckling gunboat diplomacy has met with strong opposition from the democratic forces who demand that genuine economic and political democracy be instituted in the developing countries and that conciliation be the instrument to ease international tensions.

The economic underdevelopment of the Caribbean is the inevitable consequence of an uninterrupted dependency relationship of the Caribbean region with Western Europe, North America, and others. This relationship continues to drain the region of its natural wealth, sap the strength of its human resources, and stultify its productive capacity. It was first given legal sanction with the passage of the English Navigation Acts in the seventeenth and eighteenth centuries, and parrotted by other colonial powers. Its spirit is reflected in the "Puerto Rican Model" of development, the "Caribbean Basin Initiative (CBI)", and the "Enterprise of the Americas".

Under the pretext of investment, growth, productivity, and so forth, the Puerto Rican Model, the CBI, the Enterprise of the Americas and their successors, the International Monetary Fund and the World Bank with their structural adjustment strategy – all of which have had the same substance and aims – put at the disposal of American corporate interests the local and international markets, the human and natural resources, and the revenues and finance systems of the Caribbean and other developing countries. They institute US businesses in privileged positions; frustrate and strangle local initiative, enterprise, and productivity; discourage spending on educational, cultural and social development and, thereby reduce the countries to a state of perpetual financial, commercial and aesthetic dependency.

Theoretically, all countries have the option to reject these economic models. In practice, however, both economic intervention by way of control over credit, finance and assistance programs, and covert or overt military intervention are the types of punishment that have been meted out to any country whose people or government opt for a path of socioeconomic self-development that subordinates the interests of the multinational corporations and the "global economy" to the country's own national interest. Father Aristide's Government in Haiti is a somewhat recent example of this type of intervention.

In 1990, Jean Bertrand Aristide, a liberation theologian, received a popular mandate to cleanse Haiti, the first colony, the second republic, and the poorest country in the hemisphere, of corruption, institutionalized violence, bribery and official thievery. In the seven months in which he was in office, Aristide successfully routed the death squads, placed scores of corrupt bureaucrats in jail, obliged others to go on the run, and dismissed hundreds of superfluous officials whose employment was based solely on nepotism. He introduced a literacy program and agrarian reform and was able to realize a surplus from hitherto failing government concerns like the flour mill, power plants and cement company.

Aristide believed in and practised humility. He declined a $10,000 per month presidential salary and maintained a humble existence. He placed his people before those who oppressed them and scorned any deals that ignored or were prejudicial to their interests. He fervently believed in and lived by his motto: "It is better to succeed with the people than to 'win' without them." His uncompromising stand on behalf of the poor and downtrodden resulted in his overthrow by the military and local business interests with the support of the upper clergy and international corporatism.

The contradiction within the Roman Catholic Church was laid bare when on March 30, 1992 the Papacy – the seat of Roman Catholicism – became the only state in the world to recognize the military regime that overthrew the democratically elected Roman Catholic president.

The Caribbean educational system – a product of the dominant Western philosophy and theology – was used by the Christian Churches to promote a culture of subservience to the interests of the metropolitan ruling classes. Like the political system, its purpose was not to satisfy the intellectual needs of the people, but rather to obtain acquiescence in their own state of exploitation and oppression. The result of this system was the creation of a large illiterate and semi-literate laboring class and a small "intelligentsia", largely non-Caribbean in character and orientation, lacking the capacity to relate to the people, and devoid of any connection with them or their social institutions. The educational system was designed to ensure the intellectual underdevelopment of the Caribbean people and to make them dependent on the metropolitan countries not only for their economic, social and technological needs, but also for their intellectual and aesthetic needs – their art, music, literature, craft, poetry, drama, and so forth. It was intended to make them dependent on the metropolitan countries for their cultural identity.

Some people, religious and otherwise, express the view that the economic and social development of the Caribbean cannot be attained without the active assistance of the United States, France, Britain, and other Western countries. They deny that there is any connection between the subjugation of the non-White and poor White peoples of the world and the oppression and discrimination of their counterparts within the metropolitan countries. This view, however, is inconsistent with the proposition that a country cannot oppress the people of another country unless it has the national consciousness to do so, that is, unless it oppresses its own people. The metropolitan countries, for example, cannot oppress Africans, Latin Americans, Arabs, Indians and other Asians living within their own borders and, at the same time, show love and affection to their siblings in other parts of the world. Otherwise one would have to look to a "Dr. Jekyll and Mr. Hyde" theory for an explanation of what would undoubtedly be deemed the political and social schizophrenia of the Western countries. Indeed it would be too tedious and painful to recount the abuses and crimes committed, and still being perpetrated against poor white and non-white citizens of the United States, Britain, France, the Netherlands, Portugal, Spain, and other European countries by their respective ruling classes.

The Soviet Union and the world socialist community no longer exist. The checks and balances they once provided in the world political arena are no longer available. The democratic, the poor and disenfranchised people of the world, in general, and people of color in particular are now at the mercy of the Western countries, which characterize as "terrorism" any criticism or opposition to their world hegemony. In fact the United States now exercises a power that even Britain at the height of its glory was unable to attain. It now dominates the world without having standing armies in the countries under its influence. Stephen Green's commentary in the February 12, 1993 issue of the *Christian Science Monitor,* in reference to the United States' influence within the United Nations, underscores this point: "Some [people], however, are beginning to notice that the White House waves the UN flag only when it is perceived to serve US policy to do so. When it does not, as in the case of Israel's deportation of Palestinians from the occupied territories, one hears very little about the sanctity of [United Nations] Security Council resolutions."

The world's democratic forces, particularly those within the religious institutions, have an awesome responsibility of ensuring that this enormous secular power is not abused. In fact, this responsibility is the singularly most important political and social imperative in the Caribbean and the world today. It is not only heretical but also criminal for the religious institutions, given the profound influence they exercise over the masses of our people, to ignore the serious crises facing humanity in our times. The days of sitting on the fence or remaining silent in the face of flagrant injustice are no longer acceptable. Not only is it incumbent upon the churches to incessantly reaffirm hope among the people, they must also decide whether the fraternity of humanity can be achieved by making common cause with the rulers and perpetrators of iniquities, or by struggling to eradicate such iniquities.

Christianity – Roman Catholicism and Protestantism – came to the New World as conquerors. It was used to justify and rationalize evil and iniquities. Its representatives were often apologists for and beneficiaries of imperial arrogance, territorial plunder, human enslavement, genocide, and other horrible crimes. Some elements of Christianity have today been partially transformed, in a general sense, into their opposite. In particular, the Christian Church in the Caribbean has been deserting the path of imperialist collaboration for the new highway of redemption by discarding the theology of oppression in favor of the theology of liberation. Increasingly, Christian religious leaders are making a valiant effort to correct the errors of their predecessors. By repudiating the absurd, apologetic argument of the separation of the material and spiritual interests of the poor and according respect to the non-Christian religious beliefs and institutions of the people, they are attempting to save the "soul" of the Christian Church from apostasy while simultaneously seeking a reconciliation between the theory and practice of contemporary Christianity and the revolutionary-democratic and humanistic teachings of Jesus Christ.

REFERENCES

1. Jordan, p. 7

2. Ibid. p. 9

3. Ibid. p. 23

4. Coke, Vol. I, p. 86

5. William F. Keegan, *The People Who Discovered Columbus*, University Press of Florida, Gainesville, Florida (1992), p. 8

6. Coke, Vol. I, p. 104

7. Bell, p. 9

8. Ibid. p. 8

9. Coke, Vol. I, pp.104-105

10. R. M. Walters, *The Pre-Columbian Caribbean Societies,* Department of Sociology, University of the West Indies, St. Augustine, Trinidad (1978), p. 17

11. Keegan, p. 103

12. Id.

13. Bisnauth, p. 2

14. Coke, Vol. I, p. 113

15. Ibid. p. 115

16. Ibid. p. 117

17.   Ibid. p. 119

18.   Bisnauth, p. 5

19.   Walters, p. 39

20.   Keegan, p. 9

21.   Coke, Vol. I, p. 165

22.   Manuel Maldonado-Denis, *Puerto Rico: A Socio-Historic Interpretation*, (translated by Elena Vialo), Vintage Books, Division of Random House, New York, (1972), p. 14

23.   Coke, Vol. I, p. 85

24.   Rodman, *Quisqueya*, p. 11

25.   Roger Bastide, *African Civilizations in the New World*, Harper and Row Publishers, New York (1972), p. 77

26.   Young, p. 64

27.   Bisnauth, p. 84

28.   Young, p. 65

29.   Ibid. p. 67

30.   Ibid. p. 71

31.   Roger Bastide, *The African Religions of Brazil*, Johns Hopkins University Press, Baltimore-London (1978), pp. 82-83

32.   Bastide, *African Civilizations in the New World*, p. 90

33.   Bisnauth, pp. 87-88

34. Bastide, *African Civilizations*, p. 103

35. Bisnauth, pp. 89-90

36. Schuler, p. 33

37. Ibid. p. 36

38. Mervyn Alleyne, *Africa: Roots of Jamaican Culture*, Frontline Distribution International, Inc., Chicago, Illinois (1989), p. 85

39. Id.

40. Schuler, p. 32

41. Alleyne, p. 96

42. Duany, (Glazer), *Ethnicity in the Spanish Caribbean*, p. 23

43. Hesketh Bell, *Obeah*, Negro Universities Press, Westport, Connecticut (1970) (originally published in 1889), p. 12

44. Donald Wood, *Trinidad in Transition*, Oxford University Press, London (1968), p. 167

45. Mats Lundahl, *Toussaint L' Ouverture and the War Economy of Saint-Domingue, 1796-1802,* ("Caribbean Freedom: Economy and Society from Emancipation to the Present"), edited by Hilary Beckles and Verene Shepherd, Markus Weiner, James Currey, Ian Randle, Princeton, London, Kingston (Jamaica), 1993, p. 2

46. Ibid. pp. 7-8

47. Ibid. p. 8

48. John Edwin Fagg, *Cuba, Haiti, & the Dominican Republic*, Prentice-Hall, Inc., Englewood Cliffs, New Jersey (1965), p. 125

49. Leyburn, p. 134

50. Ibid. p. 137

51. Milo Rigaud, *Secrets of Voodoo*, City Lights Books, San Francisco, California (1985), p. 31

52. Ibid. p. 33

53. Rodman, *Haiti: The Black Republic*, p. 73

54. Rigaud, p. 44

55. Leyburn, p. 147

56. Bastide, *African Civilizations in the New World*, p. 140

57. Ibid. p. 142

58. Leyburn, p. 144

59. Dana G. Munro, *The United States and the Caribbean Area*, World Peace Foundation, Boston (1934), pp. 144-145

60. Leyburn, p. 126

61. Munro, pp. 145-146

62. Leyburn, p. 127

63. Bastide, *African Civilizations in the New World*, pp. 53-54

64. *Ibid. p. 59*

65. George Eaton Simpson, *Black Religions in the New World*, Columbia University Press, New York (1978), p. 205

66. Rosemary and Gary Brana-Shute, *Crime and Punishment in the Caribbean*, Center for Latin American Studies, University of Florida, Gainesville, Florida (1980), p. 117

67. Bastide, *African Civilizations in the New World*, p. 60

68. Cornelis Goslinga, *The Dutch in the Caribbean and the Guyanas, 1680-1791*, Van Gorcum, Assen Maastricht, the Netherlands (1985), p. 367

69. William Van de Poll, *Surinam, the Country and its People*, W. Van Hoeve Ltd., the Hague, Netherlands (1951), p. 6

70. Goslinga, p. 379

71. Bastide, *African Civilizations in the New World*, p. 54

72. Van de Poll, p. 6

73. Alleyne, p. 95

74. Id.

75. Edward Seaga, *Revival Cults in Jamaica*, Institute of Jamaica, Kingston, Jamaica, (1982 ed.), p. 5

76. Ibid. p. 13

77. George Eaton Simpson, *Religious Cults of the Caribbean: Trinidad, Jamaica and Haiti*, Institute of Caribbean Studies, University of Puerto Rico, Rio Piedras, Puerto Rico (1980), p. 128

78. *Daily Gleaner,* April 5, 1899; Jamaica Journal (Quarterly of the Institute of Jamaica) Vol. 8, No. 4 (1974), p.30

79. W. F. Elkins, *Warrior Higgins, A Jamaican Street Preacher*, Jamaica Journal (Quarterly of the Institute of Jamaica), Vol. 8, No. 4 (1974), p. 30

80. Moya Pons, p. 47

81. Peter Wiernik, *History of the Jews in America*, the Jewish Publishing Company, New York (1931), pp. 29-30

82. Ibid. p. 32

83. Ibid. p. 35

84. Ibid. p. 38

85. Bisnauth, p. 69

86. Long, *The History of Jamaica,* Vol. 2, p. 293

87. Ibid. p. 296

88. Patrick Hylton, *The Struggles of the Caribbean People*, Billpops Publications, Inc., Washington, D.C. (1984), p. 24

89. Bisnauth, p. 70

90. Id.

91. Wiernik, p. 45

92. Ibid. p. 44

93. Ibid. p. 45

94. Ibid. p. 46

95. Goslinga, *The Dutch in the Caribbean and the Guianas*, p. 383

96. Ibid. p. 385

97. Wiernik, pp. 47-48

98. Goslinga, *The Dutch in the Caribbean and the Guianas,* p. 385

99. Wiernik, p. 48

100. Ibid. p. 47

101. Bisnauth, p. 74

102. Wiernik, p. 52

103. Bisnauth, p. 72

104. Wiernik, p. 53

105. Ibid. p. 57

106. Long, *The History of Jamaica*, Vol. II, pp. 295-296

107. Frances P. Karner, *The Sephardics of Curacao*, Royal Van Gorcum Co., Assen, the Netherlands (1969), p. 23

108. Ibid. p. 36

109. Ibid. p. 49

110. Rev. Harricharan, p. 3

111. Hylton, p. 39

112. Rev. Harricharan, p. 2

113. Bisnauth, p. 82

114. Bastide, *African Civilizations in the New World*, p. 47

115.   Bisnauth, p. 156

116.   Knight, p. 116

117.   Bisnauth, pp. 159-160

118.   Brimsley Samaroo, *Two Abolitions: African Slavery and East Indian Indentureship*, India in the Caribbean, Hansib Publishing Limited, London (1987), p. 27

119.   Edward Dew, *The Difficult Flowering of Surinam*, Martinus Nijhoff, the Hague-Boston-London (1978), p. 42

120.   Encyclopedia of World Cultures, Vol. VIII, *Middle America and the Caribbean: Indians in Trinidad*, G. K. Hall & Co., Boston, Massachusetts (1995), p. 107

121.   Federal Research Division, *Guyana and Belize*, Library of Congress, Washington, (1993), p. 49

122.   Encyclopedia of World Cultures, p. 107

123.   Gosine, p. 48

124.   Bisnauth, p. 156

125.   Gosine, p. 46

126.   Federal Research Division, p. 48

127.   Glasgow, p. 77

128.   Ibid. p. 82

129.   Federal Research Division, p. 48

130.   Glasgow, p. 81

131. Samaroo, p. 47

132. Encyclopedia of World Cultures, p. 105

133. Swan, p. 50

134. Encyclopedia of World Cultures, p. 105

135. Id.

136. Gosine, p. 51

137. Ibid. p. 49

138. Dew, pp. 60-61, (alt. cit. R.M.N. Panday, *"Agriculture in Surinam, 1650-1950: An Inquiry into the Causes of its Decline,"* Amsterdam (1959), pp. 72-74)

139. Gosine, p. 52

140. Daly, p. 148

141. Cheddi Jagan, *The West on Trial: The Fight for Guyana's Freedom,* Seven Seas Publishers, Berlin (1980 ed.), p. 119

142. In its November 28, 1953 issue, the U.S. weekly magazine, *The Nation,* wrote:
"The measures planned were not Socialist, let alone Communist, in essence. Its planned labour legislation was derived from the Wagner Act. Under the system to be set up, inquiries and polls could be held in any industry to decide on the union to be officially recognized. The inquiries and polls were to be conducted by a British official.

What is more, a new union challenging the position of an established bargaining agent would have to get 65 percent of the workers' votes before it could be recognized.

It was under these conditions that the PPP-supported union, the Guiana Industrial Workers' Union, hoped to replace the existing Man-Power Citizens' Association as the official organization in sugar and elsewhere."

143.   Jagan, p. 114

144.   Id.

145.   Dew, p. 150

146.   Rev. Harricharan, p. 7

147.   Excerpts from an essay entitled *The Crisis in Trinidad and Tobago*, prepared by Dessima Williams, former People's Revolutionary Government of Grenada, (PRG) ambassador to Washington, for presentation to the Conference of Caribbean Unity on the attempted coup in Trinidad-Tobago on July 27, 1990

148.   Bisnauth, p. 155

149.   Federal Research Division, p. 49

150.   Glasgow, p. 87

151.   Thomas A. Shaw, *To Be or not to Be Chinese*, (Stephen Glazer, "Caribbean Ethnicity Revisited"), Gordon and Breach Science Publishers, New York, London, Paris, Montreux, Tokyo (1985), p. 77

152.   Eric Williams, *History of the People of Trinidad and Tobago*, Andre Deutsch Limited, London (1964), p.85

153.   Turner, p. 134

154.   Ibid. p. 136

155.   Ibid. p. 134

156.   Wood, p. 162

157. Ibid. p. 165

158. Turner, p. 136

159. Wood, p. 160

160. Turner, p. 135

161. Shaw, p. 180

162. Id.

163. Historical Sketches, p. 32

164. Daly, p. 149

165. Wood, p.166

166. Shaw, p. 77

167. Ibid. p. 76

168. Horace Campbell, *Rasta and Resistance*, Africa World Press, Inc., Trenton, New Jersey (1987), p. 77

169. Ibid. p. 73

170. Ibid. p. 75

171. Robert Hill, *Leonard P. Howell and Millenarian Visions in Early Rastafari*, Jamaica Journal, (Quarterly of the Institute of Jamaica), Vol. 16, No. 1, 1983), p. 34

172. Ibid. p. 38

173. Campbell, p. 107

174. Id.

BIBLIOGRAPHY

Alleyne, Mervyn, *Africa: Roots of Jamaican Culture*, Frontline Distribution International, Inc., Chicago, Illinois (1989).

Anderson, William A., and Dynes, Russell R., *Social Movements, Violence and Change*: Ohio State University Press, Columbus, (1975).

Ayearst, Morley, *The British West Indies,* New York University Press, United Kingdom (1960).

Bastide, Roger, *African Civilizations in the New World:* Harper and Row Publishers, New York, (1972); *The African Religions of Brazil:* Johns Hopkins University Press, Baltimore-London, (1978).

Beckles, Hilary, and Shepherd, Verene, *Caribbean Freedom: Economy and Society from Emancipation to the Present,* Markus Weiner, James Currey, Ian Randle, Princeton, London, Kingston (Jamaica), 1993.

Bell, Hesketh, *Obeah:* Negro Universities Press, Westport, Connecticut, (1970, originally published in 1889).

Bell, Ian, *The Dominican Republic*, Westview Press, Boulder, Colorado (Ernest Bell, London)(1981).

Bisnauth, Dale, *History of Religions in the Caribbean,* Africa World Press, Inc., Trenton, N.J. (1996).

Brana-Shute, Gary and Rosemary, *Crime and Punishment in the Caribbean,* Center for Latin American Studies, University of Florida, Gainesville, Florida (1980).

Burns, Sir Alan, *History of the British West Indies*, George Allen and Unwin Limited, London (1965).

Caldecott, A., *The Church in the West Indies:* Frank Cass and Company, Limited, London (1970).

Campbell, Horace, *Rasta and Resistance*, Africa World Press, Inc., Trenton, New Jersey (1987).

Coke, Thomas, *A History of the West Indies:* Vol. I, Nuttall, Fisher, and Dixon,Oxford, U.K., 1808 (Reprinted by Mnemosyne Publishing Company, Miami, Florida, 1969); Vol. II, Frank Cass and Company Limited, London (1808-1811), reprinted 1971.

Cook, Sherburne F., and Borah, Woodrow, *Essays in Population History: Mexico and the Caribbean*, Vol. I, University of California Press, Berkeley (1971).

Corwin, Arthur P., *Spain and the Abolition of Slavery in Cuba, 1817-1886*, Institute of Latin American Studies, University of Texas Press, Austin (1967).

Courlander, Harold, and Bastien, Remy, *Religion and Politics in Haiti,* Institute for Cross-Cultural Research, Washington, D.C., 1966.

Daly, Vere T., *A Short History of the Guyanese People,* Macmillan Education Limited, London, 1975; *The Making of Guyana*, Macmillan Education Limited, London, 1974.

Dew, Edward, *The Difficult Flowering of Surinam*, Martinus Nijhoff, the Hague, Boston, London, 1978.

Dookhan, Isaac, *A History of the British Virgin Islands*, Caribbean Universities Press, in Association with Booker Publishing

Company, Essex, England, 1975.

Duany, Jorge, *Ethnicity in the Spanish Caribbean: Notes on the Consolidation of Creole Identity in Cuba and Puerto Rico, 1762-1868*, (Stephen Glazer, "Caribbean Ethnicity Revisited"), Gordon and Breach Science Publishers, New York, London, Paris, Montreux, Tokyo, 1985.

Eaden, John, *Memoirs of Pere Labat,* Frank Cass and Company Limited, London, 1931.

Elkins, W. F., *Warrior Higgins, A Jamaican Street Preacher*, Jamaica Journal (Quarterly of the Institute of Jamaica), Vol. 8, No. 4, 1974.

Fagg, John Edwin, *Cuba, Haiti, & the Dominican Republic*, Prentice-Hall, Inc., Englewood Cliffs, New Jersey, 1965.

Fiske, Amos Kidder, *The West Indies,* G.P. Putnam's Sons, New York-London, 1899.

Foner, Philip S., *A History of Cuba and its Relations with the United States,* Vols. 1 & 2, International Publishers, New York, 1962.

Gardner, William, *A History of Jamaica,* E. Stock, London, 1873.

Glasgow, Roy Arthur, *Guyana: Race and Politics Among Africans and East Indians*, Martinus Nijhoff, the Hague, Netherlands, 1970.

Gosine, Mahin, *East Indians and Black Power in the Caribbean*, African Research Publications, New York, 1986.

Goslinga, Cornelis, *A Short History of the Netherlands Antilles and Surinam,* Martinus Nijhoff, The Hague, 1979; *The Dutch in* the Caribbean and the Guyanas, 1680-1791, Van Gorcum, Assen Maastricht, the Netherlands, 1985.

Harricharan, Rev. J. T., *The Work of the Christian Churches Among the East Indians in Trinidad During the Period of Indentureship, 1845-1917*, Tunapuna, Trinidad, 1975.

Hill, Robert, *Leonard P. Howell and Millenarian Visions in Early Rastafari*, Jamaica Journal (Quarterly of the Institute of Jamaica), Vol. 16, No. 1, 1983.

Hylton, Patrick, *The Struggles of the Caribbean People*, Billpops Publications, Inc., Washington, D.C., 1984.

Jacob, C. M., *Joy Comes in the Morning*, Caribbean Historical Society, Port-of-Spain, Trinidad, 1996.

Jagan, Cheddi, *The West on Trial: The Fight for Guyana's Freedom*, Seven Seas Publishers, Berlin (1980).

Jordan, Winthrop D., *White Over Black*, Penguin Books, Inc., Baltimore, Maryland 1969.

Karner, Frances P., *The Sephardics of Curacao,* Royal Van Gorcum Co., Assen, The Netherlands (1969).

Keegan, William F., *The People Who Discovered Columbus*, University Press of Florida, Gainesville, Florida, 1992.

Knight, Franklin W., *Slave Society in Cuba During the Nineteenth Century*, the University of Wisconsin Press, Madison, Milwaukee and London, 1980.

Leyburn, James G., *The Haitian People*, Yale University Press, New Haven and London, 1996.

Long, Edward, *The History of Jamaica,* Vol. II, Frank Cass and Company Limited, London, 1970; (first edition 1774).

Lopez, Adalberto, *The Puerto Ricans: Their History, Culture, and Society*, Schenkman Publishing Company, Inc., Cambridge, Massachusetts (1980).

Maldonado-Denis, Manuel, *Puerto Rico: A Socio-Historic Interpretation*, (translated by Elena Vialo), Vintage Books, Division of Random House, New York, 1972.

Morales-Carrión, Arturo, *Puerto Rico and the Non-Hispanic Caribbean*, University of Puerto Rico, 1971.

Munro, Dana G., *The United States and the Caribbean Area*, World Peace Foundation, Boston, 1934.

Poll, William Van de, *Surinam, the Country and its People*, W. Van Hoeve Ltd., The Hague, Netherlands, 1951.

Pons, Frank Moya, *Caribbean Consciousness: What the Caribbean is Not*, Vol. 5, No. 3, San Jose, Puerto Rico, 1978.

Pratt, Julius W., *A History of United States Foreign Policy,* Prentice-Hall, Inc., New Jersey, 1975.

Rigaud, Milo, *Secrets of Voodoo*, City Lights Books, San Francisco, California, 1985.

Rodman, Selden, *Haiti: The Black Republic*, the Devin-Adair Company, New York, 1954; *Quisqueya: A History of the Dominican Republic*, University of Washington Press, Seattle, 1964.

Samaroo, Brimsley, *Two Abolitions: African Slavery and East Indian Indentureship, India in the Caribbean*, Hansib

Publishing Limited, London, 1987.

Schuler, Monica, *Alas, Alas, Kongo*, Johns Hopkins University Press, Baltimore and London, 1980.

Seaga, Edward, *Revival Cults in Jamaica*, Institute of Jamaica, Kingston, Jamaica 1982.

Shaw, Thomas A., *To Be or Not to Be Chinese*, (Stephen Glazer, "Caribbean Ethnicity Revisited"), Gordon and Breach Science Publishers, New York, London, Paris, Montreux, Tokyo, 1985.

Simpson, George Eaton, *Black Religions in the New World*, Columbia University Press, New York, 1978; *Religious Cults of the Caribbean: Trinidad, Jamaica and Haiti*, Institute of Caribbean Studies, University of Puerto Rico, Rio Piedras, Puerto Rico, 1980.

Southey, Captain James, *Chronological History of the West Indies*, Frank Cass and Company Limited, London, 1968.

Swan, Michael, *British Guyana, the Land of Six Peoples*, Her Majesty's Stationery Office, London, 1957.

Underhill, Edward B., *The West Indies: Their Social and Religious Condition*, Jackson, Walford, and Hodden: London, 1862.

Walters, R. M., *The Pre-Columbia Caribbean Societies*, Department of Sociology, University of the West Indies, St. Augustine, Trinidad, 1978.

Wiernik, Peter, *History of the Jews in America*, the Jewish Publishing Company, New York, 1931.

Williams, Eric, *British Historians and the West Indies,* Andre

Deutsch Limited, London, 1972; *History of the People of Trinidad and Tobago*, Andre Deutsch Limited, London, 1964; *Race Relations in Caribbean Society*, Caribbean Studies: A symposium, Institute of Social and Economic Research, University of the West Indies, 1931.

Wood, Donald, *Trinidad in Transition,* Oxford University Press, London, 1968.

Young, Josiah U., *Black and African Theologies*, Orbis Books, Maryknoll, New York, 1990.

*****

Board of Education of Great Britain, *Educational Systems of the Chief Colonies Of the British Empire: Special Reports on Educational Subjects,* Vol. IV, (Her Majesty's Stationery Office, London, 1901).

Encyclopedia of World Cultures, Vol. VIII, *Middle America and the Caribbean: Indians in Trinidad*, G. K. Hall & Co., Boston, Massachusetts, 1995.

Federal Research Division, *Guyana and Belize*, Library of Congress, Washington, D.C., 1993.

Society for the Propagation of the Gospel in Foreign Parts, *Historical Sketches,* No. IV - Guiana, Westminster, 1900; *Historical Sketches*, No. VI, SPCK, London, 1900.

The Christian Science Monitor

The Jamaican Daily Gleaner

INDEX

A

Asian ... 3, 5, 35, 64, 73, 76, 79-80, 83, 84, 97, 106, 116, 123, 132, 237, 241, 246, 248, 259, 261,268, 269, 270, 340

B

D

73, 76, 79, 93, 97, 102-103, 105, 112, 115, 120, 157,
160-161, 166, 168, 174-175, 200, 202, 222-224, 229,
231-232, 236-237, 246, 254, 259-260, 275-279, 332
Duvalier, Francois("Papa Doc");
Jean-Claude("Bebe Doc") 111-112, 124-126

E

East Indian 3, 64, 65, 76, 98, 99, 100, 102, 105, 107, 118,
208, 225, 242-246, 248-250, 252-274, 276-280, 282, 299
Ecclesiastical 5, 11, 20, 22, 31, 34, 40, 42, 59, 221
Education . 6, 36, 44, 45, 49, 61, 92, 94-98, 100-107,110- 112,
127, 134, 196, 205, 218, 235, 256, 260, 264, 271, 320, 323
Educational System 6, 98, 103, 106, 109, 112, 114, 339
Emancipation 5, 51, 54, 56, 59, 62, 67, 69-73, 80, 83,
92-94, 96-97, 107-108, 130, 173, 204, 207, 208, 218, 228
England 14, 23, 32-35, 37-39, 42, 47-49, 56, 62, 65, 81,
84-85, 88-89, 93, 98, 158, 161, 184, 216, 224, 226, 280, 295
English 13-14, 23, 35, 95, 144, 157, 160, 179, 219,
224, 227, 229, 250, 282, 337
Enslavement 1, 3, 14, 16-21, 37, 43, 47, 134, 146,
171, 335, 341
Episcopal Church 91, 108, 110
Established Church 5, 29, 32, 34, 39, 47, 48, 49, 54, 59,
62, 64, 65, 89, 90, 117, 118, 214, 328, 329
Ethiopia 145, 147, 189, 216, 284, 285, 288-290, 293-297,
306, 313, 329
Ethiopian 145, 189, 287-290, 293-295, 297, 299, 307,
313, 315, 320
Europe 3-4, 6, 9, 14-15, 20, 27-28, 39, 68, 98, 113, 125,
197, 220, 222-223, 225, 234, 254, 295, 332, 337
Evangelical 47-48, 54, 56, 216
Evangelism 53, 99, 205, 306
Exploitation 3, 5, 6, 15, 77, 93, 119-120, 123, 129, 240,
242-243, 269, 330, 334, 339
Eyre, Edward John 84-88, 237

F

G

H

I

M

N

S